Food and cooking have interested Jenny Baker ever since as a small child she was allowed to help in her grandmother's kitchen. As an adult, she and her husband James lived for a while in the Middle East where she first became aware of the diversity of foreign dishes. On their return to England, they ran a private catering business, brought up their children and spent as much time as they could in a small, French farmhouse set on a hillside, overlooking the valley of the Ardèche. It was here, in La Marie-Thomas, that she found her inspiration for this book.

Jenny Baker's most recent book, *Kettle Broth to Gooseberry Fool*, won the 1997 Guild of Food Writers' Michael Smith Award.

by the same author

THE STUDENT'S COOKBOOK (new edition)
THE STUDENT'S VEGETARIAN COOKBOOK (new edition)
SIMPLY FISH:
a guide to identifying, buying and eating fish
KITCHEN SUPPERS
JENNY BAKER'S CUISINE GRANDMÈRE:
from Brittany, Normandy, Picardy and Flanders
KETTLE BROTH TO GOOSEBERRY FOOL:
a celebration of simple English cooking

Simple French Cuisine

From Provence and Languedoc

JENNY BAKER

Illustrated by James Baker

ff

faber and faber

First published in 1990
by Faber and Faber Limited
3 Queen Square London WC1N 3AU
First published in paperback in 1992
This paperback edition first published in 1999

Printed in England by Clays Ltd, St Ives plc

All rights reserved
© Jenny Baker, 1990
Illustrations © James Baker, 1990

Jenny Baker is hereby identified as author of this
work in accordance with Section 77 of the Copyright,
Designs and Patents Act 1988

*This book is sold subject to the condition that it shall not,
by way of trade or otherwise, be lent, resold, hired out or
otherwise circulated without the publisher's consent in any
form of binding or cover other than that in which it is
published and without a similar condition including this
condition being imposed on the subsequent purchaser.*

A CIP record for this book
is available from the British Library

ISBN 0-571-20067-2

2 4 6 8 10 9 7 5 3 1

To Jean-Pierre and Monique
who rescued us and have
guarded us ever since

Acknowledgements

My thanks to all the people whom I have met through the Marie-Thomas, who have helped me in so many different ways. I would like to mention the Ayrtons, and especially Stephen for his kindness and generosity; and then some of those who have made us feel as if we really belonged to the place: the Fabres, to whom this book is dedicated, and their extensive family; Dominique and Roseline Feijoo; Emile and Henri Lacour; Cathy and Claire Pesenti and Dorothy Deeks; Monique Garcia and her husband Angel who brings us snails, wild boar and cherries; John and Dorothee Ramsay; and Jean Sahli from Switzerland. Thanks, too, are due to friends and family in England on whom I experimented, not forgetting Lynda Johnson who let me pick her green walnuts, and David Graham who brought home the galleys. I would like to mention, too, all the people at Faber and Faber who put so much into the production side and special thanks to Rosemary Goad and Kate Hobson who encouraged me in the beginning and to Tracey Scoffield who inherited me so enthusiastically.

Contents

Map viii
Introduction, 1

THE FLAVOUR
Garlic, 11
Thyme and savory, 27
Rosemary and sage, 37
Fennel, anise and mint, 45
Basil, 55
Anchovies, 63

SPRING AND SUMMER VEGETABLES
Tomatoes, 81
Aubergines, 93
Swiss chard to asparagus, 101

FRUITS OF SUMMER AND AUTUMN
Cherries to quinces, 119
Figs and honey, 131
Grapes and wines, 141
Chestnuts, 157

AUTUMN AND WINTER MATTERS
The olive, 171
Mushrooms and a black truffle, 185
Juniper and la chasse, 201
Pumpkins to beans, 213

CHEESE, 225

ETCETERAS, 237
From breadcrumbs to a
chocolate mousse . . . by
way of a hedgehog

Bibliography, 247
Index, 250

VIVIERS

L'ARDÈCHE

PONT St. ESPRIT

CÈZE

BAGNOLS

ALÈS

UZÈS

GARD

REMOULINS

NÎMES

MONTPELLIER

RHÔNE

CAMARGUE

Introduction

'Why don't you go and stay in our farmhouse in France?' our friends said one summer, when we had two small children and not much money. We looked at the map and found it was somewhere in the Rhône valley, not far from Orange and near the Ardèche. So we took them up on it and like many before us almost immediately fell under the spell of the place.

We reached the village of St Paulet-de-Caisson in the middle of an August afternoon. We had instructions to collect the key from Monsieur Rodrigo and found him sitting in his vest outside the local bar. Our French was very limited. His was better but spoken with such a heavy accent – he was one of the refugees from the Spanish Civil War – that we couldn't understand a word he said. After a while, he realized his shouting was getting us nowhere, so clutching the key in his hand and with much arm-waving, he indicated he would show us the way. He squeezed into a decrepit Deux Chevaux and we followed him out of the village.

Feeling distinctly foreign and far from home we felt we were being led into the middle of nowhere. The road was narrow, the tarmac soon giving way to a cart-track. The orchards around the village were left behind and we twisted and turned between vineyards and fields of asparagus and sunflowers, passing the occasional farmhouse. We reached the summit of the hill, turned sharply and drove through a small copse and then out into the light.

The house was almost completely hidden. All we could see was the roof of Provençal tiles and a bit of limestone wall, which seemed to grow out of the fields of sun-dried grass and wild flowers which surrounded it. We turned off the cart-track down the drive which was even more overgrown and discovered the house was much bigger than we thought. The side of the hill had been cut into broad steps and the house, sheltered by a mulberry tree, was built against one of these terraces. We followed Monsieur Rodrigo through a battered door, over which someone had painted the name, La Marie-Thomas, and found ourselves in the courtyard.

The floor was covered with fresh gravel. There was a fig tree growing out of the wall in one corner, and against the house were young lilacs and vines. Opposite the house was a concrete wash-stand and a pump. This, Monsieur Rodrigo demonstrated, was our water supply. Inside a note of welcome, a bottle of *pastis*, beds to sleep in and, best of all, a fridge, a cooker and all we needed to begin to cook.

This was the beginning, twenty-three years ago, of my love affair with that area on the edge of the Rhône, sandwiched between Provence and Languedoc. Like everyone who falls in love with a place they visit on holiday, I longed to be able to transport home something of its magic. Stones, leaves, pressed flowers soon become sad. Food was much better. Olive oil and garlic could last us through the winter. The market offered us dried herbs and olives, jars of anchovies and honey and there were books I could buy full of interesting recipes.

As we got to know the place, so we got to know the people and from them learnt more about the cooking. First there was Jean-Pierre who saved us when our car broke down and then introduced us to his family. His father was a chef and his grandmother once cooked for an ambassador in London. His wife, Monique, cooks twice a day for the family and has shared many of her recipes with me. Amongst others there is Cathy, the Englishwoman who became a farmer's wife, and the schoolmaster-turned-painter Dominique Feijoo and his wife Roseline, and then there are Emile and Henri. They are middle-aged bachelors, who live together in a large, decaying farmhouse and tend the land around us, which is now no longer grass and wild flowers but vineyards. They speak with country accents which even Jean-Pierre says he can hardly understand, but somehow we get along. They like to talk and will repeat each story several times and as their stories often concern food, this is a great help to my collection of recipes.

Like many people I used to think that French cooking was far from simple. I thought it was all dependent on long, slow-cooked sauces, exquisite pastries, stockpots simmering all day, elaborate garnishes and impossible techniques. And, of course, it is all those things when it is done by master chefs who train for years before they are even allowed to stir the pot.

But France isn't populated by master chefs. It is full of ordinary people who cook but have to work, so the everyday cooking has to be simple. It also has to be good. The French still love their food and almost everyone eats very well. You don't have to be rich or educated, or middle-class or any class to know about good food. Everyone is mad about it, especially the men who keep their wives on their toes and persuade them to cook dishes just like grandmother used to do.

People are so interested and so knowledgeable about what they like that shops and supermarkets wouldn't dare foist anything on them but the best. There would be a public outcry. Convenience foods are just that – of very high quality and convenient for the public, not just for the manufacturers. So very few people ever have to think about making a cake or bread or even pastry and no one feels guilty when they take shortcuts.

There are many reasons why France has such a tradition of good food. It remained largely a nation of country people and peasants while England became an urbanized society. It is every Frenchman's right, provided he has the necessary licence, to eat off the land, while British laws regarding game prohibit ordinary people. The French had a revolution and began to believe in liberty, equality and fraternity, whereas the other side of the Channel had puritanism, an industrial revolution and the trap of class structure.

The real joy of cooking French is the discovery that its roots are firmly based in simple country traditions. Its emphasis is on seasonal produce, vegetables and flavourings. Food is never just something to fill the stomach but an important daily ritual of shared pleasure. Dishes are discussed with gusto, both those that are in the process of being eaten and those that have been eaten or are about to be. Try saying 'wait and see' to a French person and they will be as offended as if you had told them to mind their own business.

The recipes in this book are for people cooking in Britain or perhaps when on holiday in France. When I am there, I spend a lot of time poring over cookery books and gathering recipes from friends and neighbours to add to my collection. It is when I come home that the fun begins. The recipes must be tried and tested in my Wandsworth kitchen. Most of the things I need to buy are readily to hand. Supermarkets now stock a wide variety and there are the small shops, delicatessens and street markets. Ethnic shops often supply the more elusive ingredients.

The choice of recipes has been selective. For reasons of space alone, it would be impossible to include all the dishes of Provence and Languedoc, so I have made a geographical limit as well as a personal one. We go northwards into the Ardèche, southwards to the Camargue, westwards to the Cévennes and eastwards to the Rhône Alps.

Because I have already covered many of the fish dishes in *Simply Fish* I have limited the number included in this book.

I have divided the book into sections. The first introduces the essential flavours, garlic, herbs and anchovies. Then come the seasons, each one covering a different aspect of cooking. All sections include an assortment of recipes, including starters and main courses, fruit dishes and desserts. I wanted to get away from the usual format which puts soups, meat, fish, sauces, desserts etc. in separate sections. I like to begin with one ingredient, say a plant of basil, and explore all the possibilities it offers. I hope by introducing this idea, it will inspire you to experiment and try out less familiar things.

You don't need any special or expensive equipment to follow the recipes in this book. Of course electric food processors and so on are useful but often the washing-up involved seems out of all proportion to the work they do. Apart from the usual array of kitchen utensils, I would suggest you master the art of the pestle and mortar and buy two or three in different sizes. Use a mouli-légumes to sieve soups and to purée whole, cooked garlic cloves. Have a pair of kitchen shears and two or three very sharp knives and a good cutting board. Wooden spoons and forks are indispensable. Invest in one or two cast-iron enamelled pans which can be used on top of the stove or in the oven, as well as a small and large frying pan. In earthenware, you will need a shallow gratin dish and one good-sized casserole.

The recipes are basically for four people, unless otherwise stated. It is important to realize that cooking is an ever-changing art. No two cooks cook the same. A recipe is a guide. Quantities are given in exact measures because that is useful the first time you do it, but taste as you go. Only you can decide if there is quite enough salt or whether you have been too stingy with the garlic. Ovens vary, so allow for the idiosyncrasies of yours. No two people like exactly the same methods, so the method in the recipe is useful but is not obligatory and there is no reason why you should not change it.

Jenny Baker
La Marie-Thomas and Wandsworth

The Flavour

The cooking of both Provence and Languedoc is flavoured with garlic, herbs, the olive and its oil. It uses fresh seasonal vegetables, nuts and fruit, honey, juniper, capers and spices, fish from rivers and sea, mushrooms and farm-produced cheeses. There is meat from hillside sheep and much of the beef comes from the Camargue where the cattle are allowed to roam freely. Pork is popular. Everyone used to keep their own pig and the annual slaughter took on something of the ritual of a religious sacrifice. Still to be found are masses of different sausages and pork produce sold in markets and *charcuteries*. There are chickens fed on maize, guinea fowl and quail and, in season, rabbits and hares as well as roe deer, wild boar and game birds.

Every Saturday morning, we and everyone else for miles around go to the market at Pont St Esprit. Frédéric Mistral, Provence's most famous poet, called the town the golden gate to Provence. In fact it stands beside the Rhône right on the edge of Languedoc. On the other side of the bridge, which was built by monks in the thirteenth century, is Provence. The river between the two regions is wide and treacherous and the bridge opened the way between two cultures. People could travel freely. Produce and customs were traded and a style of cooking developed which was influenced by both sides. Nowadays guide books and visitors to the Rhône valley generally refer to the whole region as Provence and it takes a local to gently point out that on the west bank, they are in Languedoc.

It is an area of small villages and towns shaded in summer by plane trees especially pruned and trained to provide a canopy over the boulevards. Chestnuts and lime trees flourish in the squares. There are large areas of forest which overlook the valleys which are criss-crossed with vineyards, and fields of corn, rape and sunflowers, orchards, plantations of olives and market gardens. In spring, the stony scrubland, the *garrigue*, is vibrant with broom and gorse. In summer the air smells of herbs and lavender which attract butterflies and bees. The colours are so intense that when it rains it seems as if the light has literally been switched off.

The herbs that are to go into the pot grow everywhere. Fennel and anise hold their umbrella flowers above clumps of wild thyme and in the few shady spots apple mint releases its scent beneath your feet. Sage and rosemary grow side by side and as you run your fingers along a spiky branch, there is an elusive aroma of camphor and pines.

Fortunately for the cooking, all is not sweetness and light. It is far from a perpetual summer. There is rain in the autumn and a great deal more in spring when it is distinctly chilly. The winter, though short, is very cold, sometimes with snow and often with frost. The land is ruled by the *mistral*, that notorious wind which blasts its way southwards down the funnel of the Rhône. It blows for three days, six days or nine days at a stretch, or so they say, lightening the heat of summer but freezing the temperature in winter and making everyone slightly mad. Villages and houses are built with their backs to the wind, facing the sun. The landscape is marked with wattle fences and tight rows of cypresses or poplars which act as wind-breaks. In summer the sun burns the *garrigue* to straw, until the heat is broken by dramatic autumn storms which can flood the vineyards and turn the village streets into streams. Overnight the grass turns green and there is a brief second spring when all the flowers come out again.

This varied climate has resulted in a varied diet, one which has evolved to suit all weathers, which makes it particularly attractive to foreign appetites. It is day-to-day cooking, food produced for the family with nothing pretentious about it, using what is in season or readily to hand and making something of it.

Some of the recipes have curious names which seem to owe little to French. This is because the south of France (which the French call the Midi) used to be quite separate from the north. It had its own language, known as *Oc* or *Occitan*, which is hardly spoken now. A few writers and poets keep it alive and country people use it as a private way of communicating, sometimes just father to son. Nearly all the regional dishes owe their names to this old language. Names like *boui-abaisso, aigo-bouido, aïoli, risto, ratatouia, broufado, cri-quette* and so on may have a slightly different spelling from their French equivalents but the root is obvious.

It is this background of flavours, climate and country traditions which makes the cooking of the region so fascinating. It is food produced with love, both to nourish and give pleasure. All we need is a little skill and imagination to produce the same sort of simple, tasty dishes that grandmothers in Provence and Languedoc have handed down to daughters and granddaughters for generations.

Garlic

Garlic bread

Croûtons with garlic

Garlic toasts

Garlic soup

Garlic butter

Garlic omelette

Baked potatoes with garlic

Sausages with garlic

Casserole of lamb from Avignon

Chicken with forty cloves of garlic

Dominique's lamb on the fire

Roast lamb with garlic sauce

Golden cream of Languedoc

Salt cod with *aïoli*

Monkfish stew with *aïoli*

Rouille

Monique's fish soup

Squid with *rouille*

Eel stew

Provence garlic is renowned for its sweet flavour and it is used in almost every dish, from just a hint to with absolute abandon. There is a belief there that the more you eat, the less you reek of it, and it is certainly true that a sliver of raw garlic has a much greater effect than eating several cloves which have been gently stewed until you can mash them with a fork.

At the beginning of May the new crop begins to appear in the market, labelled *aulx* (the plural of *ail*). As the season progresses it is on sale everywhere and the peak is reached with the garlic fairs of midsummer. If you think of buying it by the head, you are in for a big surprise. It is sold in giant bundles by the kilo, or plaited into tresses of twelve or twenty-four heads. Early garlic is attached to long, green stalks but the locals advise it is better to wait until the green is tinged with yellow.

The bulk of the crop is left to dry until the stalks turn to straw. Don't begrudge the money you spend on the stalks because they help to preserve the garlic through the winter. Bring it home and hang it in a dry place, out of too much heat and light and it will last you until the spring. You can choose from three varieties: the white and violet, which both have heads the size of golf balls, or the smaller but highly prized rose pink. They say the white will keep till after Christmas, the violet until Easter and the rose pink until May.

When buying garlic, go for firm, fat heads. Insist on feeling them and reject any that are wrinkled, bruised or discoloured or are beginning to sprout. Be wary of plaits on sale in the New Year, as these are often only useful for decorating the kitchen. If you have a well-drained, sunny garden with rich light soil, you could always grow your own. Plant individual cloves pointing upwards about 4 cm (1½ in) deep. Try an autumn as well as a spring planting. Nip off the flower heads as they appear and as the stalks become long and straggly, tie them down like daffodils after flowering. Harvest them when the leaves turn yellow, lifting each bulb gently from the ground. Remove roots and outer leaves but not the stalks. Tie the heads in bunches and hang to dry in a cool, well-ventilated place.

Garlic that is to be crushed or chopped should first be peeled. Any brown patches should be removed and in spring, when it begins to sprout, cut out the green centre which can be bitter. Crush it either in a garlic press or pestle and mortar, or by flattening it with the blade of a heavy knife.

If the cloves are to be used whole, there is no need to peel them. Once cooked, they are easy enough to eat; just press them with a fork, and the skin will split open and the soft garlic ooze out. In recipes which call for the garlic to be puréed, use a mouli-légumes, and the skins will be left behind in the grater.

The pungent flavour of garlic disappears when it is cooked, but be careful not to burn it as it turns bitter. For this reason it is often added at the end of any frying process. Herbs such as thyme, mint, basil and parsley all help to banish the smell of garlic on the breath and raw chopped garlic which is to be added at the last minute to a cooked dish is invariably mixed with parsley, a mixture known as *persillade*.

Garlic bread
Pain à l'aïllade

This method of making garlic bread uses olive oil instead of butter. The flavour is quite special and it is very quick to prepare.

French bread   olive oil
1–2 cloves garlic, crushed

Heat oven to Gas 7/425°F/220°C. Slice the bread and oil a baking sheet. Lay the bread on it in a single layer and sprinkle with the chopped garlic and olive oil. Bake for 5–10 minutes until the bread is golden.

Croûtons with garlic
Croûtons à l'ail

Croûtons are best made with day-old French bread. By then it becomes quite dry and when rubbed with garlic acts like a grater, releasing all the juices. Croûtons are used in various ways. They can be cut into cubes and added to a salad, or put into the cavity of a chicken which is to be roasted. The bread soaks up all the juices and the chicken becomes subtly flavoured with garlic. Most often croûtons are eaten with soups or fish stews. The actual pieces of bread were originally

known as *soupes* and were the inevitable accompaniment to the simple
evening meal (*souper*) of the peasant. Later the name was given to the
soup itself and even today there is a certain snobbery associated with
it. People who don't consider themselves peasants eat *potage*.

slices French bread   olive oil (optional)
1–2 cloves garlic

Cut garlic cloves in half and rub the cut side vigorously all over the
bread.

If adding to a salad either cut into cubes and turn them over and over
in the dressing before adding and tossing the salad itself; or cut into
cubes and fry in hot olive oil and add to the salad right at the last
minute.

If adding to a chicken, simply put a slice of the rubbed bread into the
bird's cavity; season with salt and pepper, sprinkle the bird with olive
oil and roast in an oven Gas 6/400°F/200°C, allowing 20 minutes per
450 g (1 lb) and 20 minutes over. Baste and turn the bird over every 20
minutes.

If eating croûtons with soup or a fish stew, the bread can either be
fried in hot olive oil until it is crisp or sprinkled with oil and put into a
hot oven (Gas 7/425°F/220°C) for 5–10 minutes until it is golden.

Garlic toasts
Rôties à l'ail

Peel 10 garlic cloves, put them into a pan and just cover with water,
bring to the boil, simmer for 5 minutes then drain. Melt 25 g (1 oz)
butter in the pan, add garlic and fry gently until soft but not coloured.
Meanwhile make 150 ml (¼ pint) of thick bechamel sauce (see Index).
Mash garlic and mix with the sauce. Spread on to slices of toast,
sprinkle with breadcrumbs and brown under a hot grill or in the oven.

Garlic soup
Aïllade languedocienne

Garlic is reputed to give you strength and this version of garlic soup is
very fortifying. It is pale, the colour of straw, tasty and satisfying. The
method appears somewhat bizarre but is quick and easy. It is
thickened with mayonnaise.

whole head garlic
6–7 tablespoons olive oil
2 eggs
1 litre (1¾ pints) water
1 teaspoon salt

freshly milled black pepper
sprigs of thyme and sage
bay leaf
French bread

Separate the garlic into cloves, peel and cut into quarters. Heat 2
tablespoons of the oil in a saucepan and cook the garlic very gently to
release its flavour. It must not brown or blacken or it will be bitter.
Take the pan off the heat. Separate the eggs, putting the yolks into a
mortar or deep bowl. Add egg whites to the pan, stirring vigorously.
They will cook and at this stage look fairly unprepossessing. Pour the
water into the pan and add salt, pepper and the herbs and bay leaf tied
together in a bunch. The egg white will form a white snow on top. Boil
uncovered over a medium heat for 15 minutes. Meanwhile, beat the
egg yolks and gradually beat in the remaining oil, at first a few drops at
a time and then a little more rapidly until you have a thick mayonnaise.
When the soup is ready, stir it a tablespoon at a time into the
mayonnaise. Once this sauce has thinned to a cream, you can pour it
directly into the soup without fear of it curdling, but don't let it boil.
Serve with fried croûtons – but don't bother to rub them with garlic.

Garlic butter
Beurre d'ail

Garlic butter can be eaten with *crudités* – raw vegetables such as
carrots, cauliflower, radishes etc. Or use it to spread on bread or to
flavour steaks. The garlic is first boiled to lose its harshness, becoming
sweet and nutty. Separate a head into cloves and put them into a pan of
boiling water. Boil until they are soft, which takes about 20 minutes.
Put them through a mouli-légumes. Season with salt and pepper and
mix with 225 g (8 oz) unsalted butter.

Garlic omelette
Omelette à l'ail

Use garlic to flavour an omelette. Allow one or two cloves per person,
peel them, crush them and soften them gently in butter without letting

them brown. Once they are transparent, add to the beaten eggs and make the omelette in the usual way.

Baked potatoes with garlic
Trufets à l'ail

When potatoes arrived in Languedoc from the New World, they gave them the same name as the truffle, because both are dug from the ground, hence the name of this dish. Then truffles were familiar to every peasant; nowadays, of course, they fetch such big money that no one can afford them. However, this garlicky recipe turns baked potatoes into a feast.

4 medium potatoes	salt
24 whole cloves garlic	freshly milled black pepper
4 tablespoons crème fraîche	4 tablespoons grated cheese

Heat oven to Gas 6/400°F/200°C and bake the potatoes in their jackets for about an hour, until they are soft. Meanwhile put the garlic cloves into a pan of salted water, bring to the boil and cook for 20–30 minutes until soft. Drain and put through a mouli-légumes. Take the potatoes out of the oven and raise the heat to Gas 7/425°F/220°C. Cut potatoes in half lengthwise and, holding them in a clean cloth, use a teaspoon to scoop the flesh into the bowl with the puréed garlic. Mix well with a fork, mash in the crème fraîche and season with salt and pepper. Fill the potato skins with the mixture. Top each with grated cheese and return to the oven to brown for 5–10 minutes.

Sausages with garlic
Saucisses à l'ail

French sausages are spicier and meatier than most on sale in Britain, although you may be lucky and have a local shop which sells them. Otherwise go for the best you can find, such as ones flavoured with herbs or any made by a good butcher.

450 g (1 lb) sausages	1 tablespoon olive oil
24 cloves garlic	freshly milled black pepper
salt	

...mmer the garlic for 20–25 minutes in salted water. Heat the oil in a heavy-based pan and brown the sausages on all sides. Drain the garlic cloves but save the water and add about a cupful of it to the sausages. Watch out as it can splutter and burn you. Season with pepper and salt, lower the heat, cover the pan and simmer for 20 minutes. Add the garlic cloves and a little more of the water if necessary and cook for a further 5 minutes.

Casserole of lamb from Avignon
Daube avignonnaise

Most *daubes* (slow-cooked casseroles) of the region are made with beef, but in this recipe from Avignon lamb is used instead. If you want to use beef, follow the same method, but use red wine instead of white and fry two or three rashers of chopped bacon with the meat.

900 g (2 lb) stewing lamb
2 large onions, sliced
2 carrots, sliced
8 cloves garlic
bay leaf
finely pared peel of 1 orange

sprigs of thyme *or* 1 teaspoon
    dried
2 cloves
6 tablespoons olive oil
600 ml (1 pint) dry white wine
salt
freshly milled black pepper

Cut lamb into chunks and put it in a large china or glass bowl or dish. Add the onions, carrots, unpeeled cloves of garlic, bay leaf, orange peel, thyme, cloves, 2 tablespoons olive oil and the wine. Leave to marinate until the next day, turning the meat over once or twice during this time.

Remove the meat from the marinade and dry it well with kitchen paper. Heat the remaining olive oil in a heavy-based pan and fry the meat on all sides until brown, in two or three batches if necessary. Transfer it to a clean casserole and keep warm. Heat the marinade with all its ingredients and pour over the meat. Add salt and pepper, cover, and simmer gently for at least 4 hours until the meat is tender.

Traditionally, these *daubes* are served with a dish of small pasta.

Chicken with forty cloves of garlic
Poulet aux quarante gousses d'ail

Forty is not a magic number – it can be thirty, or twenty or even one hundred. The garlic melts and is so sweet and soft that however many cloves, there are never enough. This recipe is best with one of those French maize-fed chickens, or one that is farm reared rather than frozen. You need a lidded ovenproof pot just large enough to hold the chicken.

1½ kg (3–3½ lb) chicken
salt
freshly milled black pepper
6 tablespoons olive oil
fresh sprigs of rosemary, thyme,
   sage, parsley

bay leaf
1 stick celery
40 cloves garlic, more or less
1 tablespoon flour

Heat the oven to Gas 5/375°F/190°C. Put salt, pepper and a sprig of thyme inside the chicken. Put the olive oil into the pot and add the herbs, celery and unpeeled cloves of garlic. Lay the chicken on top and turn it over and over so that it is coated with the herbs and oil. Mix the flour with enough water to form a thick paste. Dip your finger in it and run it all round the inside edge of the lid and put it on the pot. The paste acts as a seal, so no steam can escape and the chicken cooks in its own juices. Cook for 1½ hours. Bring the pot to the table so that the perfume of garlic and herbs is released as you unseal the lid.

At table, squash each clove flat with your fork and scrape out the juicy flesh.

Dominique's lamb on the fire

You need a shoulder of lamb, plenty of garlic and fresh thyme and a fire which is glowing hot and built with oakwood. Insert slivers of garlic into the meat and rub it well with thyme, salt and pepper. Put the lamb on a rack over the glowing wood and turn it as it cooks – at first very often because you don't want to burn the skin over the hot fire. It is done when you prick it with a knife and the blood does not run, which takes 30 minutes or a little longer. It is very simple and very good.

Roast lamb with garlic sauce
Aïado

A simple way of roasting lamb is to add a handful of whole unpeeled
garlic cloves to the roasting pan 15 minutes before the meat is cooked.
At table everyone simply mashes the cloves with their fork, squeezing
out the succulent purée. The following is more work for the cook but
worth the trouble. The garlic sauce is also delicious with simply grilled
lamb chops.

leg or shoulder of lamb   150 ml (¼ pint) dry white wine
2 heads garlic   salt, pepper
3–4 tablespoons olive oil   sprigs of rosemary or thyme
150 ml (¼ pint) water

Heat oven to Gas 6/400°F/200°C. Put the meat into a roasting tin,
pierce it with the point of a knife and insert one clove of the garlic
(there's no need to peel it). Pour over the olive oil. Roast for 20 minutes
per 450 g (1 lb) and 20 minutes over, basting every 20 minutes. Fifteen
minutes before the end of cooking time add the rosemary or thyme.
   Meanwhile, make the garlic sauce, the aïado. Put the unpeeled garlic
cloves into a saucepan over a high heat. Let them just begin to change
colour, shaking the pan constantly. Off the heat add the water and
wine; it will sizzle immediately, so take care not to burn yourself.
Season with salt and pepper. Simmer, covered, for 20–30 minutes until
the garlic is soft. Put through a mouli-légumes. Return to the pan.
When the meat is done, add a tablespoon or two of the roasting juices
to the garlic purée, reheat sauce gently and serve separately in a small
bowl.

Golden cream of Languedoc
Aïoli

This pungent sauce, known as la crème d'or in Languedoc or the
golden butter of Provence, is indeed deep gold when made in the Midi.
I can never decide if this is due to the startling yellow of egg yolks
produced by maize-fed chickens or to a trick of sunlight. It is never so
golden in England, but the flavour adds the taste of the south to all
sorts of dishes. It can be eaten with raw or cooked vegetables and adds
a fillip to an otherwise bland dish of chick peas or haricot beans. It is

delicious with baked fish, shellfish or snails and is added to fish soups to both thicken them and give them pungency.

It is important to crush the garlic first to release its oils, before working in the breadcrumbs, egg yolks and oil. Recipes which suggest adding chopped garlic to a finished mayonnaise are not the real thing. A pestle and mortar is ideal, or if you wish you can use a food processor following the method for making mayonnaise. As with any mayonnaise-type sauce, make sure all ingredients are at room temperature.

6 cloves garlic	2 egg yolks
1 tablespoon breadcrumbs	300 ml ($\frac{1}{2}$ pint) approx. olive oil

Peel the garlic, slice into slivers and pound to a paste. Mix in the breadcrumbs and egg yolks. Beat in the olive oil, at first drop by drop and then, as the mixture begins to thicken and resemble mayonnaise, add more liberally but never in a heavy stream. It is ready when it resembles a thick, creamy mayonnaise.

Salt cod with *aïoli*
Aïoli garni

Salt cod was Friday fare, and with typical ingenuity the people of the Midi transformed it into a feast. This dish, in which *aïoli* is the main feature, is perhaps the most famous. The cod is first soaked for a couple of days to rid it of its saltiness and then is gently poached and served surrounded with a garnish of vegetables, some raw, some cooked. Tiny snails and halved hard-boiled eggs complete the picture. (This recipe, along with others using salt cod, is included in *Simply Fish*.)

Monkfish stew with *aïoli*
Bourride

Bourride is a traditional fish stew, but unlike the *bouillabaisse* of Marseille is not dependent on unobtainable Mediterranean fish. It is made using almost any sort of white fish, either one kind or an assortment. Monkfish (*baudroie*, otherwise known as *lotte*) is a favourite. The fish is poached on a bed of onions or leeks and the cooking liquid is thickened at the last moment with an enriched *aïoli*.

The following recipe comes from Sète, the principal fishing port of Languedoc. Serve it with freshly boiled potatoes. Dried bitter orange peel is sold in France, but it's easy to dry your own (see Index). Failing this, use a piece of lemon peel plus a piece of fresh orange peel.

450 g (1 lb) leeks, finely sliced
1 bulb fennel, finely sliced
3 tablepoons olive oil
piece of dried orange peel
bay leaf
sprigs of thyme
700 g (1½ lb) monkfish steaks, skinned

white wine and water, to cover
salt
freshly milled black pepper
aïoli, made with 4 extra egg yolks
croûtons

Clean and slice leeks, wipe and slice fennel. Heat the olive oil in a large pan and cook the leeks and fennel for 5 minutes or so, over a medium heat, stirring from time to time. Add the orange peel, bay leaf and thyme. Lay the fish steaks on top. Cover with an equal quantity of wine and water. Add salt and pepper. Bring to the boil, lower the heat and barely simmer for about 10 minutes. Meanwhile make the *aïoli* and stir in the extra egg yolks. Carefully remove the fish and vegetables to a warm serving dish. Strain the stock and stir a little into the *aïoli* a spoonful at a time. When the sauce has become quite liquid, stir all of it into the stock. Put back on to a low heat and stir until it becomes thick and creamy and coats the back of the spoon. It must not boil or it will curdle. Serve the liquid in a soup tureen at the same time as the fish. Shallow soup plates are ideal, as everyone helps themselves to the soup, fish and potatoes, and the whole is mopped up with the croûtons.

Rouille

Rouille is a spicy version of *aïoli* and is principally used to give fire to fish soups. The following recipe is the modern version. In the old days stale bread soaked in water was usually used in place of eggs, and at the end of the cooking time some of the potatoes from the soup were crushed and added to the sauce. As with any mayonnaise-type sauce, make sure all ingredients are at room temperature. Use a pestle and mortar or, if you prefer, a food processor.

8 cloves garlic

2 red chillies *or* 1 teaspoon
cayenne or hot chilli powder

1–2 egg yolks

300 ml (½ pint) approx. olive oil

Peel garlic, cut into slivers and crush with the chillies. Stir in the egg
yolks and begin to beat in the olive oil, drop by drop. As the mixture
thickens, add the olive oil more rapidly, beating well all the time, until
you have a thick mayonnaise-type sauce.

Monique's fish soup
Soupe de poisson

Fish soup eaten with *rouille*, grated cheese and croûtons of bread is so
filling that you need only the lightest of main courses to follow. Make
it ahead of time. The preparation is straightforward but the sieving is a
messy process, best done when you are not being harassed by hungry
mouths. On the market stalls in France you will come across piles of
small fish labelled *soupe de poisson*, and fishmongers in Britain often
sell fish heads and inexpensive pieces for soup. Choose white fish –
nothing oily like mackerel or herring. Serve the soup with one bowl of
grated cheese (mature Cheddar does well), another of *rouille* and
plenty of croûtons.

2 tablespoons olive oil

2 leeks, sliced

2 onions, chopped

1 can chopped Italian tomatoes

700 g (1½ lb) fish pieces

2 fish heads

350 g (12 oz) potatoes, peeled
and quartered

1 clove garlic, crushed

bay leaf

piece of dried orange peel

sprig of fennel *or* 1 teaspoon
seeds

salt

freshly milled black pepper

few strands saffron *or* ½ teaspoon powder

grated cheese

croûtons

rouille

Heat oil in a large saucepan and cook the leeks and onions for several
minutes over a medium heat, stirring from time to time. Add the
tomatoes, fish pieces and heads and cook a few more minutes, then
add potatoes, garlic, bay leaf, orange peel, fennel, salt, pepper and
saffron. Cook briskly for 20 minutes until potatoes are soft. The soup
must then be sieved twice – once to break up as much of the fish as

possible, and again with all the bones discarded so that it becomes
creamy and smooth. You can use a mouli-légumes, or a sieve over a
bowl with a wooden spoon. Instead of the second sieving, a food
processor or liquidizer can be used.

There are no rules about how to eat the *rouille* with the soup. Some
people just put a spoonful of it into the bowl, while others spread it
first on to the croûtons.

Squid with *rouille*
Rouille de calmars

Squid (or cuttlefish, *seiches*, if you can get them) are delicious with
rouille. You need 700 g (1½ lb), cleaned and cut in rings (see Index for
how to prepare them). Put them into a pan, cover with water, add salt,
a chopped onion, a couple of crushed cloves of garlic, thyme, a bay
leaf, parsley and a generous sprinkling of freshly milled black pepper.
Bring to the boil and simmer for an hour. Add a spoonful of the liquid
to the *rouille*. Lift out the fish using a slotted spoon, put it in a warm
serving dish, stir in the *rouille* and eat with croûtons which have been
baked in the oven.

Eel stew
Catigot d'anguilles

From the Camargue comes this dish of freshwater eels, a cross between
a stew and a soup. Like *bouillabaisse* it must be fiercely boiled to mix
the oil and water. Eels are sold live and as killing and skinning them
can be a gruesome task, ask the fishmonger to do it for you and cut
them into pieces about 8 cm (3 in) long.

8 tablespoons olive oil	700 g (1½ lb) eel(s), skinned and
2 onions, chopped	cut into chunks
1 can chopped Italian tomatoes	salt
sprig of celery	freshly milled black pepper
bay leaf and thyme	300 ml (½ pint) red wine
1 red chilli *or* ½ teaspoon chilli	300 ml (½ pint) water
powder	French bread croûtons fried in
6 cloves garlic	oil

Heat the oil in a large heavy pot, add the chopped onions and let them brown over a high heat. Add tomatoes, celery, bay leaf, thyme, chilli, garlic and pieces of eel. Cook over a medium heat for 5 minutes, stirring from time to time. Add salt and pepper. Heat wine and water to boiling point in another pan and pour into the pot. Leave to boil for 20 minutes to reduce the liquid, and serve with the croûtons.

Thyme and savory

Chicken liver salad with thyme

Artichokes with thyme

Leek and potato soup with thyme

Potato gratin with thyme

Chicken with thyme and garlic

Potatoes with pork and thyme

Roast kid

Madame Boeuf's thyme liqueur

Broad beans with savory

Rabbit with savory

Thyme is the most widely used of all the herbs both on its own and sharing a place with parsley and bay leaf in a *bouquet garni*, the bunch of herbs which is a part of all French cooking. Wild thyme (*farigoule*) has a flavour very like our own garden thyme and is to be found in every sort of dish from soups to casseroles, sprinkled over grills and rubbed into joints of lamb for roasting. It can be dusted over cooked vegetables and crushed into salad dressings. But always use thyme with discretion, the flavour must never overpower. Dried thyme especially must be used with care.

Thyme, like parsley, basil and mint, acts as a mild antidote to the strong effect of garlic. The essential oil is used as a component in toothpastes and mouthwashes. It is used in herbal remedies as an antiseptic and digestive and is reputed to cure a stiff neck if dried in a pan, then wrapped in gauze and applied to the sore spot.

Savory (*sarriette*) is nicknamed donkey's pepper, *pèbre d'ai*, in the Occitan language – perhaps because it made grazing donkeys sneeze. This is summer savory, milder and less bitter than the related winter savory which sometimes gives an unpleasant flavour to dishes. Savory is used with meat, fish and poultry, in egg dishes and with vegetables and dried beans. It can also be used in recipes instead of thyme.

Both savory and thyme are easy to grow from seed, and thyme can be increased by separating established plants. Summer savory is an annual, but once planted in the garden will seed itself, thus ensuring a supply year after year. They both like a sunny spot and prefer a chalky soil. They dry beautifully or they can be frozen. Dry the stalks, spread out in wooden trays in the sun, bringing them in at night. If there is no sun, hang them in bunches from the ceiling, stalks uppermost, or put them in the airing cupboard. Once dry, it is easy to pull the leaves from the stalks and store in airtight jars. If you are buying them dried, remember the well-worn but good advice to buy only small quantities because they lose their scent and flavour over a few months.

Chicken liver salad with thyme
Salade aux foies de volaille au thym

In the past this first-course salad was most often made with pork liver, but nowadays you are more likely to come across this version. It is served at La Sarrasine in the village of Aiguèze which is the last bastion between Gard and the Ardèche. We were with our wine-grower friends, Emile and Henri, and while they piled our plates high, they discussed how to make it. The next time they came to lunch, we tried it out. Emile insisted on helping by mixing the hot livers with the salad. We all agreed later this was a mistake because it cooked the salad. Somehow I was to blame – Emile had forgotten his part.

225 g (8 oz) chicken livers	salt
1 tablespoon flour	freshly milled black pepper
Cos or lamb's lettuce	25 g (1 oz) butter
1 teaspoon mustard	1 tablespoon brandy
1 tablespoon vinegar	1 clove garlic, chopped
6 tablespoons olive oil	thyme

If livers are frozen, defrost, drain and wipe with kitchen paper. Cut into bite-sized pieces and put them in a paper bag with the flour. Shake to coat the pieces evenly. Wash and dry the lettuce. Mix the mustard and vinegar in a salad bowl, add 5 tablespoons olive oil, salt and pepper. Put the lettuce on top. Heat the butter with remaining tablespoon of oil, add livers and toss over a medium heat until they are brown all over. Heat brandy in a ladle and when it lights, pour over the livers. When flames die down, add garlic and thyme. Toss the lettuce, pile livers on top and serve at once with plenty of French bread.

Artichokes with thyme
Artichauts en barigoule

Bouquets of small, violet artichokes with sharp, barbed leaves are on sale in the markets in the early spring, their stalks (which are tender enough to eat) secured with an elastic band. These young artichokes can simply be grilled by liberally brushing them with olive oil and flavouring them with thyme, salt and pepper. Or they can be eaten raw with *anchoïade* (see Index), or *à la poivrade* (with olive oil and lashings of black pepper). They are found in omelettes or *salade niçoise* or as part of a *pan bagnat* (see Index for recipes). Do buy them in France if you have the chance, as they are rarely found in England. I have followed this Provençal method successfully using the large, globe Breton artichokes. Variations of this recipe appear in all the region's cookery books – its name is a mystery as some recipes feature *barigoule*, the local name for a wild mushroom, the *lactaire délicieux*, but in others there's not a whiff of it. I suppose it is one of those recipes from which you add or subtract what is to hand.

8 violet *or* 4 Breton artichokes	several sprigs of thyme
juice of ½ lemon	6 tablespoons olive oil
2 onions, sliced	150 ml (¼ pint) dry white wine
2 carrots, sliced	150 ml (¼ pint) water
2 cloves garlic, crushed	salt
2 rashers streaky bacon, chopped	freshly milled black pepper

Break off the stems of each artichoke (breaking rather than cutting pulls out the inedible fibres from inside the heart). Put each artichoke into a bowl of water and add the lemon juice. This prevents them from going black as well as coaxing out any insects. Choose a pan large enough to stand the artichokes upright in one layer and in it make a bed of the onions, carrots, garlic, bacon and thyme. Put in the artichokes, moisten them with the oil, pour over the wine and water and season with salt and pepper. Bring to the boil, cover, lower the heat and simmer gently for 1½–2 hours. They can be eaten hot or cold. Serve surrounded by the sauce which has formed from the other vegetables.

Leek and potato soup with thyme
Porrosalda

This pale green leek soup differs from the well-known *vichyssoise* because it is not puréed but cooked long enough for the potatoes to melt and thicken the broth. It is flavoured with bacon and thyme.

 spoons olive oil
(4 oz) streaky bacon,
  opped
7 0 g (1½ lb) leeks
450 g (1 lb) potatoes
1 heaped tablespoon flour
1 litre (1¾ pints) water

1 clove garlic, chopped
salt
pinch of nutmeg
freshly milled black pepper
2–3 sprigs of thyme
4 tablespoons grated cheese

Heat the oil in a large saucepan and fry the bacon until it begins to colour. Wash the leeks well under running water, discard most of the green tops and slice finely. Add to the pan. Mix well. Peel and cut the potatoes into small dice. Add them to the pan, cover and allow the vegetables to sweat over a medium heat for about 10 minutes. Remove lid, stir well and sprinkle in the flour. Cook for a couple of minutes, stirring all the time. Pour over the water, bring to the boil and add garlic, salt, nutmeg, pepper and the thyme. Simmer, covered, for 30–40 minutes until the leeks and potatoes are soft and mushy. Serve sprinkled with grated cheese.

Potato gratin with thyme
Gratin aux pommes de terre au thym

This gratin is quick to prepare. Peel and slice the potatoes and put them straight into the frying pan as you go, as soaking them will release too much of their starch. Cut them as finely as you can with a sharp knife. A food processor saves time, but I find it makes them turn grey and watery and stick to the pan.

3–4 tablespoons olive oil
700 g (1½ lb) potatoes
bay leaf
2–3 sprigs of thyme

300 ml (½ pint) hot water
salt
freshly milled black pepper

Heat oven to Gas 5/375°F/190°C. Put oil into a flameproof gratin dish or frying pan, and add the potatoes as you prepare them. Fry over a medium heat, stirring the slices about from time to time. When all the potatoes are in the pan, cook until they begin to turn transparent and golden. Add the bay leaf and thyme, and pour over the hot water – it splutters so take care it doesn't burn you. Season with salt and pepper.

If you are using a frying pan, transfer the contents into a gratin dish at this point. Put into the oven for 45–60 minutes.

Chicken with thyme and garlic
Poulet au thym et à l'ail

This dish from Languedoc takes only minutes to prepare and is ready in less than an hour. It comes swimming in a pale, winey sauce flavoured with the subtle blend of thyme and garlic. In Provence they would add a few skinned, chopped and de-seeded tomatoes, and perhaps throw in a handful of olives at the end. Use a free-range or maize-fed chicken if you can.

1½ kg (3–3½ lb) chicken, cut into
  8 pieces
2 tablespoons olive oil
8 cloves of garlic

several sprigs of fresh thyme
salt, pepper
150 ml (¼ pint) dry white wine

Skin the chicken pieces. Heat the oil in a wide pan and brown them on all sides, in two batches if necessary. Add the unpeeled cloves of garlic, the thyme, a good pinch of salt, plenty of freshly milled black pepper and the white wine. Bring to the boil, lower heat and simmer, covered, for 30–40 minutes. Remove the chicken to a warm dish. Boil the sauce vigorously to reduce, pour over the chicken and serve.

Potatoes with pork and thyme
Bombine

This dish, which comes from the Ardèche, like many traditional recipes depends on the individual cook for its interpretation. When times are lean, the chops are omitted and only the bacon used. At other times mushrooms might be added, or tomatoes and olives. You could use the same recipe with lamb chops instead of pork.

2 tablespoons olive oil
4 lean pork chops or boned
  escalopes
2 onions, chopped
700 g (1½ lb) potatoes
several sprigs of thyme
bay leaf

2 cloves garlic
salt
freshly milled black pepper
8 rashers unsmoked streaky
  bacon
150 ml (¼ pt) white wine

Heat oven to Gas 6/400°F/200°C. Heat the olive oil in a heavy-based casserole and brown the meat on both sides, in two batches if necessary. Remove to a plate. Fry the chopped onions for a few minutes. Peel and finely slice the potatoes. Cover the base of a large gratin dish with half the sliced potatoes and half the fried onions. Lay the chops on top. Add thyme, bay leaf, garlic (leave whole and unpeeled) and season with salt and pepper. Cover with the remaining potatoes and onion, and season again with salt and pepper. Lay the bacon rashers on top and pour on the wine. Top up with water so ingredients are barely covered. Bake for 1 hour until potatoes are soft.

Roast kid
Chevreau rôti

The meat of an adult goat is tough and stringy, but kid, known as *broutard* or *cabri* in Occitan, is sweet and tender, and with the increased production of goat cheeses it is becoming more widely available in Britain. You can find it in ethnic shops or markets, in specialist butchers or the food halls of large department stores. It can be cooked like lamb, and in fact the head of both is considered a feast in Provence and Languedoc. (The head is split in two and placed in a roasting tin, care being taken not to damage the tongue and brains. It is then roasted in the oven, seasoned with salt, pepper, chopped garlic and parsley and liberally sprinkled with olive oil.) Whole kid are spit-roasted and sprinkled towards the end of cooking with thyme, savory and bay. Or try this recipe for a leg – you can substitute sprigs of rosemary for the thyme and savory, if you prefer.

leg of kid	6 tablespoons white wine
4 cloves garlic	salt
6–8 tablespoons olive oil	freshly milled black pepper
several sprigs of thyme and	juice of 1 lemon
savory	chopped parsley

Heat oven to Gas 6/400°F/200°C. Slice one clove of garlic finely. Make small incisions in the leg and insert one sliver in each. Put into a roasting tin and sprinkle with a little oil. In a small bowl mix the thyme and savory with remaining oil, wine and 2 crushed cloves of garlic. Roast the leg for 15 minutes, season it with salt and pepper and baste with the mixture of oil and wine. Roast for 15 minutes per 450 g (1 lb) with 15 minutes over if you like pink meat, 20 minutes for well done. Baste every 15 minutes with the oil and wine mixture. Remove the leg from the oven, put on a serving dish, squeeze over the lemon juice and dust with the remaining garlic (finely chopped) and the parsley.

Madame Boeuf's thyme liqueur
Riquiqui or *la farigouleto*

After an enormous *bouillabaisse* cooked by Grandmother Boeuf she poured us some of her special *riquiqui* as a *digestif*. For several years afterwards, she always sent a bottle to us as a present, and then when she was around ninety, she decided she would give me the recipe. When I'm in St Paulet in May, I pick the flower heads from the thyme growing in the courtyard and steep them in eau-de-vie. I have made it in England, too, from our softer but strongly flavoured garden thyme, using vodka as the alcohol. It is very soothing after a rich meal, and so far has never given us a hangover. The alternative name stems from the Provençal word for wild thyme. Follow the same method to make liqueurs from the leaves and flowers of sage, myrtle, verbena or St John's wort.

80+ thyme flower heads   1 litre (1¾ pints) eau-de-vie or
80 sugar lumps   vodka

Pick the flowers when they are dry on a sunny day, never after rain. Put them into a 1 litre (2 lb) preserving jar. There must be enough to fill it completely. Add the sugar lumps which will compress the flowers. Pour in sufficient eau-de-vie or vodka to come right to the top. Seal and leave for at least two months. The sugar gradually dissolves and the liquid turns a pale gold. Strain and pour into a bottle. Leave for two or three months to age.

Broad beans with savory
Fèves fraîches à la sarriette

Simmer shelled broad beans for 10–15 minutes in water flavoured with several sprigs of savory. Drain them, return to the pan with 2 tablespoons olive oil. Add a ladleful of water and heat through, then take off the heat and quickly stir in an egg yolk or two to thicken the sauce.

Rabbit with savory
Lapin au pèbre d'ai

In this dish a jointed rabbit is cooked on a bed of onion flavoured with savory. The liver, which is considered (and is indeed) a delicacy, is added at the last moment.

3 tablespoons olive oil
1 rabbit, cut into 8 pieces, plus the liver
4 onions, chopped
300 ml (½ pint) dry white wine

1 tablespoon white wine vinegar
6–8 cloves garlic
salt, pepper
3 or 4 sprigs savory

Heat 2 tablespoons of the oil in a heavy-based pan and brown the pieces of rabbit over a high heat, in two batches if necessary. Remove and keep warm. Add the remaining oil and the onions to the pan and let them brown, stirring them so they do not stick. Return the rabbit pieces to the pan, add wine, vinegar, whole garlic cloves, salt, pepper and the savory. Bring to the boil, reduce heat, cover and simmer for 1¼ hours. Add the liver and cook for 5 minutes more.

Rosemary and sage

Courgettes with rosemary

Pork with rosemary and aubergines

Spring chicken grilled with rosemary

Rosemary and herb teas

Partridge with rosemary

Pork in milk with sage

Quail with sage

Life-saving soup with sage

As a herbal remedy rosemary is said to counteract rheumatism, so perhaps that is why, when steeped in eau-de-vie, it gained a reputation as an elixir of youth. The ladies of the court of Louis XIV were mad about it. The story went that in the fourteenth century, Elisabeth of Poland drank it so that she could seduce the King of Hungary and become his queen. It was much more romantic to believe that an arthritic old lady could turn herself into a young girl than that the king had married her simply for gain.

If you can find a sunny spot, sheltered from the wind, rosemary is easy to grow and can be propagated in the autumn by breaking off ripened shoots and planting them straight in the ground. The leaves are spiky so for cooking whole sprigs are usually used which can be removed at the end of cooking time. If you cannot get fresh rosemary, use dried but with discretion because the dried leaves are especially pungent and needle sharp. Fortunately it is an evergreen.

Rosemary is ideal in a marinade for lamb, pork or fish. Put chops or fish steaks in a glass or china dish, add sprigs of rosemary, a tablespoon or two of olive oil, a squeeze of lemon juice and some freshly milled black pepper and leave for an hour or two. Trout is delicious grilled with sprigs of rosemary in the cavity.

Sage, with its pale, grey leaves and violet-blue flowers thrives well in chalky soils, attracting all sorts of insects including bees. A bunch of the leaves can be dried at the end of summer to be used during the coming months. The Romans credited it with health-giving properties and an old superstition has it that if you grow sage in your garden, you will never die. Really it is the sage which in a sense never dies because it is propagated by taking cuttings.

The flavour of sage can be musty and quite overbearing so it is used sparingly, giving a subtlety to pork and small game birds such as quail. The flowers and leaves can also be used to make a soothing *digestif*, made like the version given for thyme (see Index).

Courgettes with rosemary
Flan de courgettes au romarin

This simple *flan*, similar to a quiche but minus the pastry, is a favourite at many of the local restaurants, either as a starter or as a vegetable course.

700 g (1½ lb) courgettes   salt
1 tablespoon olive oil   freshly milled black pepper
sprig of rosemary   pinch of nutmeg
1 egg, beaten   4 tablespoons grated cheese
4 tablespoons crème fraîche

Slice the courgettes very thinly. Put them and the olive oil into a saucepan, top with the rosemary and put over a high heat until they begin to sizzle. Lower the heat, cover and simmer for about 30 minutes until soft. Drain in a colander and discard the rosemary. Heat oven to Gas 6/400°F/200°C. Put courgettes into a gratin dish, mix in the beaten egg and crème fraîche, season with salt, pepper and nutmeg and top with the grated cheese. Bake for 25–35 minutes.

Pork with rosemary and aubergines
Porc au romarin et aux aubergines

A spectacular looking dish of pork and sliced aubergines with an orange coloured topping, simple to do but good enough for a dinner party. The rosemary flavours the meat deliciously and the aubergines melt to a sweet purée.

4 lean pork chops or escalopes   groundnut oil for frying
2 tablespoons olive oil   2 eggs
4 sprigs of rosemary   2–3 tablespoons water
freshly milled black pepper   1 tablespoon tomato purée
700 g (1½ lb) aubergines   50 g (2 oz) grated cheese
salt

Marinate the chops for an hour or two with the olive oil, rosemary and a generous seasoning of black pepper. Peel and cut the aubergines into thin slices lengthwise, sprinkle them with salt and leave for an hour. Dry with kitchen paper. Pour enough groundnut oil into a frying pan to cover the base generously. Heat and fry the aubergine slices over a high heat until golden on both sides. They will need to be done in several batches, adding more oil if necessary. As you cook them drain them on a plate interleaved with pieces of kitchen paper and keep warm. Heat oven to Gas 6/400°F/200°C. Fry the pork chops in the same pan, pouring over the marinade, lowering the heat a little and cooking them for 8–10 minutes on each side, until they are cooked through. Test with the point of a knife – the juice should be golden and not pink. Lay the chops in a gratin dish, cover with aubergine slices, and season with salt and pepper. Beat the eggs with the water and tomato purée, season with salt and pepper and pour over chops and aubergines. Sprinkle with the cheese and bake for 10–15 minutes until the top is golden.

Spring chicken grilled with rosemary
Poussin grillée au romarin

Allow 1 spring chicken for two people. Cut in half lengthwise and flatten slightly by beating it with a wooden spatula. Moisten with olive oil, season with salt and pepper. Heat the grill for 5 minutes. Oil the grid and grill the chicken on the middle rung for 20–30 minutes. Turn every 5 minutes and halfway through the cooking time put a sprig of rosemary on each piece. The chicken is done when pierced with a skewer and the juices run clear, not pink.

Rosemary and herb teas
Tisanes

Teapots are not a feature of southern France, so their recipes for herb teas, *tisanes*, tell you to put sprigs of herbs in a saucepan with water, bring to the boil and simmer for 10–15 minutes. It is easier to make them using our time-tested method for making ordinary tea. Apart from rosemary, other herbs to use include the flowers of thyme, lime (*tilleul*), camomile, verbena or St John's wort, or leaves of thyme, mint, sage (fresh or dried), or fennel seeds, rosehips or lavender seeds.

Warm a teapot, add the herbs (a sprig of flowers or leaves, or a teaspoon of seeds per cup), top with boiling water and leave to infuse. Sweeten with a little honey or sharpen with a slice of lemon.

Partridge with rosemary
Perdreaux au romarin

This is an old Provençal recipe. The birds are plucked and drawn and a sprig of rosemary put inside each cavity. They are then wrapped in bacon and sautéed in olive oil with chopped onion, more rosemary and sprigs of thyme. Once browned on all sides, a glass of rosé wine is added and the birds are simmered gently for a further 15 minutes. They are served on a dish surrounded by the sauce, which is reduced by fast boiling and then strained.

Pork in milk with sage
Porc au lait et à la sauge

A joint of pork, delicately flavoured with sage, is succulent and tender cooked this way in milk.

1½ kilo (3–3½ lb) rolled joint of pork	salt
6 sage leaves	freshly milled black pepper
2 tablespoons olive oil	450 ml (¾ pint) milk
4 onions, chopped	½ teaspoon paprika

Make incisions at intervals in the pork with the point of a knife and insert a sage leaf in each. Heat the olive oil in a heavy-based pan and brown the meat all over. Add the chopped onions and continue to cook until they are golden. Season with salt and pepper. Pour over the milk, and bring to the boil. Lower the heat, add the paprika and cover the pan. Simmer very gently for about an hour until the meat is cooked. Test with the point of a skewer: the juice should run yellow, not pink.

Quail with sage
Cailles à la cévenole

One summer evening we went with Jean Sahli, a Swiss who had come to France to paint, to a restaurant in Le Garn run by a farmer's wife. High in the hills above the Ardèche gorge, we went through a courtyard where row upon row of boars' trotters were nailed to a wall and hunting dogs panted behind bars. Madame Raoux cooked a wonderful dish of pancakes flavoured with truffles and then produced quail, plump little birds, their sad heads tucked under. Jean laughed at my squeamishness. He chopped off and crunched the head with gusto, declaring it was the best bit. In England quail are usually sold headless and I feel more comfortable though a bit hypocritical because they are delicious and quick to prepare. Quail are very meaty and one bird is sufficient per person but they are moreish and few people will refuse the chance of being offered two.

4–8 quail	8 cloves garlic, unpeeled
8–16 sage leaves	salt
8–16 rashers streaky bacon	pepper
25–50 g (1–2 oz) butter	3 tablespoons dry white wine
2 tablespoons olive oil	

Put one sage leaf inside each quail, the other on the breast and wrap each bird securely in two strips of bacon, stretching it slightly so it clings firmly. Secure with string or cotton. Melt the butter with the oil in a heavy-based pan, brown the birds all over, add the whole garlic cloves, salt, pepper and wine, put on the lid and cook very gently for 25–30 minutes, when the birds will be done. Cut and remove the string before serving on a platter with the garlic and the cooking juices poured over.

Life-saving soup with sage
Aigo bouido

Versions of this soup appear in every cookery book of the region, always quoting the pithy saying *l'aigo bouido sauvo la vido* (which roughly means 'the life-saving boiling water'). Boiling water maybe, but it is the sage with its health-giving properties, not to mention the garlic, which restores even the most fragile stomach after a night on the tiles. Some people add a bay leaf and thyme and thicken it with egg yolks, or it becomes the boiled water of the rich, by adding grated cheese and spoonfuls of mayonnaise at table. It is very good indeed.

1 whole head garlic	salt
1 litre (1¾ pints) water	4 slices French bread sprinkled
4 sprigs of sage	with olive oil
2 tablespoons olive oil	

Separate the garlic into cloves, peel them and crush them lightly. Put into a saucepan with the water, sage, olive oil and salt, bring to the boil and simmer briskly for 15 minutes. Heat the grill and lightly toast the bread sprinkled with olive oil. Put a slice into each bowl. Remove the sprigs of sage and pour the soup over the bread.

Fennel, anise and mint

Mussels with *pastis*

Lord Clive's original mincemeat pies

Mackerel with fennel

Cuttlefish salad with fennel

Nectar of the gods

Courgettes and tomatoes with fennel

Fish stew with fennel

Beef stewed with fennel

Melon with apple mint and honey sauce

Almond spread with mint and anchovies

The flavours of fennel (*fenouil*) and anise (*anis*) are sometimes difficult to distinguish, as both have a scent akin to liquorice. Fennel is often used to flavour fish, most famously in the recipe for grilled sea bass which is cooked over a bed of dried fennel stalks and vine shoots, and the seeds or feathery leaves feature in many fish stews and soups as well as giving a subtle flavour to green olives. Florentine fennel is the bulb-like stalk base of a related plant and is used raw in salads with lemon juice and olive oil, or cooked as a vegetable, quartered and blanched for a few minutes before being fried in olive oil and seasoned with salt and pepper. It is often one of the vegetable ingredients of fish or meat stews.

Fennel, which can be grown from seed, dries well. Hang the leafy stalks upside down and use sprigs as required. Anise is principally used as an essential component of the famous aperitif *pastis*, a glass of which, mixed in the ratio of one to five of water, is perhaps the most evocative reminder of the golden evenings of a Provence summer.

Spearmint, which is our garden mint, thrives in damp climates and plays little part in the local cooking. But apple mint, with its round, downy leaves, was first used by the Romans to make mint sauce and does appear in an occasional dish. It makes a soothing tea, infused in the same way as rosemary (see Index).

Mussels with *pastis*
Moules au pastis

In this recipe the mussels are first steamed open and then stuffed with crème fraîche flavoured with garlic and *pastis*. (If you like you can put the cooked mussels into snail dishes which can be bought from specialist kitchen shops.) *Pastis* is aniseed-based with a strong and powerful flavour, and apart from being drunk as an aperitif, it is wonderfully handy in the kitchen as a flavouring for fish dishes. If you haven't any *pastis*, add a teaspoon of crushed anise or fennel seeds.

1 kg (2 lb/1 quart) mussels   handful chopped parsley
1 tablespoon flour or bran   1 tablespoon *pastis*
225 g (8 oz) crème fraîche   freshly milled black pepper
4 cloves garlic, chopped   6 tablespoons breadcrumbs

Wash mussels in several changes of water, scrub them and use a knife to break off the barnacles, and pull out the beards. Discard any that are open and won't close if tapped sharply – these are dead. Leave them to soak for an hour or two in water with a tablespoon of flour or bran. As they open to feed, they release any lurking grit or sand. Heat oven to Gas 7/425°F/220°C. Put mussels into a saucepan over high heat until they open. Drain off liquid they will have exuded and pull off one shell from each. Mix all the other ingredients. Fill each mussel with the mixture and put into gratin dishes. Bake for 10 minutes, until hot and bubbling. Bring to the table with plenty of bread to mop up the juices.

Lord Clive's original mincemeat pies
Petits pâtés

Legend has it that these small pies were created in the eighteenth century for Lord Clive of India when he visited the south of France. Several towns have their own versions; some with mutton, others with beef; some sweetened with raisins, others with citrus peel. As their origin is English, I felt free to adapt the recipe to suit myself, and add a dash of *pastis* just to remind me of Provence. You could use brandy instead. These amounts will be sufficient for 12 pies.

225 g (8 oz) puff pastry   1 tablespoon mixed peel
75 g (3 oz) minced lamb or beef   1 tablespoon soft brown sugar
25 g (1 oz) suet   1 tablespoon *pastis*
1 tablespoon raisins   1 egg yolk, beaten

If using frozen puff pastry, let it thaw. Heat oven to Gas 7/425°F/ 220°C. Roll out the pastry and cut out 12 bases and 12 slightly smaller lids, using pastry cutters or two glasses. (The first rolling won't yield enough, so gather up the bits and roll out again.) Mix all the other ingredients except the egg in a bowl. Line a tray of individual tart tins with the bases, fill each with a heaped teaspoon of the mixture, dampen the edges of the pastry lids with water and cover the pies. Seal the edges by marking all round with the prongs of a fork. Cut a small slit in each pie for the steam to escape, brush with the beaten egg, using a pastry brush or simply your fingers and bake in the oven for 15–20 minutes until pastry is crisp and turning golden. Eat hot.

Mackerel with fennel
Macquereaux au fenouil

In this recipe the mackerel are left overnight in the *court bouillon* in which they are poached and are then served cold.

4 mackerel	2 teaspoons fennel seeds
salt	freshly milled black pepper
2 onions, sliced	300 ml (½ pint) white wine
2 carrots, sliced	vinegar
4 slices lemon	

Ask your fishmonger to clean and gut the fish for you. Put them in a shallow dish and salt them lightly. Leave for an hour or two, then wipe dry with kitchen paper. In a wide, shallow pan make a bed of onion and carrot, lay fish on top, put a slice of lemon on each, add the fennel seeds, season with black pepper, add the vinegar and just cover with water. Bring gently to the boil. As soon as the first bubble appears, remove the pan from the heat. Allow the fish to cool in the liquid. Transfer to the fridge and leave until the next day. Carefully remove the fish to a serving plate.

Cuttlefish salad with fennel
Salade de suppion

Suppion, tiny cuttlefish, are sold already cleaned in French markets or at fish counters. They can be rolled in flour and deep-fried like whitebait or make a delicious fish starter flavoured with fennel. In this recipe you can use squid if you can't get cuttlefish. Buy about 700 g (1½ lb). Clean them (see Index), cut in rings and gently poach them for 20 minutes or so in water flavoured with white wine, a bay leaf, parsley, black peppercorns and fennel seeds. Drain well, season with plenty of black pepper and lemon juice. Serve cold, sprinkled with olive oil, chopped garlic and parsley.

Nectar of the gods
Nectar des dieux

This is reputed to be an elixir of long life. Whether or not this is so, it makes a splendid aperitif. Vanilla pods may seem expensive, but after use, they can be rinsed, dried and used again. Follow the age-old rule and store them in a jar of caster sugar, thus scenting the sugar beautifully.

300 ml (½ pint) eau-de-vie or
   vodka
2 tablespoons coriander seeds
1 tablespoon aniseed
1 whole clove

1 stick cinnamon
150 g (6 oz) caster sugar
150 ml (¼ pint) water
vanilla pod
300 ml (½ pint) dry white wine

Pour the eau-de-vie or vodka into a preserving jar, add the coriander, aniseed, clove and cinnamon. Seal and leave for 30 days. At the end of this time, dissolve the sugar in the water with the vanilla pod and simmer gently for 5 minutes. Leave to cool, remove vanilla pod. Add this syrup and the white wine to the alcohol. Strain and bottle. Leave to age for two or three months.

Courgettes and tomatoes with fennel
Tian de courgettes et tomates au fenouil

Tian is the Provençal name for a shallow, earthenware gratin dish. In the days when an open fire was the only source of heat, the tian would find its way to the baker's oven to be cooked. Vegetable tians taste good whether hot or cold and no one ever tires of them. There's a story of four friends going on a picnic, each brought a special dish to try to outdo the others and all four arrived with a tian.

4 tablespoons olive oil
1 onion, chopped
450 g (1 lb) courgettes, sliced
450 g (1 lb) tomatoes, skinned
   and sliced or 1 can chopped
   Italian tomatoes
salt

freshly milled black pepper
1 clove garlic, chopped
2 sprigs of fennel or 1 teaspoon
   seeds
4 tablespoons grated cheese
4 tablespoons breadcrumbs

Heat oven to Gas 5/375°F/190°C. Heat 1 tablespoon of the oil in a frying pan, add the onion and cook for several minutes over a medium heat until it is soft. Spread it over the base of a gratin dish. Top with half the courgettes and half the tomatoes, season with salt, pepper, garlic and fennel. Cover with remaining courgettes and tomatoes, season again with salt, pepper, garlic and fennel. Sprinkle over 2 tablespoons of oil. Top with grated cheese and breadcrumbs and sprinkle over the remaining tablespoon of oil. Bake for 30 minutes.

Fish stew with fennel
Pot au feu de poissons

This fish stew can be made without those anxieties that affect most of us when trying to come up with an authentic *bouillabaisse* (the recipe for which is given in *Simply Fish*). I have suggested using readily obtainable kinds of fish but you can make it more exotic by including a couple of red mullet and some black sea bream. It is robust and filling and a marvel on a cold evening.

450 g (1 lb/1 pint) mussels
1 tablespoon flour or bran
2 tablespoons olive oil
2 fish heads
450 g (1 lb) fish pieces, plus 1 kg (2¼ lb) assorted white fish such as haddock, cod, coley, hake, dogfish etc.
1 large onion, chopped
4 carrots, sliced
1 teaspoon fennel seeds

450 g (1 lb) leeks, sliced
1½ litres (2½ pints) water
1 teaspoon salt
freshly milled black pepper
1 bulb fennel, sliced
1 can chopped Italian tomatoes
700 g (1½ lb) potatoes, quartered
croûtons
rouille (see Index)

Prepare mussels as in recipe for Mussels with *pastis* (see Index) and leave them soaking in water with the flour or bran. Heat the oil in a large pan, put in the fish heads and fish pieces (the rest of the fish is added later), the onion, 1 sliced carrot, fennel seeds, and the green part of the leeks. Add water, salt and a generous amount of pepper. Bring to the boil and simmer for 15 minutes. Strain the liquid into another pan using a sieve or mouli-légumes to crush the cooked fish and vegetables and extract the bones. Bring to the boil and add the white parts of the leeks, remaining carrots, fennel bulb, tomatoes, potatoes and more

ling, simmer for 15 minutes. Add the fish, simmer for a further
5 minutes. Five minutes before the stew is ready, put the mussels
a pan, set them on a high heat to cook and open. Remove fish and
put on a warmed platter. Drain the mussels and arrange them around
the fish. Put vegetables into a deep bowl and the broth into another.
Serve the *rouille* separately. Eat with French bread or croûtons.
Everyone helps themselves as they wish to fish, vegetables and broth,
and either stirs in the *rouille* or spreads it on the bread.

Beef stewed with fennel
La Gardiane

This stew comes from the region of salt lakes and marshes famous for
its black bulls, white horses and pink flamingoes, ruled by the
gardians, the cowboys of the Camargue. Fennel, orange peel and
anchovy combine to give it a certain savage flavour. It needs long, slow
stewing. If you have a slow-cook pot, it can be prepared in the morning
and left to cook until the evening. Serve with plain boiled rice.

700 g (1½ lb) stewing beef	parsley, thyme and bay leaf
4 tablespoons olive oil	2 tablespoons tomato purée
100 g (4 oz) smoked streaky bacon, chopped	finely pared rind of 1 orange
	freshly milled black pepper
2 carrots, chopped	2 cloves garlic, chopped
1 onion, chopped	100 g (4 oz) black olives
2 sticks celery, chopped	25 g (1 oz) butter
1 bulb fennel, sliced	2 anchovy fillets
2 tablespoons flour	1 teaspoon *pastis*
150 ml (¼ pint) water	salt
300 ml (½ pint) red wine	

Cut the beef into large cubes. Heat the oil in a heavy-based casserole
and brown the meat all over on a high heat. Add bacon, carrots, onion,
celery and fennel, mix well and cook until they are beginning to
colour. Lower the heat, dust in the flour and mix well. Cook for a
couple of minutes and stir in the water followed by the wine. Add a
bouquet garni of parsley, thyme and a bay leaf tied in a bunch, tomato
purée, orange rind, pepper and garlic. Bring to the boil, lower the heat
and simmer, covered, for 3 hours. Alternatively, cook in a cool oven,
Gas 2/300°F/150°C, for the same length of time. Check occasionally,

and if it is becoming too dry, add a little water. By this time the meat should be tender. If it is not, continue cooking for a further 30 minutes. Add olives and cook for another 15 minutes. Mash the butter with the anchovies and *pastis* and, off the heat, add in small pieces to the stew, stirring all the time. Remove bouquet garni, taste and, if necessary, add salt.

Melon with apple mint and honey sauce
Melon à l'aigre-douce

For a first course, cut a ripe melon into thick slices and serve with this sauce which is not so far removed from ordinary mint sauce. The apple mint and the red wine sweetened with honey give it a more delicate flavour.

3 tablespoons chopped apple mint
4 tablespoons red wine
1 tablespoon honey
1 teaspoon vinegar
salt
freshly milled black pepper

Put chopped mint leaves into a small serving bowl or jug. Pour the wine into a saucepan with the honey and vinegar and gently heat, stirring until the honey melts. Cool and pour over the mint. Add salt and plenty of black pepper.

Almond spread with mint and anchovies
Lou saussoun

Eat this unusual combination on squares of toast or small biscuits as an appetizer. The flavour of the almonds is subtly enhanced by that of mint, fennel and anchovies. You can use ready-ground almonds but for better flavour buy whole almonds in their skins. To skin them, simply put them in a bowl, pour over boiling water and leave for a few minutes, after which the skin will wrinkle and rub off between your fingers. Grind in a mincer or food processor.

4 sprigs of fresh mint
½ teaspoon fennel seeds
25 g (1 oz) anchovy fillets, chopped
50 g (2 oz) ground almonds
1–2 tablespoons olive oil
salt to taste

Use a pestle and mortar (or food processor). Put leaves from 3 sprigs of mint and the fennel seeds into the mortar, pound well, add anchovies and pound to a paste. Mix in the ground almonds. Beat in sufficient olive oil and water to make a thick paste. Taste and, if necessary, add a little salt. Put the spread into a pot and garnish it with the remaining sprig of mint. Cover and keep in a cool place.

Basil

Courgette salad with basil

Tomato salad with basil

Basil sauce

Soup with *pistou*

Warm potato salad with basil

Salade niçoise

Lamb chops with basil

Chicken with basil

Basil wine pick-you-up

Basil came to Europe from India where its ability to conjure dreams has earned it a place as a sacred plant. In the West it became the symbol of fertility. It has a sweet and heady smell which fills a room with a peppery fragrance.

Buy a plant from supermarket, nursery or greengrocer, bring it home and keep it moist and warm, perhaps on a sunny windowsill. Or grow it from seed. Eat when the leaves are young and fresh and replace plants with new ones rather than encouraging one plant to produce for the whole summer.

Basil is used to flavour stews, sauces and salads, grilled meats and fish and all kinds of vegetables, from aubergines to sweet peppers and most especially tomatoes. You can turn an omelette or scrambled eggs into something special by adding a few chopped leaves just when the eggs are set and if you also include a few tomatoes, roughly chopped and softened in a little olive oil, you will have a dish fit for that proverbial king. There are many varieties, some with leaves as small as thyme which are strong and pungent and used only in small quantities. The best are those with long, silky leaves. It is said to be addictive and once used you won't be able to do without it.

It is frequently added to a dish right at the last minute and I often use it instead of parsley to garnish vegetable dishes, salads, etc. It won't survive the frost and it doesn't dry well but can be preserved by filling a clean jar with the chopped leaves and topping with olive oil. Kept in the fridge it solidifies, so you can take a spoonful as you need. Eventually it looks a bit murky but the flavour is not impaired. Add a few sprigs to a bottle of red wine vinegar, let it steep for a week or so, then use the flavoured vinegar in salad dressings.

Courgette salad with basil
Courgettes au basilic en salade

Slice small courgettes very thinly, season with salt, pepper and a squeeze of lemon juice, sprinkle with olive oil and a handful of chopped basil leaves.

Tomato salad with basil
Salade de tomates au basilic

Basil's affinity with tomatoes is renowed, as each enhances the taste of
the other. Simply put 2–3 tablespoons of olive oil into a bowl, add salt
and some chopped basil. Cut tomatoes in quarters and remove the
seeds. Just before serving, add them to the bowl turning them over to
coat them evenly. This salad is especially good eaten with curd cheese
or a mild, fresh goat's or ewe's cheese such as Banon.

Basil sauce
Pistou

This violent and sublime concoction of garlic, sweet basil, cheese and
olive oil is similar to (and often confused with) Italian *pesto*, which is
made in the same way but with the addition of crushed pine nuts.
Pistou is used to give an aromatic flavour to a soup of summer
vegetables, which in the old days would have been simmered in an
earthenware pot on the corner of the fire. Like *pesto*, it can also be
eaten with spaghetti or other pasta with plenty of freshly milled black
pepper. It is delicious with poached fish or shellfish. It freezes well, so if
you are feeling especially energetic make double the quantity and
freeze half for another time. It is also worth buying jars of basil sauce
(usually sold as *pesto*). While being less robust than the real thing, they
nevertheless provide a pleasant standby for adding zip to soups, salads
or pasta sauces. The cheese to be used in the sauce might be Parmesan
or Gruyère but it works well with a mixture of Roquefort and goat's
cheese or a dry Edam or mature Cheddar. The cheese is cut into
matchstick strips – grating, so rumour has it, will alter the flavour.

4 cloves garlic, quartered	100 g (4 oz) hard cheese, cut in
25–50 g (1–2 oz) fresh basil	matchstick strips
leaves	4–5 tablespoons olive oil

You can use a food processor but the sauce has a rougher, more
authentic texture made in a mortar which can be brought to the table
and thus will also cut down on the washing-up. Put garlic cloves into
the mortar and pound to a paste with the pestle, holding this
comfortably, like a pencil or a paintbrush. Let the weight of it do the
work rather than pounding heavily. Tear the basil leaves into pieces

and add a few at a time to the mortar. Continue to pound, until you have a dark green paste. Add the matchsticks of cheese a little at a time, and pound until the mixture has the consistency of soft butter. Gradually beat in the oil until finally the sauce is like a coarse mayonnaise.

Soup with *pistou*
Soupe au pistou

Everyone has their own version, and this one comes from Charles Fabre, who was a Savoy chef and later worked in Nice. It is filling enough to provide a complete meal for lunch or supper. Fresh *haricots rouges* and *blancs* can be used but canned or dried do as well and I often make it using canned flageolets.

225 g (8 oz) carrots, chopped
225 g (8 oz) leeks, chopped
2 courgettes, chopped
225 g (8 oz) French beans,
    chopped
sprig of celery, chopped
4 medium potatoes, chopped
salt, pepper

450 g (1 lb) tomatoes, peeled
    and chopped *or* 1 can
    chopped Italian tomatoes
225 g (8 oz) dried haricot beans,
    soaked and cooked *or* 1 can
    haricot or flageolet beans
handful small pasta such as
    vermicelli (optional)
bowl of *pistou*

If using dried beans, these must either be soaked overnight in cold water or brought to the boil in a pan of water, removed from the heat and left to steep for at least an hour. Drain, put into a pan of fresh water and simmer for about 1 hour. Drain again. Put all the vegetables except tomatoes and the haricot beans into a large saucepan, add sufficient water to cover, put on the lid, bring to the boil and simmer for 30–45 minutes. Add the tomatoes and haricot beans, season with salt and pepper and simmer for a further 15 minutes. If using pasta add at this point and cook 5–10 minutes longer. Once the soup is ready, stir a tablespoon or two into the *pistou* sauce which can then either be brought to the table for everyone to add as they wish to their helping of soup, or you can stir it all into the soup pot before serving, but don't let it boil as the cheese, especially if it is Gruyère, will become tough and stringy.

77

Warm potato salad with basil
Salade de pommes de terre au basilic

Plainly boiled potatoes sprinkled with basil have a sweet, peppery flavour. In this dish the flavour is sharpened with white wine vinegar and the potatoes are good eaten in the cool of a summer's evening with an omelette; or create a simple winter starter by piling the potatoes on a dish surrounded by slices of garlic sausage or other cold meat. If basil is not to hand use parsley or thyme instead.

450 g (1 lb) potatoes
salt
1 clove garlic, chopped
1 tablespoon white wine vinegar

2 tablespoons olive oil
freshly milled black pepper
handful chopped basil

Boil potatoes in their skins in salted water until they are soft but still firm. Drain and peel them as soon as they are cool enough to handle, slicing them into a salad bowl. Stir in the garlic. Sprinkle over the white wine vinegar and olive oil and season generously with salt and pepper. Garnish with the chopped basil.

Salade niçoise

People argue about this salad and its ingredients. Essentially it consists of raw vegetables, which might include tiny broad beans, black olives, garlic, tuna fish and/or anchovies with a liberal dressing of olive oil, all topped with tomatoes and fresh chopped basil. Sometimes hard-boiled eggs are included. It is ideal for those summer days when it is just too hot to cook. Below is just one of many versions.

6–8 firm, ripe tomatoes,
    quartered
fine salt
1 green pepper, finely chopped
150 g (6 oz) mange-tout
can broad beans or flageolets
4 spring onions, chopped

1 clove garlic, crushed
225 g (8 oz) can tuna in oil
3–4 anchovy fillets
handful black olives
freshly milled black pepper
3 tablespoons olive oil
1 tablespoon chopped basil

Sprinkle the quartered tomatoes with fine salt and set aside to drain some of their moisture. Put chopped green pepper into a deep salad

bowl. Slice mange-tout. Drain and rinse the broad be.
add to the bowl. Add chopped spring onions and gai
and cut anchovies into small pieces and add. Mix. Sca.
over and season with pepper. Just before serving, arrange \
on top, sprinkle over the oil and garnish with the basil.

Lamb chops with basil
Côtelettes d'agneau au basilic

This is a quick and easy way of preparing lamb using either chops or
steaks. They should be lean and at least 3 cm (1 in) thick.

4 lamb chops or steaks	150 ml (¼ pint) white wine
1 tablespoon olive oil	2 tablespoons chopped basil
1 tablespoon tomatoe purée	salt
1 clove garlic, chopped	freshly milled black pepper

Heat the oil in a frying pan and fry the chops over a medium heat for 5
minutes on each side. Remove and keep warm. Add the tomato purée
and garlic to the pan and stir in the wine. Add basil, salt and pepper
and return the chops. Cover, lower the heat and cook for a further 5–
10 minutes. Test by piercing with a skewer; if you like to eat lamb
underdone, the juice should run pale pink. Otherwise continue to cook
until the juices run clear. Serve the chops with the sauce poured round
them.

Chicken with basil
Poulet sauté au basilic

In this simple chicken dish flavoured with tomatoes, the basil is added
right at the end so that it loses none of its pungency. Use a maize-fed or
free-range chicken if you can.

1 chicken, cut into 8 pieces	150 ml (¼ pint) dry white wine
3 tablespoons olive oil	2 cloves garlic
1 onion, chopped	salt, pepper
1 tablespoon tomato purée	handful chopped basil
3–4 tomatoes, skinned and chopped	

Ɪᴋin chicken pieces. Heat 2 tablespoons of olive oil in a heatproof casserole and add the chicken pieces. Let them brown and turn golden over a medium heat for about 5 minutes on each side. If necessary do this in two batches. Remove and keep warm. Add the onion, let it soften, add tomato purée and tomatoes, mix well and pour in the wine, let it bubble until reduced by about half. Add garlic cloves (whole and unpeeled), salt and pepper, stir and return the chicken pieces. Simmer, covered, for about 40–45 minutes until the chicken pieces are cooked. Add basil and the last spoonful of olive oil. Mix and simmer for a further 5 minutes.

Basil wine pick-you-up
Le vin de basilic

There are many different recipes for herb wines, those not always soothing drinks which really fall into the same category as the bottle of brandy kept for medicinal purposes in my grandmother's wardrobe. Basil has long been renowned for aiding stomach upsets so this is one to enjoy after a stint of over-indulgence. Unlike many things supposed to do you good, this one also tastes good.

1 bottle light red wine	piece of dried orange peel
handful basil leaves, with	20 sugar lumps
flowers if possible	150 ml (¼ pint) water

Put the wine, basil and dried orange peel (see Index) into a 1 litre (2 lb) storage jar. Put sugar and water into a saucepan and heat it gently until the sugar dissolves. Let it cool. Pour into the jar. Seal the top and leave for a week. Take a little in a glass as and when required.

Anchovies

Anchovy butter

Anchovies on French bread

Anchovies and egg on French bread

Rice salad

Stuffed eggs

Anchovy salad dressing

Celery with hot anchovy sauce

Courgettes with anchovy

Cardoons with anchovies

Gratin of artichoke hearts with anchovies

Anchovy pastry

Stuffed vegetables

Sweet peppers with anchovies

Rabbit in a piquant sauce

Beef stew with capers, gherkins and anchovies

Guinea fowl with anchovies and capers

Fresh anchovies

Cured Mediterranean anchovies are the star ingredient in many simple and tasty dishes. The curing process, which can last from one to eighteen months, turns their grey flesh to varying shades of mud-red. Once, everyone salted and cured their own supply, but nowadays most people buy them ready prepared, packed tightly together in jars or cans. Some people insist that salted anchovies are the only ones worth using but there are just as many who prefer the milder flavour of those kept in oil. If you have the chance, experiment and decide which are right for you.

They are used to give flavour to stews and sauces, vegetable dishes and salads. Canned fillets in oil are ready to use but those preserved in salt must be soaked in water or milk for half an hour or so before using and as they are whole, need to be split and the sharp backbone removed. You will seldom want to use a jarful at once but it saves time if you soak the whole lot and return those you don't use to the jar, cover them with olive oil and use as needed.

Anchovies can give character to salads. Mix small pieces with diced beetroot, chopped garlic and olive oil – the saltiness of the anchovies contrasts beautifully with the sweetness of the beetroot. Or slice a cabbage and mix it with 4 or 5 anchovy fillets, a clove or two of chopped garlic, season with freshly milled black pepper and sprinkle with a dressing made from olive oil and a little vinegar. The traditional Easter salad, *salade de Pâques*, consists of hard-boiled eggs cut in half lengthwise, laid on a bed of lettuce and coated with a dressing made from crushing the yolks from two more hard-boiled eggs, 4–5 crushed anchovy fillets and chopped spring onions mixed with 4–6 table-spoons olive oil.

Anchovy butter
Beurre d'anchois

This butter is good served with roast beef, grilled steaks or fish and is lovely with baked jacket potatoes. Make ahead of time and keep in the fridge to use as needed.

6 anchovy fillets   1 teaspoon flour
1 tablespoon olive oil   2–3 basil leaves, chopped
100 g (4 oz) butter

Pound the anchovies with the oil. Melt butter in a small pan and stir in
the flour, cook for 2–3 minutes over a low heat, stirring constantly.
Gradually add the anchovy mixture and the basil. Pour into a small
bowl and leave to set.

Anchovies on French bread
Les quichets

This is perhaps the simplest way of using anchovies and is delicious as
a lunchtime snack or appetizer.

1 clove garlic   8 anchovy fillets
4 slices stale French bread   fennel seeds
olive oil

Heat grill or oven to Gas 7/425°F/220°C. Cut the garlic clove in half
and rub it over both sides of the bread slices. Lay them in the grill pan,
or on a baking sheet, sprinkle with oil and top each with 2 anchovy
fillets and a pinch of fennel seeds. Grill until golden or bake at the top
of the oven for 5–10 minutes.

Anchovies and egg on French bread
Rousdito à l'anchoio

Vary the above recipe by pounding the anchovy fillets in a mortar until
you have a paste. Mix in an egg yolk. Sprinkle the bread slices with
olive oil and spread with the anchovy and egg paste. Grill or bake as
before.

Rice salad
Salade de riz

In recent times much of the marshland of the Camargue has been
reclaimed and rice is grown, not on a scale grand enough for export
but sufficient to satisfy local demand. If you buy it, cook it in your
favourite way, but allow rather less liquid than for the long-grain rice
available at home. I often cook more than I need so that I have enough
for a rice salad the following day.

300 g (8 oz) long-grain rice
salt
4 eggs
1 tablespoon wine vinegar
1 teaspoon ready-made mustard
1 clove garlic, chopped
handful chives, snipped
1 teaspoon fresh thyme *or* ½
   teaspoon dried

pinch of nutmeg
6–8 tablespoons olive oil
225 g (8 oz) can tuna, flaked
4 tomatoes, chopped
1 small green pepper, finely
   sliced
handful black olives
50 g (2 oz) anchovies

Put rice and 600 ml (1 pint) of water into a saucepan, bring to the boil, add salt, stir with a fork, cover and simmer for 20 minutes. Remove from heat and leave without raising the lid for 10 minutes. Set aside to cool. Boil the eggs for 12 minutes. Put them under running cold water, crack the shells, peel and leave in cold water until ready to use. (Cold water prevents the yolks from turning grey.) Make a vinaigrette in the salad bowl by pounding the vinegar, mustard, garlic, chives, thyme and nutmeg together before gradually beating in the oil. Tip in the rice and mix well. Add tuna, tomatoes, green pepper and the olives. Mix lightly. Garnish with the anchovies arranged in a criss-cross pattern and top with the hard-boiled eggs cut in quarters.

Stuffed eggs
La Berlingueto

There are many versions of this dish of hard-boiled eggs stuffed with anchovies. This is the simplest. Others suggest laying the eggs on a bed of blanched spinach, perhaps mixed with sorrel, or placing them on a layer of sliced tomatoes.

4 eggs
2 tablespoons fresh breadcrumbs
50 g (2 oz) anchovies, chopped
1 clove garlic, chopped
3 tablespoons chopped parsley

2–3 tablespoons milk
freshly milled black pepper
dried breadcrumbs
olive oil

Boil the eggs for 12 minutes and treat as in previous recipe. Heat oven to Gas 5/375°F/190°C. Cut each egg in half lengthwise. Remove the yolks, chop them and put into a bowl. Mix in the fresh breadcrumbs, anchovies, garlic and parsley, and add enough milk to make a soft paste. Season with pepper (no salt because of the anchovies). Fill each egg white with the anchovy mixture. Oil a gratin dish, put any remaining filling in the base, lay the eggs on top, sprinkle with dried breadcrumbs and olive oil. Put into the oven for 10–15 minutes to heat through and brown.

Anchovy salad dressing
Anchoïade

I watched Grandpa Fabre make this dressing which has a subtle flavour that brings out the taste of salad ingredients. (Serve it with green salad or as a dip with raw vegetables such as celery, with which it has an affinity.) He held a garlic clove between his finger and thumb and used a knife to shave it into slivers straight into the salad bowl. He added 4 or 5 anchovy fillets, crushing them with a wooden spoon before beating in a tablespoon of vinegar and 5 or 6 tablespoons olive oil and then he seasoned the dressing with a few turns of freshly milled black pepper. You can add chopped herbs if you wish – parsley, thyme or basil – and if you want a thicker sauce, try adding a couple of hard-boiled egg yolks, crushing them well before beating in the vinegar and oil. Some people add a tablespoon or two of capers and a squeeze of lemon juice.

Celery with hot anchovy sauce
Céleri à l'anchoïade

People's eyes light up when they talk about celery dipped in this hot anchovy sauce. Perhaps they believe it really does have aphrodisiac properties as suggested in the Provençal saying: *le céleri pour les petits maris.*

1 head celery	150 ml (¼ pint) olive oil
2–3 cloves garlic	few drops vinegar
50 g (2 oz) anchovies	freshly milled black pepper

Wash the celery, separating the stalks and removing any stringy fibres. To make it crisp, soak for an hour in cold water in the fridge. Boil the garlic in salted water for 5–10 minutes until soft. Remove and skin. Crush the anchovies with the garlic in a heatproof bowl, gradually beating in the olive oil and vinegar. Season with pepper, and stand the bowl in a pan of hot water. Bring the water just to boiling point, and keep hot until the point of serving. Bring to the table with the drained celery. Everyone dips their pieces of celery into the hot *anchoïade*.

Courgettes with anchovy
Courgettes à l'anchoïade

Anchovies are used to add saltiness to many vegetable gratins. This one with courgettes is suitable for a first course. It can be eaten hot or cold.

900 g (2 lb) courgettes	freshly milled black pepper
2 tablespoons olive oil	2 tablespoons chopped parsley
50 g (2 oz) anchovies	3–4 tablespoons breadcrumbs
2 cloves garlic, chopped	

Wash and slice the courgettes very thinly. Heat the oil in a frying pan, add the courgettes and let them soften over a medium heat, turning them over from time to time so they do not burn. This will take about 15 minutes. In the meantime heat oven to Gas 6/400°F/200°C. Empty the courgettes into a gratin dish. Put the anchovies into the frying pan and cook until they soften, crushing them with a wooden spoon. Turn off heat. Add chopped garlic, pepper, parsley and breadcrumbs and mix all together. Spread this mixture over the courgettes. Sprinkle with olive oil and bake for 15–20 minutes.

Cardoons with anchovies
Cardons de Noël

I long to try this traditional Provençal Christmas recipe for cardoons, which are related to artichokes, but I am never there when they are in season. The purple-centred flowers which resemble giant thistles dry well, and look beautiful in a vase. The leaf stalks are edible but the prickly outer stems and leaves must be cut away to reveal the inner stalks and heart. Cut these into 12 cm (5 in) lengths, putting them into water with a little vinegar as you go, to prevent them blackening. Blanch them for 5 minutes in boiling salted water. Drain. Make a béchamel sauce using olive oil (see Index); flavour with a few chopped anchovies. Put the cardoons into a gratin dish, pour over the sauce, add pepper, dust with grated cheese and bake for 15–20 minutes at Gas 6/400°F/200°C.

Gratin of artichoke hearts with anchovies
Tian d'artichauts aux anchois

Prepare this the day before because it is to be served cold either as a
first course or as part of a summer lunch. The mixture of artichoke
hearts, tomatoes, anchovies and olives is similar to a pizza topping.
Artichokes are never cheap in Britain, so use the canned variety,
rinsing them under running cold water before using.

1 can artichoke hearts	12 black olives
450 g (1 lb) tomatoes, sliced	sprigs of fresh thyme and savory
freshly milled black pepper	2–3 tablespoons breadcrumbs
50 g (2 oz) anchovies	olive oil

Heat oven to Gas 4/350°F/180°C. Oil an earthenware gratin dish.
Drain and rinse the artichokes and lay them on the base. Top with the
sliced tomatoes. Season with the pepper. Lay the anchovies in a lattice
pattern on the top, add olives and herbs. Sprinkle over the breadcrumbs and moisten with olive oil. Bake for 30 minutes and leave to
get cold.

Anchovy pastry
Fougasse aux anchois

On Saturdays we go to the market in Pont St Esprit. It is the weekly
ritual that no one misses. Everyone stocks up for the week, meets
friends and has a gossip. Often I go in search of a *fougasse*, which is
traditionally made with the leftovers of bread, brioche or pastry
dough. The ones I buy are like flat breads with a crisp, golden crust and
springy interior and are made in a lattice-work shape like a butterfly.
They are flavoured with anchovies or black olives or, most common of
all, *gratons* (sometimes called *gratterons* or *graillons*), the small,
frizzled cubes of pork left over from making lard which are salted
while hot. It is hard to reproduce these simple treats without a curved
brick or stone oven under which a fire is lit and into which the dough is
slid on long wooden paddles. Few French people would try. But a
pastry *fougasse* is a different matter and takes no time at all, especially
if you use ready-made puff pastry. It makes a most satisfying snack at
any time, or for delicious cocktail snacks, make a couple and divide
each into eight strips before baking.

100 g (4 oz) puff pastry   freshly milled black pepper
50 g (2 oz) anchovies in oil   beaten egg yolk or a little milk

Heat oven to Gas 7/425°F/220°C. Roll pastry into a square with sides roughly 20 cm (8 in) (or use a sheet of ready rolled pastry). With the blunt side of a knife mark it into thirds. Crush the anchovies with the oil from the can, add a few turns of pepper and spread half this paste over the centre third of the pastry. Fold one third over, and spread the remaining anchovy paste on top. Fold over the remaining third. Using a rolling pin, roll firmly once each way to seal the edges. Brush with beaten egg or milk and bake on an oiled baking tray for 20 minutes. Cut into slices and serve hot.

Stuffed vegetables
Légumes farcis

Stuffed aubergines, courgettes, tomatoes and peppers are a feature in Provence. Either use one variety or a mixture and never mind if you make more than you can eat, they are just as good cold as part of a lunch or picnic. In this recipe anchovies are used but you can if you wish substitute minced cooked meat or ham.

4 courgettes, large tomatoes or peppers *or* 2 aubergines *or* a mixture of vegetables
4 tablespoons olive oil
2 onions, chopped
2 tablespoons tomato purée
50 g (2 oz) anchovies, chopped
8 tablespoons cooked rice or fresh breadcrumbs
2 cloves garlic, chopped

freshly milled black pepper
1 tablespoon chopped basil or parsley
2 eggs, beaten
4 tablespoons grated cheese
4 tablespoons dried breadcrumbs
150 ml (¼ pint) water or stock or tomato juice

Heat oven to Gas 6/400°F/200°C. Cut vegetables in half and, using a teaspoon, scoop out and reserve the flesh (in the case of peppers, simply remove and discard the seeds). Sprinkle the inside of tomatoes or aubergines with salt and turn them upside down to drain. Chop the flesh. Heat the olive oil and fry the onions until soft, stir in the tomato purée, chopped flesh of the vegetables, anchovies, rice or fresh breadcrumbs, garlic, pepper and herbs. Salt should not be necessary because of the anchovies. Add the beaten eggs. Pour sufficient oil into shallow oven dishes to cover the base and arrange the halved vegetables in a single layer on top. Fill each half with stuffing and top with grated cheese and dried breadcrumbs. Carefully pour round water, stock or tomato juice and put into the oven. Courgettes, tomatoes and peppers will take about 30 minutes, aubergines up to an hour. Baste from time to time and if they are getting too brown but are still not soft, cover with a piece of foil and lower the heat to Gas 5/ 375°F/190°C.

Sweet peppers with anchovies
Filets de poivron aux anchois

This is a pretty starter or light lunch dish, especially if you mix red peppers with yellow or green. If fresh peppers are unobtainable or you are pressed for time, you can use instead a can of Spanish red pimientos, as they are ready skinned and cooked and only need to be sliced.

2 sweet peppers	olive oil
2 hard-boiled eggs	1 lemon
50 g (2 oz) anchovies	chopped basil or parsley

Wash the peppers. Heat grill. Line the grill pan with foil and lay the peppers on top. Grill them, turning from time to time until the skin chars and blackens when it will come away paper thin. Or you can toast them, turning them round and round over a gas flame. Cut them in half, remove and discard seeds and cut the peppers into thin strips. Put them in a shallow dish, add the eggs cut in quarters and arrange the anchovies in a lattice pattern on top. Moisten with oil and the juice of the lemon, sprinkle over the basil or parsley. Serve cold.

Rabbit in a piquant sauce
Lapin en saupiquet

In this aromatic recipe, the rabbit is marinated in plenty of olive oil and herbs before being tossed in flour and cooked in white wine. At the end it is flavoured with a mixture of the chopped liver, anchovies, capers, garlic and parsley. The list of ingredients may seem long, but the method is very straightforward and quick.

1 rabbit, cut into 8 pieces, plus
   the liver
300 ml (½ pint) olive oil
3–4 sprigs of thyme
3–4 sprigs of rosemary
2 bay leaves
2–3 tablespoons flour
2 onions, chopped

5 cloves garlic
300 ml (½ pint) dry white wine
25 g (1 oz) anchovies
1 tablespoon capers
freshly milled black pepper
handful chopped parsley
12 black olives

Marinate the rabbit (except the liver) with half the olive oil, thyme, rosemary and bay leaves for 24–48 hours in a deep china or glass bowl. Turn the pieces over twice each day. During this time keep the liver, moistened with a tablespoon of vinegar, covered in the fridge.

When you are ready to begin cooking, remove the rabbit from the oil and coat the pieces with the flour by shaking them together in a bag. Strain the marinade into a heavy-based casserole large enough for all the rabbit pieces to fit snugly in one layer. Put over a medium heat and then add the rabbit, chopped onion, 4 whole cloves garlic and pour in the wine. Raise the heat and as soon as it boils, lower the heat, cover and simmer gently for about 1 hour or until tender. Meanwhile, crush the anchovies in a mortar (or use a food processor), chop remaining clove of garlic and add rinsed capers, the rabbit's liver, a generous amount of pepper and the parsley. Crush all to a paste. Heat the remaining oil in a small saucepan, add the paste and cook, stirring for several minutes. Set aside. When rabbit is ready, remove the meat to a serving dish and keep warm. Stir the paste into the sauce in which the rabbit was cooked, add the olives and pour over the rabbit.

Beef stew with capers, gherkins and anchovies
La Broufado

The *mariniers du Rhône*, the boatmen of the Rhône, are credited with inventing this warming stew. In this version the meat is marinated for 24 hours before being slowly simmered in white wine in a round, lidded earthenware pot known as a *poêlon*. You can, if you prefer, use a cast-iron casserole. Halfway through the cooking time the stew is flavoured with capers and gherkins. Finally the sauce is lightly thickened with a mixture of flour and olive oil and the chopped anchovies are added.

700 g (1½ lb) good quality
  stewing beef
2 tablespoons wine vinegar
2 onions
sprigs of thyme, parsley and
  marjoram or ½ teaspoon of
  each, dried
bay leaf
2 tablespoons brandy
150 ml (¼ pint) olive oil

1 clove garlic, chopped
salt
freshly milled black pepper
300 ml (½ pint) dry white wine
1 tablespoon capers
4 gherkins, sliced
1 tablespoon flour
4 anchovy fillets, chopped
2–3 tablespoons chopped
  parsley

Cut the beef into cubes and marinate for 24 hours in a china or glass dish with the vinegar, 1 chopped onion, the herbs, bay leaf, brandy and half the olive oil.

Heat 3 tablespoons of olive oil in a flameproof casserole. Chop the second onion and soften over a medium heat; when it is golden push to one side. Dry the pieces of meat with kitchen paper (keep the marinade) and brown them all over, in two or three batches if necessary. Add garlic, season with a little salt and pepper, pour in half the wine and all of the marinade. Cover and simmer slowly over a very low heat or in the oven Gas 3/325°F/160°C for 1 hour. At this point add the capers (rinsed) and sliced gherkins. After a further hour add remaining wine and continue to simmer for 45 minutes. In a small bowl mix the flour with the remaining 2 tablespoons olive oil, remove the casserole from the heat and stir this mixture into the sauce. Return to the heat, stir until the sauce thickens and add the chopped anchovies. Simmer for 5–10 minutes. Dust with parsley and serve.

Guinea fowl with anchovies and capers
Pintade aux anchois

Guinea fowl flavoured with anchovies, capers and lemon juice is quick and simple to prepare and makes a very tasty main course for a small dinner party, one bird feeding four comfortably.

1 guinea fowl
25 g (1 oz) butter
1 tablespoon olive oil
1 onion, finely chopped
4 anchovy fillets, chopped
1 teaspoon flour

150 ml (¼ pint) white wine
1 tablespoon capers
freshly milled black pepper
juice of 1 lemon
salt to taste

Cut the guinea fowl into four pieces. Kitchen shears come in handy for this job. Heat the butter and oil in a heavy-based casserole and brown the pieces all over. Remove. Add the onion and cook until golden. Stir in the chopped anchovies followed by the flour. Cook gently, stirring for a couple of minutes before gradually mixing in the white wine. Return the pieces of guinea fowl, add capers (rinsed), pepper and the lemon juice. Cover the pan and simmer gently for 30–40 minutes. Taste and if necessary add a little salt.

Fresh anchovies
Anchois frais

Fresh anchovies are found in French markets from spring through to autumn. They have burnished silver scales tinged with olive-green which once they are out of the water gradually darken to blue. Savour them when you can and handle with care. Wash under the tap and snap off the heads which come away with most of the innards. They are so soft, they can be filleted with a finger nail. They are delicious simply grilled or baked, sprinkled with herbs and olive oil, at Gas 5/375°F/190°C for about 10 minutes.

Anchovies and other small fish such as sardines, red mullet and boops (a small Mediterranean sea bream with big eyes) are delicious spiced and preserved in vinegar to be eaten cold, *en escabèche*. They keep several days in the fridge and make an ideal starter. Although they are usually first fried, you can equally well use fish that have been grilled or baked.

6 tablespoons olive oil	2 red chillies
2 onions, chopped	150 ml (¼ pint) red wine vinegar
2 cloves garlic, chopped	150 ml (¼ pint) water
1 bay leaf	900 g (2 lb) fresh anchovies
sprigs of thyme and rosemary	2–3 tablespoons flour

Heat 3 tablespoons of oil in a small saucepan. Fry the onions over a medium heat, add garlic, bay leaf, herbs and chillies. When the onions are golden and soft pour over the vinegar and water and simmer gently for 10 minutes. Meanwhile, flour the fish. (The easiest method is to put flour in a paper bag, add fish and shake well.) Heat remaining oil in a frying pan and fry the fish quickly until golden on both sides. Lay the fish in a shallow dish, pour over the contents of the saucepan. Leave to get cold, cover and put in the fridge. Serve cold.

Spring and Summer Vegetables

At the Saturday morning market in Pont St Esprit, the town is filled to bursting with people and parked cars. Not even the pedestrian crossings are spared. The boulevards are one long traffic jam and the Allées and the Place de la République, with their double rows of plane trees, are crammed with stalls arranged in four long lines – two gangways formed by setting the two centre lines of stalls back to back facing the outer lines. People pass backwards and forwards in a continuous flow. It's like the High Street crush on Christmas Eve only much better humoured. Everyone is there and it's impossible not to meet someone you know, which means stopping and exchanging the three obligatory kisses, repeated again on saying goodbye. There are babies in pushchairs, dogs on leads and old ladies banging people's ankles with their cumbersome shopping trolleys. The women are intent on the serious business of shopping while the men come for the stroll. The cafés are doing a roaring trade, especially the one by the Fontaine du Coq, which is everyone's rendezvous.

Anything you want to buy, you can buy in the market. It is the hub of everyone's lives. Even the local shops have stalls there. The plan appears to be haphazard but the regulars all have their time-honoured places. Some stalls are just trestle tables brought in by farmers selling honey or goat's cheese or fresh-dug vegetables, while the professionals have specially converted vans and trailers which unfold like a conjurer's box to reveal their produce, protected from the weather by canopies which open like giant umbrellas.

There is an abundance of everything, especially of vegetables, all displayed in boxes or baskets. There are peas and all kinds of beans, fat carrots and leeks, onions of every kind, tomatoes, aubergines, cour-gettes and green and red peppers piled alongside each other, asparagus sold loose by weight or in kilo bundles and radishes crammed between heaps of white-stalked Swiss chard and spinach. Potatoes are to be had by the sack and there is even a stall selling nothing but lettuce, three for a song.

Everyone helps themselves, filling the plastic or aluminium bowls provided by the stallholders with as much or as little as they want. Prodding, feeling and rejecting all but the best, aided and abetted by the stallholders, most of whom would be affronted if they thought they had sold you something substandard, which is astonishing after the look-but-don't-touch attitude of most English markets.

We tend to think of meat as being the centre of French cooking and certainly when you read a menu in the south of France, meat features in almost every dish. This is strange because meat used to be a luxury and traditional recipes lay a much greater emphasis on vegetables. Everyone grew their own and anyone who has a plot of land or an allotment continues to do so. When we are there, our neighbours Emile and Henri never visit us empty-handed and Cathy plies us with salad leaves from her garden in front of the farm. Everyone has far more than they can possibly eat and there is a huge variety of ways of making sure no one could ever possibly grow tired of them.

Tomatoes

Fried eggs with tomatoes

Tomato omelette

Tomatoes stuffed with tuna

Baked or fried tomatoes

Pizza with pastry

Iced tomato soup

Eiderdown soup

Snails in tomato sauce

Fresh tomato sauce

Rosy cauliflower

Chicken liver mousse with fresh tomato sauce

Frogs' legs

Red mullet with tomatoes

Squid pie

It is impossible to cook in the manner of Provence or Languedoc without the tomato. There are two kinds: the small, plum-shaped variety and those which are huge and misshapen, some as big as fists, almost bursting with dense, juicy flesh.

Apart from using them in salads, their sweetness gives flavour to all sorts of dishes from fish to eggs, poultry, game and meat casseroles, soups and dried beans, vegetable dishes and the pizza which has been adopted by the southern French. This flavour is almost impossible to capture if we use those tasteless imports, which apparently are specially grown for the British market. The big suppliers have decreed that all we want are perfect-shaped, uniform-sized tomatoes and that the flavour is of least importance. Fortunately, the recipes can be made very successfully using canned Italian tomatoes, the self-same little plum tomatoes which thrive in the warm Mediterranean climate. I often buy the chopped variety because they save time.

Of course if you have a sunny garden or greenhouse it is not difficult to grow your own. Go for varieties with plenty of flavour (a good nursery will be able to advise you). They might sell seeds of the incomparable Marmande tomato, or you could bring back packets from France. Or, if time is short, buy some tomato plants. If you see odd-shaped, home-grown tomatoes on sale, the chances are they will have good flavour and recently some supermarkets and shops have been selling tomatoes imported from Provence. Their flavour is less intense than those bought on their home ground but they improve if left to ripen for a day or two.

Tomatoes are easy to skin if covered for a few minutes in boiling water. Many French recipes also specify de-seeding. If the tomatoes are fleshy, they can be squeezed like a sponge to release the seeds, otherwise scoop them out with a spoon or knife.

Fried eggs with tomatoes
Oeufs à la tomate

Fried eggs with a difference, gently cooked on a bed of garlicky tomatoes for a satisfying light lunch or supper. Peel and quarter 450 g

(1 lb) tomatoes. Heat sufficient oil to cover the base of a frying pan and fry the tomatoes with a garlic clove cut in two and a handful of chopped parsley. When the tomatoes are soft and form a bed over the base of the pan, break 4 eggs on top and cook gently over a low heat until they are set.

Tomato omelette
Omelette aux tomates

An omelette with the summery freshness of tomatoes can be made very simply by adding slices of raw tomato just at the moment when the eggs begin to set. The omelette is folded in half and the tomatoes themselves retain all their sweet juiciness. But for mild-flavoured tomatoes try the following:

For one person:

2 tablespoons olive oil	salt
2 tomatoes, peeled and chopped	freshly milled black pepper
bay leaf	3–4 basil leaves, chopped
2 eggs	1 clove garlic, crushed

Heat one tablespoon of the oil and fry the tomatoes with the bay leaf over a medium heat until almost all the moisture has evaporated. Remove bay leaf. Beat the eggs in a bowl, add salt, pepper, basil and garlic and stir in the tomato mixture. Wipe out the pan with kitchen paper, heat the remaining oil, pour in the mixture and cook briskly, lifting the edges of the omelette as it cooks so that the uncooked mixture runs underneath. As soon as it is set, fold in half and slide on to a warm plate.

Tomatoes stuffed with tuna
Tomates au thon

In summer when you can't bear to cook, halved tomatoes can be prepared with a filling of tuna fish topped with mayonnaise, or stuffed with *tapenado* (see Index). Cut the tomatoes in half, remove the flesh with a teaspoon, sprinkle with salt and turn them upside down for 30 minutes to drain before adding the filling. Stand them on a bed of lettuce and garnish with olives and gherkins.

Baked or fried tomatoes
Tomates à la provençale

Good quality tomatoes are delicious either fried or baked and flavoured with garlic and parsley. Cut them in half and scoop out the seeds.

Fry them in olive oil, cut side down to evaporate their water, turn them over, add more oil, season with salt, pepper and a little sugar. When they are soft, sprinkle over a clove or two of chopped garlic mixed with a handful of chopped parsley.

Alternatively, bake them in an oven heated to Gas 7/425°F/220°C. Arrange the tomato halves in an oiled gratin dish. Put a pinch of salt, a sliver of garlic and some chopped parsley on each. Sprinkle with breadcrumbs and olive oil and bake in the oven for 10–15 minutes.

Pizza with pastry
Pizza provençale

Pizzas are as popular in the south of France as they are in Britain. Special vans parked by the roadside, on beaches and riverbanks, in village squares and markets, offer fresh pizzas to order, and the air is scented with that mouthwatering combination of tomatoes and herbs. No one needs to make them, but if they do it is never a chore, because the dough can be bought from the baker's shop, or they will follow the Provence tradition and make it with pastry. This can be home-made or bought – frozen puff pastry works very well. The topping can of course be varied to suit yourself.

225 g (8 oz) pastry, short or puff
1 teaspoon mild mustard
1 tablespoon tomato purée
450 g (1 lb) ripe tomatoes, sliced
chopped oregano or basil
freshly milled black pepper
6–8 anchovy fillets
12–18 black olives
75–100 g (3–4 oz) grated Cheddar or Gruyère
olive oil

Roll out the pastry and line a 30 cm (12 in) flan tin. Prick the base all over with a fork and put back in the fridge for 30 minutes to firm up. Heat the oven to Gas 7/425°F/220°C. Spread the mustard and the tomato purée over the pastry base and cover with the sliced tomatoes, sprinkle over the oregano or basil and season with black pepper. Arrange the anchovies and olives on top and cover with the grated cheese, sprinkle with olive oil and bake for 25 minutes.

Iced tomato soup
Soupe glacée à la tomate

A perfect soup for a supper party in high summer, to be made a day ahead and served straight from the fridge.

3 tablespoons olive oil
2 leeks, sliced
900 g (2 lb) tomatoes, peeled *or*
   1 can Italian tomatoes
1 tablespoon tomato purée
sprigs of thyme
bay leaf

1 clove garlic
1 litre (1¾ pints) water
salt
freshly milled black pepper
5–6 ice cubes
handful chopped chives and
   basil

Heat the oil in a saucepan and add the sliced leeks. Cook over a medium heat for 5 minutes. Cut tomatoes in half, and add to leeks, together with the tomato purée, herbs and the whole garlic clove. Mix well and add the water, salt and pepper. Bring to the boil, cover and simmer for 30 minutes. Liquidize or put through a mouli-légumes. Taste and if necessary add more salt and pepper. Leave to cool, put in the fridge. Serve in a tureen with the ice cubes and sprinkle with the chopped chives and basil.

Eiderdown soup
Tourrin à l'édredon

A *tourrin* (also known as *tourain*, *tourril* or *thourin*) is a soup of onions or garlic, or a mixture of the two, softened in oil before being simmered in a flavoured stock or water, or sometimes milk. At the last moment it is thickened with egg yolks, and is often served with grated cheese. Tradition has it that enough was made for two meals. After lunch, the tureen was slid under the eiderdown to keep hot for supper. The following is a rather luxurious version using white wine and tomatoes, but if you have no white wine or even tomatoes, make a basic version by leaving them out; and if you have no onions, use 5 or 6 cloves of garlic instead – different but still very good. Or add 100 g

(4 oz) of raw ham or bacon at the point when the onions have been softened; or include a few diced potatoes; or throw in a handful of vermicelli 5 minutes before the end of cooking time.

2 tablespoons olive oil
900 g (2 lb) onions, finely sliced
2 cloves garlic, chopped
1 teaspoon sugar
1 heaped tablespoon flour
1 can chopped Italian tomatoes
1 litre (1¾ pints) water
150 ml (¼ pint) white wine
2 sticks celery, chopped

sprig of fennel *or* 1 teaspoon
   seeds *or* ½ teaspoon nutmeg or
   cinnamon
1 teaspoon salt
freshly milled black pepper
2 egg yolks
slices of stale French bread
bowl of grated cheese

Heat the oil in a large saucepan and add the onions and garlic. Cover the pan, lower the heat and cook until they are soft and golden but not brown. This will take 30–40 minutes. Stir in the sugar and flour, followed by tomatoes, water, wine, celery, fennel (or nutmeg or cinnamon), salt and pepper. Bring to the boil, lower the heat, cover and simmer for 30 minutes. Taste and adjust seasoning. Put the egg yolks into a bowl, mix well and gradually beat in 5 or 6 tablespoons of the soup. Off the heat, stir this mixture into the soup. You can gently reheat, but be careful not to let it boil as it will curdle. The soup is traditionally ladled into soup plates each of which contains a slice of bread, and grated cheese is handed round separately to be sprinkled over the top.

Snails in tomato sauce
Escargots à la suçarelle

The snails prized in the south of France are *le petit gris* (the same species as our garden snail) and the smaller, flat glass snail. It is forbidden to collect them during the mating season but on grey, drizzly days in autumn they creep out from the stones under which they have hibernated during the long, hot summer and are gathered into sacks.

Before they can be eaten they must be kept in a container and purged for at least a fortnight because they are partial to plants which are poisonous to us. (This usually means keeping them in a ventilated but covered bucket with a supply of herbs to eat, but some purists advocate starvation.) They are then thoroughly cleaned in several changes of salted water and boiled in two stages until they are tender. This entails putting them into cold water with peppercorns, thyme, parsley and a bay leaf and boiling them for an hour. The water is thrown away and the whole process repeated. At this point, some people extract each snail and cut away the black viscera which can be bitter, though local experts insist this is only necessary with really large snails. They are then put back into the shells ready for the final stage. Snails do tend to be rubbery and this finishing process is vital to turn what is really just a free source of food for country people into a dish to tell your friends about. Restaurants mostly offer them stuffed with garlic butter, but Emile and Henri's way is to add a few potatoes to the broth and eat the lot with a sauce made by pounding 100 g (4 oz) garlic with the same amount of walnuts, beating in an egg yolk and enough olive oil to make a thick sauce. Others surround them with sorrel and anchovies, or Swiss chard and spinach flavoured with rosemary and mint.

In this recipe the snails are heated in a piquant tomato sauce. It is often made with small glass snails which are most easily eaten by piercing the shell with a needle, or acacia thorn, opposite the opening. The snail is then sucked out, and the noise this makes is the name of the dish, *suçarelle*. You can use this sauce for large snails too, or for the canned variety, in or out of their shells. (If you want to use the shells again, they can be cleaned by boiling for 30 minutes in water with a teaspoon of bicarbonate soda.) Enthusiasts will eat at least 25 fresh snails each but a can weighing around 225 g (8 oz) will do for four.

purged and boiled snails *or* 1 can prepared
2 tablespoons olive oil
1 onion, chopped
2 rashers streaky bacon, chopped

2 cloves garlic, chopped
2–3 sprigs of parsley
1 can chopped Italian tomatoes
2 whole red chillies
25 g (1 oz) breadcrumbs

Put the snails into their shells. Heat oil in a saucepan, add the onion and bacon and cook them for a few minutes over a medium heat before adding garlic, parsley, tomatoes and chillies. Bring to the boil, lower heat and simmer, covered, for 20 minutes. Remove chillies and sieve the sauce, stir in the breadcrumbs and add the snails. Stir them around and heat through gently for 20–30 minutes.

Fresh tomato sauce
Coulis de tomates

Home-made tomato sauce accompanies many dishes and in the past every household bottled vast quantities for use in the winter. It is simple to make but if you are short of time an excellent substitute is Sugocasa. This is the brand-name for a commercially produced Italian sauce, sold in jars in many supermarkets. It is made from chopped tomatoes, tomato purée and onions.

450 g (1 lb) ripe tomatoes *or* 1
   can chopped Italian tomatoes
1 tablespoon olive oil
1 onion, chopped
1 clove garlic, crushed

salt
freshly milled black pepper
sprigs of thyme and parsley
bay leaf
2 sugar lumps

If using fresh tomatoes, peel, de-seed and chop them. Heat the oil in a small saucepan and add the onion, let it soften for a few minutes over a medium heat before adding all the other ingredients. Simmer, uncovered for 30–40 minutes until the sauce is quite thick. It can be sieved or not, the choice is yours.

Rosy cauliflower
Choufleur d'églantine

A refreshing change from cauliflower in white sauce, in this recipe it is covered with tomato sauce, sprinkled with cheese and glazed under a hot grill.

1 medium cauliflower
salt
1 clove garlic, chopped

fresh tomato sauce (see recipe
   above)
75 g (3 oz) grated cheese
50 g (2 oz) butter

Divide the cauliflower into florets, chop the stalks and discard all the outer leaves. Cook in a little boiling salted water for 10 minutes. Heat grill. Drain and put cauliflower into a gratin dish and sprinkle over the garlic. Pour over the sauce, sprinkle with the grated cheese, dot with the butter and put under the grill until the top is bubbling and beginning to brown.

Chicken liver mousse with fresh tomato sauce
Gâteau aux foies de volaille au coulis de tomates

This is a favourite starter at L'Escarbille in St Martin d'Ardèche. There the tomato sauce is flavoured with crab, which is perhaps an unnecessary refinement. The little pots are turned out on to individual plates and the mousse served surrounded by its sauce.

25 g (1 oz) butter
225 g (8 oz) chicken livers
4 eggs, beaten
4 tablespoons crème fraîche or
  double cream

1 teaspoon tomato purée
salt
freshly milled black pepper
1 tablespoon brandy
bowl of fresh tomato sauce

Heat oven to Gas 4/350°F/180°C. Melt the butter in a frying pan and brown the livers quickly on all sides. Crush them and beat in the eggs, crème fraîche or cream, tomato purée, salt, pepper and brandy (or put all ingredients into a food processor or blender). Taste for seasoning. Butter four individual ovenproof cocottes and line the bases with rounds of greaseproof paper. Stand the little pots in a baking tin half-filled with boiling water. Bake for 20 minutes. Test by piercing with the point of a knife – it should come out clean. Turn the mousses out on to plates and pour a little tomato sauce around each.

Frogs' legs
Grenouilles à la provençale

Since hearing the spring mating chorus of the frogs in the river at night at St Martin d'Ardèche and walking across the beach alive with their babies, I have become less enthusiastic about eating frogs' legs, which nevertheless are delicious, tender and sweet with just a hint of fishiness. You are not very likely to find them on sale in England but just in case you come across a frozen packet in a supermarket in France, here is what to do with them.

Let them defrost, coat them in seasoned flour and fry them in very hot oil until golden brown all over, and put them on a warm serving dish. Add a little butter to the pan and throw in some chopped garlic. As soon as it begins to colour, add 4–5 peeled and de-seeded tomatoes to the pan (or use a can of chopped Italian tomatoes), let them soften and pour in a glass of white wine, let it boil fiercely, add salt, freshly

milled black pepper and a good handful of chopped parsley. Pour
sauce over the legs and serve at once.

Red mullet with tomatoes
Bécasse de mer à la marseillaise

Red mullet, nicknamed *bécasse de mer* (woodcock of the sea), has
sweet, delicate flesh and in Provence is generally eaten ungutted or at
least with its liver left intact, which adds a gamey flavour. It has big
scales, which when removed can fly all over the kitchen, so put the fish
in the sink, hold the fish by its tail and work up the fish towards the
head with the blunt side of a knife. Use short strokes which lift and
brush the scales loose without damaging the skin. In this recipe it is
simply baked with white wine and tomatoes and is delicious eaten hot
or cold.

2 tablespoons olive oil
4 red mullet
450 g (1 lb) ripe tomatoes,
   peeled *or* 1 can Italian
   tomatoes
1 onion, chopped

1 clove garlic, chopped
2–3 tablespoons chopped
   parsley
150 ml (¼ pint) white wine
salt
freshly milled black pepper

Heat oven to Gas 6/400°F/200°C. Heat the oil in a frying pan and cook
the fish for 2 minutes on each side. Remove to a shallow ovenproof
dish. Put tomatoes, onion, garlic, parsley and wine into the frying pan,
bring to the boil, pour over the fish, add salt and pepper and put into
the oven for 20–25 minutes.

Squid pie
Tielle

In the fishing port of Sète, *tielles* are as common as pasties in Cornwall.
They are small pastry turnovers with crenellated edges, filled with fish
and flavoured with parsley, garlic, tomato and red chillies, which
make a welcome snack in the middle of the day. This recipe is for one
big pie, enough for four for lunch or supper. If using frozen puff
pastry, allow it to defrost. Try to persuade your fishmonger to clean
the squid; if he won't, it is not difficult. Cut off the tentacles above the

eyes, and set aside. Pull the head from the body and discard it along with all the innards. Cut open the pouch with scissors, remove the transparent quill and wash the interior. Cut into chunks.

2 tablespoons olive oil
2 onions, chopped
700 g (1½ lb) squid, roughly
    chopped
1 heaped tablespoon flour
2 tablespoons chopped parsley
2 cloves garlic, chopped

5 ripe tomatoes, peeled *or* 1 can
    chopped Italian tomatoes
4 dried red chillies
salt
350 g (12 oz) ready-made puff
    pastry
1 egg yolk, beaten and thinned
    with a few drops water

Heat the olive oil in a saucepan and fry the onions over a medium heat for a few minutes, give them a stir and add the squid. Raise the heat to evaporate the liquid which the squid will give out, toss the pan and turn the fish over and over so it does not stick or burn. Sprinkle in the flour, mix well, lowering heat as necessary. After a couple of minutes, add parsley and garlic, the chopped tomatoes, chillies and salt. Bring to the boil, cover and simmer for 30 minutes. Heat oven to Gas 7/ 425°F/220°C. To make sure the pastry base cooks as quickly as the top, put a baking sheet in the oven to heat. Divide the pastry in two portions, one about a third larger than the other. Roll out the larger to fit the base and sides of a 20 cm (8 in) pie dish and the smaller to make the lid. Line the dish with the base pastry and pour in the contents of the saucepan. Moisten the edges of the pastry lid, lay it on top, press firmly all round. Trim away any excess pastry with a knife and pinch a crenellated pattern all round, or mark with the prongs of a fork. Cut a slit in the centre to release steam, and brush the surface all over with the egg yolk. Bake for 30 minutes. If the pastry begins to brown too soon, cover loosely with foil.

Aubergines

Preliminary preparation

Fried aubergines

Grilled or barbecued aubergines

Aubergine caviar

The Pope's aubergines

Aubergines with onions and tomatoes

The gypsies' ratatouille

Aubergine, tomato and courgette gratin

Avignon's aubergine and tomato ratatouille

Aubergines, called *merinjana* in the local tongue, came to France via Arabia and Persia, were adopted with enthusiasm, and play a key part in the cooking of Provence and Languedoc. They give a tender sweetness to many dishes. As a vegetable they are delicious with rabbit, pork, lamb and chicken. They can be fried or grilled, made into vegetable stews and gratins which often include tomatoes, green peppers or courgettes, all of which go into the famous *ratatouille*. Or try them peeled and sliced, softened in oil and then layered in a gratin dish with grated cheese (use a mature Cheddar mixed with Edam). Top with a béchamel sauce and a final layer of cheese, then put into a hot oven until the top bubbles and turns golden. Aubergines make delicious fritters, sprinkled with salt and served with a home-made tomato sauce. (A fritter recipe is given in Etceteras.)

Choose ones which are glistening and firm, and insist on feeling them. It is often easier to buy them by numbers rather than weight, allowing a whole or half a one per person depending on the recipe.

Preliminary preparation

Cut off the stem end and remove the rough and sometimes prickly calyx. The seductive, purple skin can be chewy and bitter, so peel it with a sharp knife. Many of the recipes require the aubergines to be fried and in order to prevent them absorbing an alarming quantity of oil, they must undergo an initial salting period which rids them of their excess moisture. Slice them in rings unless the recipe specifies otherwise, lay the slices in a single layer on a board or table and sprinkle with fine salt. Leave for an hour and then wipe dry with kitchen paper. Heat a frying pan, cover the base generously with olive or groundnut oil and fry a few slices at a time, over a medium to high heat, until they are soft and golden on both sides. As they are done, drain them on a plate, interleaving each layer with kitchen or greaseproof paper. Add more oil to the pan if necessary.

Fried aubergines
Risto

Fried with tomatoes, aubergines have a jammy consistency and make a
delicious vegetable eaten with roast lamb or game.

450 g (1 lb) aubergines	2 cloves garlic, chopped
2 ripe tomatoes, chopped	1–2 sprigs of thyme
freshly milled black pepper	handful chopped basil or parsley

Prepare aubergines as given under Preliminary preparation at the
beginning of this section, using olive oil to fry them. Return the fried
slices to the pan, add the tomatoes, pepper, garlic and thyme and cook
gently for about 15 minutes until the mixture is soft and pulpy, stirring
from time to time. Add the chopped basil or parsley just before
serving.

Grilled or barbecued aubergines
Chatons

Grilled aubergines are very simple to prepare. Don't peel them as the
skin is needed to hold them together. Cut them in half lengthwise,
slash them at intervals to prevent them curling, sprinkle them with fine
salt and leave to drain for an hour. Dry with kitchen paper. Sprinkle
them with olive oil, season with freshly milled pepper and grill them
over a barbecue or under, but not too close to, a hot grill, skinside up
for 5 minutes, then turn and grill a further 10 minutes, lowering the
heat. Or try pushing whole aubergines into the hot cinders beneath a
barbecue and let them cook until they blister and blacken. Split them
in half. Eat these grilled or baked aubergines sprinkled with lemon
juice and olive oil and seasoned with salt, pepper and parsley. Scoop
out the pulp with a spoon.

Aubergine caviar
Caviar d'aubergines

This is a milder spread than the caper, olive and anchovy Provençal
caviar tapenado, given in the Olive section. It is sweet and garlicky.
Make it with a pestle and mortar or, if you prefer, a food processor.

450 g (1 lb) aubergines

3 cloves garlic, crushed

2 spring onions, chopped

2–3 tablespoons olive oil

juice of 1 lemon

salt

freshly milled black pepper

handful chopped basil or parsley

Heat oven to Gas 5/375°F/190°C and bake the aubergines, left whole, for 30–40 minutes until they feel soft and the skin is brown, wrinkled and beginning to blacken. Remove from the oven and cool, split in half and scoop out the flesh with a spoon into a bowl or mortar. Add garlic and spring onions and mash or pound well, gradually beating in sufficient olive oil to make a thick, creamy paste – it must not be runny. Stir in lemon juice, salt and pepper to taste, and finally the basil or parsley. Eat on slices of toast or French bread as a snack, or as part of a cold buffet.

The Pope's aubergines
Papeton d'aubergines

This is a Provençal aubergine *flan* which legend tells was created especially for one of the Popes of Avignon. It is glorious in flavour, clerical in looks with its sombre base crowned with a golden crust of cheese, the whole surrounded by a scarlet tomato sauce. Traditionally eaten as a vegetable with rabbit or meat, it is also perfect as a vegetarian main course accompanied by jacket potatoes and a salad. It is also delicious cold as a starter.

700 g (1½ lb) aubergines

olive oil

1 clove garlic, chopped

1–2 shallots *or* 1 small onion,
  chopped

sprigs of thyme

bay leaf

salt

freshly milled black pepper

4 eggs

4 tablespoons crème fraîche

75–100 g (3–4 oz) grated cheese
  (use mature Cheddar, Red
  Leicester or Gruyère)

fresh tomato sauce (see Index)

Prepare aubergines as given under Preliminary preparation at the beginning of this section. Fry them in olive oil in a heavy-based, large casserole. When all the slices have been fried return them to the pan with the garlic, shallots or onion, thyme and bay leaf. Season with salt and pepper. Cover, lower the heat and simmer for 30 minutes, turning the pieces over from time to time. Drain them in a colander, remove bay leaf. Heat oven to Gas 6/400°F/200°C. Put the slices through the middle grater of a mouli-légumes or purée them in a food processor. Beat in the eggs one at a time, and stir in the crème fraîche. Taste and if necessary add more salt and pepper. Put the mixture into an oiled soufflé or other round, deep dish and stand it in an oven tray half-filled with boiling water. Put in the oven and bake for about 20 minutes, by which time a crust will have begun to form on top. Sprinkle over the grated cheese and bake for a further 15–20 minutes until top is golden and the *flan* is cooked through – test with a skewer, it should come out clean. Serve with the tomato sauce handed round separately.

Aubergines with onions and tomatoes
Chichoumeille

In this dish, equal quantities of aubergines and tomatoes are gently sweated with onions and a little olive oil until they are soft and tender. That is all, no other flavourings like garlic or herbs, just the three vegetables absorbing the juices of each other. Try to save a little for another meal as it is also good cold.

450 g (1 lb) aubergines
2 tablespoons olive oil
225 g (8 oz) onions, chopped

450 g (1 lb) ripe tomatoes, chopped *or* can chopped Italian tomatoes
salt
freshly milled black pepper

Prepare aubergines as given under Preliminary preparation at the beginning of this section until the point where they have been wiped dry after salting. Heat the oil in a large, heavy-based casserole and cook the onion gently for five minutes or so. Add the aubergines and chopped tomatoes. Season generously with salt and pepper. Cover and simmer for about 30 minutes. Remove lid and continue cooking for a further 10 minutes to reduce the liquid.

The gypsies' *ratatouille*
Bohémienne

This version of the well-known *ratatouille* is supposed to come from the gypsies who cooked it over the fire in which their hedgehog was baking in its covering of clay. (Any left-over *ratatouille* can be eaten cold, or put into an omelette or used as a filling for a quiche by mixing the *ratatouille* with 2 or 3 beaten eggs, a carton of curd cheese and a little milk, then baking at Gas 6/400°F/200°C for 25–30 minutes.)

6 tablespoons olive oil	1 can chopped Italian tomatoes
2 onions, chopped	*or* 450 g (1 lb) ripe tomatoes,
450 g (1 lb) aubergines, skinned	peeled and chopped
and sliced	salt
450 g (1 lb) courgettes, sliced	freshly milled black pepper
2 green peppers, finely sliced	sprigs of thyme
6 cloves garlic, chopped	bay leaf

Heat 4 tablespoons of oil in a large, heavy-based casserole and soften the chopped onion. Add all the other ingredients and simmer, covered, on a low heat for 1 hour. Remove lid, raise heat and cook until nearly all the liquid has evaporated, stirring occasionally so it does not stick. Stir in remaining oil and serve piping hot.

Aubergine, tomato and courgette gratin
Gratin languedocien

This basil-flavoured gratin of aubergine, tomato and courgettes with its crisp topping of golden breadcrumbs comes from Languedoc.

2–3 aubergines	salt
2 courgettes, sliced	freshly milled black pepper
olive oil	generous handful breadcrumbs
1 can chopped Italian tomatoes	1 clove garlic, chopped
chopped basil	

Prepare, slice and fry aubergines as given under Preliminary preparation at the beginning of this section. When all the slices have been transferred to a plate, layers interleaved with kitchen paper, add the courgettes to the pan, adding more oil if necessary, and fry them until they are beginning to turn golden on both sides. Heat oven to Gas 5/375°F/190°C. Put aubergines, courgettes and tomatoes in alternate layers in a gratin dish, seasoning each layer with a little basil, salt and pepper. Finish with a layer of tomatoes. Mix the breadcrumbs with the chopped garlic and sprinkle over the top. Moisten with olive oil and bake for 30 minutes.

Avignon's aubergine and tomato *ratatouille*
Ratatouille avignonnaise

In Avignon they make their *ratatouille* a little differently from
everywhere else – aubergines and tomatoes only are used in equal
quantities and the dish is finished off in a hot oven.

450 g (1 lb) aubergines, peeled	freshly milled black pepper
450 g (1 lb) tomatoes, peeled	2 anchovy fillets
and quartered	1 tablespoon flour
olive oil	1 tablespoon milk
1 clove garlic, chopped	handful breadcrumbs
salt	

Prepare aubergines as given under Preliminary preparation at the
beginning of this section, cutting them into slices lengthwise. Once the
frying process is complete add more oil to the pan if necessary and add
the tomatoes with the garlic, salt and pepper. Return the aubergines,
mix and cook gently until soft. Heat oven to Gas 6/400°F/200°C.
Meanwhile, put the anchovies into a small saucepan with 2 tablespoons of olive oil, dust in the flour, mix well and stir in the milk. Stir
into the vegetables and turn them into a gratin dish. Sprinkle the
breadcrumbs on top, moisten with oil and put in the oven for 10–15
minutes to brown.

Swiss chard to asparagus

Gratin of Swiss chard or spinach

Spinach or Swiss chard loaf

Spinach or Swiss chard broth with eggs

Swiss chard stalks with anchovies

Trout with sorrel and spinach

Broad beans with sorrel

Sweet spinach or Swiss chard pie

Languedoc faggots

Spinach and sorrel omelette

Top and tail radish soup

Broad bean salad

Hop shoot salad

Mixed green salad with bacon and croûtons

Asparagus with lemon sauce

Asparagus and sorrel or spinach soup

Swiss chard, sorrel and spinach are all green leafed vegetables which feature often in the cooking of both Provence and Languedoc. Each is something of an acquired taste as the leaves of all three have a degree of bitterness. It is often possible to use the leaves of one or the other though the flavour and even texture of the dish will not be the same.

Gratin of Swiss chard or spinach
Tian de blettes ou d'épinards

Swiss chard goes under all sorts of aliases. The whole vegetable, leaves and all can be *blette*, *bette*, *bléa* or *blète*, while the stalks alone are referred to as *cardes* or *côtes de poirée*. The papery leaves are usually cut away, to be used perhaps in *caillettes* or a vegetable loaf, while the white, fleshy stalks are most often served in a white or cheese sauce or flavoured with anchovies as part of the Christmas eve supper. It is not easily found in England. You need an enterprising greengrocer or ethnic shop or market.

Spinach is of course plentiful and the frozen variety is a good substitute when you cannot buy fresh. You have probably enjoyed it served simply as a vegetable with a good knob of butter. It is also good sprinkled with a little olive oil, a few drops of orange flower water and a handful of pine kernels.

Either Swiss chard or spinach can be used in this recipe. With Swiss chard you can use just the stalks or the stalks and the leaves. First snip off the leaves with scissors and wash them well under running water. Wash the stalks, remove any fibres and cut them into 5 cm (2 in) lengths. Spinach, which can be gritty, needs thorough washing in several changes of water.

900 g (2 lb) Swiss chard or
  spinach
juice of ½ lemon
salt
300 ml (½ pint) béchamel sauce
  (see Index)

nutmeg
100 g (4 oz) grated cheese
salt
freshly milled black pepper

Put the leaves of Swiss chard or spinach and 1 tablespoon water into a
saucepan over a medium heat and cook for 2–3 minutes until they
reduce and soften. Shake the pan from time to time to prevent the
leaves from sticking. Drain them in a colander. Rinse out the saucepan,
and put in the Swiss chard stalks, cover with water, add the lemon
juice and a little salt. Cover, bring to the boil and let them bubble for
10–15 minutes until they soften. Put into a colander to drain. Heat the
oven to Gas 6/400°F/200°C. Make the bechamel sauce, add a pinch of
nutmeg and 75 g (3 oz) of the cheese. Season generously with salt and
pepper. If using spinach, put it all into a gratin dish and pour over the
sauce; if Swiss chard, put the leaves into the base of a gratin dish, pour
over half the sauce, lay the stalks on top and pour over remaining
sauce. Sprinkle over the rest of the cheese and put in the oven for about
20 minutes to turn golden brown.

Spinach or Swiss chard loaf
Pain d'épinards ou de blettes

The deep speckled green of this vegetable loaf contrasts beautifully in
colour and flavour with the tomato sauce with which it is served. It can
be eaten as a starter or as a vegetarian main dish, in which case add
100 g (4 oz) grated cheese 15 minutes before the end of the cooking
time. It will turn golden and bubbling. You can if you wish make it in
individual ovenproof pots, in which case reduce the cooking time to
20–25 minutes.

450 g (1 lb) spinach or 900 g (2 lb) Swiss chard or 350 g (12 oz) spinach and 150 g (6 oz) sorrel	salt
	freshly milled black pepper
	grated nutmeg
	2 cloves garlic, chopped
50 g (2 oz) butter	thyme
1 tablespoon flour	4 eggs
4 tablespoons crème fraîche or milk	tomato sauce (see Index)

Heat oven to Gas 6/400°F/200°C. Wash the leaves (use the Swiss chard
stalks for another dish) and cook for a few minutes in a very little
salted water. (If using frozen spinach, simply defrost it, which can be
done by gently heating in a saucepan.) Drain well in a colander,

pressing out excess water with an upturned saucer. Chop. Dry the pan and melt the butter in it. When it is hot add the chopped leaves and dust in the flour. Mix well and add crème fraîche or milk, salt, pepper and grated nutmeg. Simmer gently for a couple of minutes, stirring all the time to cook the flour. Take off the heat and add garlic and thyme. Beat the eggs and stir into the mixture. Butter a round ovenproof dish, pudding basin or cake tin and turn the mixture into it. Stand it in a roasting tin half-filled with boiling water and bake for 40–45 minutes. Test by inserting a skewer, which should come out clean; if necessary give it a few minutes longer. It can be served straight from the dish with the tomato sauce served separately, or remove from the mould by setting it aside for 5–10 minutes before running a knife round the edge and turning it out on to a heated dish. Serve with some of the tomato sauce poured round, the rest handed round separately.

Spinach or Swiss chard broth with eggs
Bouillabaisse d'épinards ou de blettes

If you think *bouillabaisse* is a fish stew, you are right, but the word really describes the method of cooking, which is rapid boiling to amalgamate olive oil and water and reduce the sauce. (The recipe for the fish version is in *Simply Fish*.) The version below is based on spinach or Swiss chard leaves, is quick and easy and results in a delicious dish for lunch or supper. It can also be made with a mixture of spinach and sorrel. Serve it on toast or croûtons in wide soup bowls. Saffron should really be used, but failing that turmeric will give the dish a golden glow.

450 g (1 lb) spinach or Swiss chard leaves *or* 350 g (12 oz) spinach and 150 g (6 oz) sorrel
3 tablespoons olive oil
1 onion, chopped
450 g (1 lb) potatoes, sliced
600 ml (1 pint) boiling water
1 clove garlic, crushed

sprig of fennel *or* 1 teaspoon seeds
bay leaf
sprig of parsley
pinch of powdered saffron or turmeric
salt
freshly milled black pepper
4 eggs

Blanch the leaves in a very little water for 2–3 minutes, drain in a colander and press out all the moisture using a plate or saucer. Chop

them. Heat the oil in a wide, heavy-based pan and fry the onion until
golden, add chopped leaves and let them sweat for a few minutes, then
add the potatoes and pour in the boiling water. Add garlic, fennel, bay
leaf, parsley and saffron or turmeric. Season with salt and pepper.
Cover and simmer for about 20 minutes until the potatoes are cooked.
Carefully break the eggs on top and let them poach until the whites are
set.

Swiss chard stalks with anchovies
Cardes à l'anchoïade

The stalks alone are used for this dish which is flavoured with
anchovies. The leaves can be used in another recipe.

50 g (2 oz) anchovies   150 ml (¼ pint) water
900 g (2 lb) Swiss chard   freshly milled black pepper
juice of ½ lemon   1 tablespoon chopped parsley
1 tablespoon olive oil   2 cloves garlic, chopped
1 onion, chopped   1 egg yolk
1 heaped teaspoon flour   few drops vinegar

If the anchovies are salted, put them to soak for an hour in water or
milk. Clean the chard stalks, remove stringy fibres and cut into chunks.
Blanch them in boiling, salted water for 10 minutes with the lemon
juice which will keep them very white. Drain. Heat oil in a frying pan,
add onion and let it soften. Add anchovies, breaking them up with a
wooden spoon. Dust in the flour, mix well and gradually stir in the
water. Add chard, pepper, parsley and garlic. Cover and cook gently
for 30 minutes. Remove from heat, and thicken the sauce by mixing in
the egg yolk beaten with a few drops of vinegar.

Trout with sorrel and spinach
Truites aux herbes

Sorrel can be elusive but once I was lucky and bought it in a pot from a
supermarket and then transferred it to the garden, where it grows very
happily. You can also find it sometimes at nurseries or garden centres.
It has an acquired bitterness and is often used quite sparingly to
flavour a salad, soup or an omelette when a handful or two is gently
softened in butter until it turns to a purée to be added just at the point

when you fold the omelette over. As a sauce it is delicious with fish. Simply stir a few tablespoons of crème fraîche into a purée of sorrel and thin with a little of the cooking liquid. It is most famously used as a base for cooking shad, a bony but much prized fish which comes into the rivers of southern Europe to breed in May. Sorrel is high in oxalic acid, which over a long, slow cooking period reduces the shad's needle-sharp bones to a mush. (A detailed recipe can be found in *Simply Fish*.)

In the following recipe, the leaves of sorrel and spinach are combined with watercress, mint and chives to make a deep green filling for the trout.

4 medium trout	salt
225 g (8 oz) mixture of sorrel, spinach and watercress	freshly milled black pepper
	150 ml (¼ pint) white or rosé
25 g (1 oz) butter	wine *or* water and the juice of
1–2 tablespoons snipped chives	1 lemon to make 150 ml (¼
1 tablespoon chopped mint	pint)

Have the trout cleaned and the gills removed. Wash sorrel, spinach and watercress and put into a saucepan with half the butter. Put over a medium heat and cook until they turn soft and reduce. Meanwhile heat oven to Gas 5/375°F/190°C. Drain the vegetables well. Add chives, mint, salt and pepper. Fill the cavity of each trout. Lay them in an ovenproof dish (any remaining stuffing can be put around them). Season with salt and pepper. Pour over the wine or water and lemon juice and dot with remaining butter. Bake for 25–30 minutes, basting half-way through the cooking time.

Broad beans with sorrel
Fèves à l'oseille

The new season's beans picked when they are 5–6 cm (2 in) long can be cooked whole in their pods. Simply string them like runner beans and cook in a little salted water flavoured with parsley or savory. (Or they can be eaten raw, everyone shelling their own and dipping them into *gros sel* and butter, or you can add a chopped handful to a *salade niçoise*.) When they are older and the beans are fatter, they need to be shelled – use rubber gloves if you don't want black fingers. 900 g (2 lb) of beans in the pod will yield around 350–400 g (12–14 oz), which is enough for four as they are quite filling, but if you have big appetites, buy an extra 450 g (1 lb). If shelling beans is too much of a chore, the following recipe works well with the frozen variety. The combination of olive oil, sorrel and herbs lends an appealing bitter-sweetness.

2 tablespoons olive oil
900 g (2 lb) broad beans,
   shelled *or* 350–400 g (12–14
   oz) frozen
salt

freshly milled black pepper
25 g (1 oz) butter
handful mixed sorrel leaves,
   thyme and chives, chopped

Heat the olive oil, add the beans and cook over a medium heat, stirring from time to time, for 5–10 minutes, when they will turn from bland to bright green. Barely cover with boiling water (which splutters when added so take care it doesn't burn you). Add salt and pepper and cook until the beans are soft. Test after 10–15 minutes, as the cooking time depends on size and age. Drain, add butter, shake the pan well to coat the beans all over. Empty into a warm serving dish and sprinkle over the chopped sorrel, thyme and chives.

Sweet spinach or Swiss chard pie
Tourte d'épinards ou de blettes

If you like mince pies, this Christmas eve treat, variations of which appear from Nice to the Ardèche, will appeal to you. The filling consists of spinach or Swiss chard leaves, beaten egg and grated cheese sweetened with raisins soaked in rum, eau-de-vie or brandy plus fruit and sometimes pine nuts.

225 g (8 oz) raisins
4 tablespoons rum, eau-de-vie or
   brandy
450 g (1 lb) spinach or Swiss
   chard leaves
pinch of nutmeg
1 banana, cut in rings

225 g (8 oz) Cox's apples,
   peeled, cored and sliced
50 g (2 oz) pine nuts (optional)
2 whole eggs, beaten
50 g (2 oz) grated cheese
225 g (8 oz) puff pastry

Heat oven to Gas 6/400°F/200°C. Soak raisins in a bowl with the rum, eau-de-vie or brandy. Make filling by washing the spinach or Swiss chard and blanching it for a few moments until it softens and reduces. Drain well. Put it into a bowl and add nutmeg, the raisins and liquor, banana, apples, pine nuts, eggs and cheese. Mix. Divide the pastry into two pieces, one a third larger than the other. Roll out the larger and line a deepish 20 cm (8 in) pie dish or tin. Fill with the spinach mixture, smoothing it over. Roll out the second piece of pastry to fit the top. To make sure of a good seal, dampen the edge of the pastry lid with a finger dipped in water, lay lid on top, press the two layers together right round, then mark the border with the prongs of a fork. So that the steam may escape, cut 2 or 3 slits in the centre of the pastry lid and bake for 40 minutes. Eat hot, tepid or cold.

Languedoc faggots
Caillettes

Caillettes are similar to faggots. Perhaps they came to England via the Huguenots because *fagòt* is another of their names. The French version mixes pork and pig's liver with a vegetable which is usually Swiss chard, spinach, sorrel or lettuce but there are recipes using wild boar or even a pair of thrushes. Sometimes chestnuts are added, or earthy wild mushrooms, and if there is nothing else to hand, mashed potatoes do very well. *Caillettes* are traditionally wrapped in caul, the thin and lacy membrane known as *crépine* in French, which encloses the pig's paunch. This is hard to come by nowadays in a British butcher's. Its purpose is to act as a wrapper to hold the *caillettes* in shape and keep them moist. In its absence you can use rashers of streaky bacon and greaseproof paper. If you do get hold of caul, soak it in tepid water with a little salt or vinegar for 30 minutes. It will soften and the layers separate easily. *Caillettes* are usually eaten cold but are very good hot with a home-made tomato sauce.

450 g (1 lb) pork	2 cloves garlic, chopped
225 g (8 oz) pig's liver	pinch salt
450 g (1 lb) spinach, fresh or	freshly milled black pepper
frozen *or* a mixture of spinach	1 beaten egg
and sorrel *or* Swiss chard	piece of caul *or* 8 rashers
leaves	unsmoked, streaky bacon and
1 tablespoon olive or peanut oil	some greaseproof paper
1 onion, chopped	

Heat oven to Gas 5/375°F/190°C. Mince meat and liver (or ask your butcher to do this). Blanch spinach in a very little boiling, salted water (or defrost frozen); drain well in a colander, extracting as much liquid as possible by pressing it down firmly with a small plate or saucer. Chop roughly. Heat oil and cook onion over a medium heat until soft, stirring from time to time. Combine minced meats, chopped leaves, onion, garlic, salt and pepper. Take the mixture off the heat and stir in the beaten egg. Divide the mixture, which should be firm and moist, into 8 portions and form these into balls. Cut the caul or greaseproof paper into 8 pieces, each large enough to wrap a portion. Set each *caillette* into the centre of a piece of caul, or wrap each with a piece of bacon and set into the centre of a piece of paper. Make loose parcels and put them folded side down in a tight-packed single layer in an oiled gratin dish. Bake for 45–50 minutes.

Spinach and sorrel omelette
Omelette aux épinards et à l'oseille

This marbled green omelette tastes as beautiful as it looks and can be made with spinach or a mixture of spinach and sorrel.

350 g (12 oz) spinach, fresh or frozen *or* 225 g (8 oz) spinach and 100 g (4 oz) sorrel
1 tablespoon tomato purée
1 clove garlic, chopped
1 tablespoon chopped basil or parsley
4 tablespoons olive oil
salt, pepper
8 eggs
4 tablespoons grated cheese

Wash and blanch leaves for several minutes in a very little water, drain well and chop. Frozen spinach must be defrosted and drained well. Put the chopped leaves into a bowl and mix in the tomato purée, garlic, basil or parsley, 2 tablespoons of the oil, salt and pepper. Beat in the eggs one at a time. Put the grill on high before you begin to cook the omelette. Heat the remaining 2 tablespoons of oil in a frying pan and when it begins to smoke, pour in the egg mixture. Cook over a high heat, stirring from time to time as the egg sets. When it is quite thick, cover and cook on a low heat for 2 or 3 minutes. Remove from the heat, sprinkle with the grated cheese and set the pan under the grill for a minute or two. The top will turn a golden brown as the cheese melts and bubbles. Serve from the pan in wedges.

Top and tail radish soup
Soupe pelou

One day we ate a bowl of radishes dipped in salt and butter and Jean-Pierre remarked that his grandmother always made a soup from the leaves. When I discovered the recipe I realized it was the perfect soup for frugal grandmothers. No waste at all. The tops, tails and leaves go into the pot to make tomorrow's lunch with the addition of some slices of garlic bread. When choosing your radishes, make sure the bunch is very fresh and the leaves in good condition.

tops, tails and leaves of a bunch   salt
    of radishes   freshly milled black pepper
350 g (12 oz) potatoes, peeled   nutmeg
    and chopped   croûtons
1 litre (1¾ pints) water

Wash the tops, tails and leaves and put them in a pot with the potatoes, water, salt, pepper and a pinch of ground nutmeg. Bring to the boil, cover and simmer for 40 minutes. Put through a food processor, liquidizer or mouli-légumes. Put a croûton into each soup plate and pour over the hot soup.

Broad bean salad
Ensalado de favo

Broad beans, which tend to be bland, become interesting in a salad with fried bread croûtons. Shell the beans and mix them in a salad bowl with salt, pepper, one tablespoon vinegar and one of olive oil. Cut 2 or 3 slices of French bread into cubes. Heat 4 tablespoons oil in a frying pan and fry bread cubes until golden. Tip over the beans and serve at once.

Hop shoot salad
Salade de houblons

If you live in a hop-growing area, this is a salad to make in early spring when other salad vegetables are scarce. Wash 2–3 handfuls of the shoots, blanch them for 10 minutes in salted water, drain well and leave to cool. Serve in a bowl with a vinaigrette sauce flavoured with a little mustard.

Mixed green salad with bacon and croûtons
Lou mesclun au lard et aux croûtons

This simple mixture of wild salad leaves has a true country origin, though nowadays it has become *le snob*, appearing on many expensive menus. People would gather what they could find such as the leaves of young dandelions, rocket, sorrel and spinach, salad burnet, cresses, lettuce, nasturtium leaves, velvety lamb's lettuce, watercress and chervil. The salad becomes a feast by adding pieces of bacon and small croûtons of fried bread.

selection of salad leaves
2 teaspoons lemon juice
salt
freshly milled black pepper
4 tablespoons olive oil

100 g (4 oz) bacon, chopped
2 slices French bread, cut in
    cubes
olive oil for frying

Choose three or four different varieties of leaves, and wash and dry them. In a large salad bowl, mix the lemon juice with salt and pepper and beat in the olive oil. Tip in the leaves. Heat frying pan and cook the bacon until the fat runs and it begins to crisp. Push the bacon to one side of the pan, add a little oil if necessary, and fry the bread cubes until they are golden. Toss the salad. Tip over the bacon and croûtons and bring to the table.

Asparagus with lemon sauce
Asperges à la sauce au citron

From April through to June, handwritten notices offering *asperges* point to the farms where they are sold bunched and priced according to the size of the stalks. As we drive past the packing station at St Paulet, we glimpse bundle upon bundle trundling along the conveyor belt, waiting to be boxed and driven through the night to Paris, Germany and Belgium. It is a different variety from our green asparagus, the stalks of these are white ending in a tip of pale purple. The thinnest are the cheapest and are ideal in an omelette or cooked, drained and then put into a gratin dish, sprinkled with cheese, dotted with butter and put into a hot oven for 5 minutes or so. The fat stalks, as thick as a thumb, are the best, juicy to the last morsel. We never tire of them as a first course simply served warm or cold with either melted butter, warm olive oil or this lemony cream sauce.

Asparagus needs to be cooked upright, the stalks standing in the boiling water while the heads cook in the steam. In the absence of an asparagus kettle with its own wire basket, stand a cutlery drainer in a deep saucepan and improvise a lid with foil.

700 g (1½ lb) green or white
    asparagus
1 teaspoon mustard
1 teaspoon lemon juice
salt

freshly milled black pepper
2 tablespoons crème fraîche
150 ml (¼ pint) olive oil
handful chives

Wash asparagus. Green asparagus is usually quite smooth but the stringy fibres of white asparagus must be scraped away, so use a knife and work upwards from the cut end. Trim the stalks so that they can stand evenly upright in the pan (any left-over bits can be added to the pan). Make four bundles and tie each with string, winding round from the base to just below the heads and criss-crossing back again. (This prevents the stems sagging during the cooking process and becoming impossible to lift out without breaking.) Put the bundles into the wire basket or cutlery drainer, and lower into the pan half-filled with salted water. Bring to the boil, put on the lid and cook quite briskly until the stems are soft when tested with the point of a knife, which takes about 20–40 minutes. Lift out and drain. Cover a warm plate with a clean napkin, lay the bundles on top, cut away the string, fold over the napkin. (The napkin helps to drain the excess water as well as keeping the asparagus warm.) Mix mustard, lemon juice, salt and pepper in a mortar or a small bowl, stir in the crème fraîche and gradually beat in the oil. Snip in the chives using scissors. Eat the asparagus with fingers, dipping the heads into the sauce.

Asparagus and sorrel or spinach soup
Soupe d'asperges et d'oseille ou d'épinards

Don't throw away the asparagus water, but use it as a basis for a soup. Heat 2 tablespoons of olive oil in a saucepan, add 2 handfuls of chopped sorrel or spinach leaves and let them cook for 3–4 minutes until they reduce, stirring all the time. Add 1 litre (1¾ pints) of the asparagus water and two medium potatoes, peeled and quartered. Season with salt and pepper and cook, covered, for about 20 minutes, until the potatoes are soft. Sieve or liquidize, add a dollop of butter or

crème fraîche and serve with small croûtons of bread fried in olive oil.
A few chopped bits of crisply fried bacon are a pleasant addition.

Fruits of Summer and Autumn

There is a barn on the road to St Martin d'Ardèche where we go to buy fruit. It is next to a sleeping beauty of a house with a turret and balcony overgrown with wisteria and red-trumpeted bignonia. Both the house and barn are beginning to crumble. Inside it is dark and cool as a cave, the rafters supporting the clay nests of swallows which dip in and out, feeding their insatiable babies. Strings of onions and bunches of dried herbs, lavender and garlic hang from a beam and there are stacks of wooden slatted trays full of all the fruits of summer and autumn. Two elderly women serve behind a rickety counter which holds an ancient set of scales, a cardboard money box, and jars of their home-produced honey and jams.

Both regions are famous for their fruits. In the fertile valleys of the rivers, the farms are surrounded by orchards of cherry trees, peaches and apricots, pears and plums, apples and greengages, while along the coast the almond flourishes. As each crop ripens so the pickers can be seen, baskets tied round their waists with apron-strings, their special wide-based ladders propped against the trees. The packing station in the village works overtime to send the fruit out through the night to Paris and beyond, some of it finding its ways to shops and supermarkets in England.

Farms along the road offer soft fruits for sale and the stall facing the Fontaine du Coq is piled high with plump strawberries from Carpentras and the smaller, sweeter *fraises de montagne*, selling them in 3 kilo punnets or loose by weight. Later in the season come raspberries, melons, figs and table grapes.

The year peaks with the *vendange*, the wine harvest, which, if the weather holds, is a time of early-morning mists and golden days. The vineyards turn from green to red and gold, yellow and orange, streaked crimson as if with the juice of the grapes themselves. Chestnuts swell on the trees, and the first quinces are on sale at La Blache, the home for retired priests on the way to Pont St Esprit.

With such a surfeit, countless means have been devised to make good use of the fruits. The kitchen becomes an alchemist's pantry for liqueurs and sweet wines. The smell of jams and jellies fills the house while outside there are trays of figs drying in the sun and the windows of all the *pâtisseries* are filled with shiny open tarts of every sort of fruit.

Cherries to quinces

Cherry custard cream

Cherries in sugar syrup

Bitter-sweet cherries

Strawberries in wine

Apricot bread

Peaches in white wine

Old has-been's dessert

Rosy fruit salad

Black sausage with apples

Roast pork with apples and celeriac

Potato salad with walnuts

Greengage tart

Quince or crab apple jelly

Quince paste

Cherries are the signal that spring is turning into summer. In Provence the first to appear are the *bigarreau*, sweet and almost black and so good they are best just eaten as they are. There is a host of varieties which follow and as it is impossible to tell by their colour whether they are sweet or sour, the only thing to do is to ask to taste, which is quite acceptable in France, though frowned on in Britain. Acid cherries are ideal for cooking but you can use sweet ones too. Make sure they are bright and firm, without any sign of bruising.

Cherry custard cream
Flan aux cerises

This pale, freckled dessert with little mounds of dark cherries is the Provençal equivalent of a *clafoutis* or an English custard cream. Stone the cherries if you have the time, using an olive stoner. But if you don't, only the most hard-to-please will complain, and you can silence them by explaining it is the stones which give that elusive flavour of almonds.

450 g (1 lb) cherries
3 eggs plus 3 yolks
75 g (3 oz) caster sugar

few drops vanilla essence
600 ml (1 pint) milk
cinnamon

Heat oven to Gas 4/350°F/180°C. Wash cherries and remove stalks. Stone them if you wish and put them into a buttered oven dish. Beat whole eggs, yolks and sugar together, followed by vanilla essence and milk. Pour over the fruit, sprinkle lightly with cinnamon. Bake for 35–50 minutes, the time depends on the depth of the dish. Test with a skewer, it should come out clean. Leave to cool and serve cold.

Cherries in sugar syrup
Cerises au sirop

Cherries have a short season but they will keep for at least a year if they are preserved in syrup. Much nicer than canned, they are a useful store cupboard standby. Add them to fruit salads or use in recipes in place of fresh fruit. You need a pan deep enough to hold the jars and they should not come into contact with the base, so use a rack or improvise one with a double layer of wire-netting. Use preserving jars with rubber seals.

900 g (2 lb) cherries   600 ml (1 pint) water
225 g (8 oz) granulated sugar

Choose firm, ripe cherries. Remove the stems. Fill preserving jar(s). Put sugar and water into a pan and bring slowly to the boil. When the sugar has dissolved, simmer for 5 minutes, then leave to cool. Pour syrup over the fruit, topping up with more water if necessary to cover, and tap the jar to remove air bubbles. Seal. Stand the jar on the rack and fill the pan with water to just below the level of the rim of the jars. Cover, bring very slowly to the boil and continue to boil for 10 minutes. Lift out jars and leave to cool. Store in a cool, dark place.

Bitter-sweet cherries
Cerises à l'aigre-douce

In autumn markets on the olive stall you might come across pickled cherries which are delicious eaten with cold meats.

450 ml (¾ pint) red wine vinegar   pared rind of ½ lemon
6 coriander seeds   225 g (8 oz) soft brown sugar
3 cloves   450 g (1 lb) cherries
6 juniper berries

Put all ingredients except cherries into a saucepan, bring to the boil, cover, remove from the heat and leave for 24 hours. Use ripe, perfect fruit. Cut the stems to about 1 cm (½ in). Fill a preserving jar with the fruit. Pour over the vinegar and spices. Seal and leave for at least 30 days.

Strawberries in wine
Fraises au vin

Don't wash strawberries unless they are muddy. When you are tired of eating them just as they are with sugar and cream, try them sprinkled with freshly milled black pepper or sprinkled with a little wine vinegar. They make a beautiful deep pink liqueur, wonderful drunk at the end of a meal, or poured sparingly over ice cream (see recipe for Fruit liqueurs). Or serve them in wine as in this recipe, just on their own without any cream.

450 g (1 lb) strawberries	1 tablespoon cassis or
3–4 tablespoons caster sugar	blackcurrant juice
juice of ½ lemon	150 ml (¼ pint) rosé or white
	wine

Hull the strawberries, put them into a glass or china bowl. Sprinkle with the sugar, lemon juice, cassis or blackcurrant juice and wine. Cover and put in the fridge for an hour or two before eating.

Apricot bread
Pain aux abricots

This is a teatime treat for anyone. Apricots are brushed with raspberry glaze and baked on a bed of French bread, so that the two fruits combine and intensify each other's flavour. In France, the glaze is made with raspberry jelly, jars of which are easily found. At home I use raspberry jam, sieved to remove the pips. If you baulk at this extra chore, you could try using redcurrant or rowanberry jelly instead.

1 jar raspberry jelly or jam	stale French bread
4 tablespoons water	450 g (1 lb) apricots

Heat oven to Gas 4/350°F/180°C. Put the jelly or jam into a saucepan and add the water. Bring to the boil and boil for 2 minutes, stirring. If using jam, press through a nylon sieve to remove pips. Return to the heat and simmer for 5 minutes. Meantime cover the base of a 20 cm (8 in) flan tin with 1 cm (½ in) thick slices of French bread, filling in the gaps with odd pieces. Use a brush to paint the bread with the raspberry glaze. Cut apricots in half, remove stones and arrange the fruit, cut side down, in concentric circles on top of the bread. Paint each half-apricot with glaze, making sure it is well covered. Bake for 45 minutes, brushing every 15 minutes with more of the glaze. (As the glaze cools, it thickens and you may need to re-heat it gently before each application.) When the apricot bread is cooked, give a final coat of raspberry glaze, set aside to cool and serve cold with whipped cream, crème fraîche or fromage frais. Store any left-over glaze in a sealed jar to use another time.

Peaches in white wine
Pêches au vin blanc

There are hundreds of varieties of peaches and their smooth cousins
the nectarines, and the *brugnons* (which differ from nectarines in that
their stones are separate from the flesh). Their skin may vary from pale
to golden and red and the flesh is as varied – from white, the most
delectable, to orange stained with the crimson of the stone. In France,
they are sold in fruit trays, which prevents them from bruising, and not
quite ripe, so they must be left for a few days to soften. When buying
peaches in England, don't let anyone pile them into a bag but ask for
one of the boxes in which they arrived. This dessert is the simplest of
all. Make it about an hour before it is needed.

4 ripe peaches	4 tablespoons caster sugar
thinly pared rind of 1 lemon	300 ml (½ pint) white wine

Peel peaches by plunging them for a few minutes into boiling water.
Slit them and the skin slips off easily. Cut them into eighths from stem
to base, thus making neat segments which come away freely from the
stone. Put them into a shallow bowl, crack one of the stones and put it
in the centre, topped with the lemon rind. Sprinkle with the sugar,
pour over the wine, cover and put in the fridge for an hour. Remove
stone and rind just before serving.

Old has-been's dessert
Confiture de vieux garçon

In France, a middle-aged man left on the shelf is a *vieux garçon*. He
presumably makes this alcoholic dessert, which contains all the soft
fruit of summer, to console his lonely winter nights. The original *vieux
garçon* would have used eau-de-vie or brandy. In Britain vodka or
white rum does as well. The secret is to add each variety of fruit as it
comes into its prime, beginning with the cherries of early summer and
finishing with the first grapes of autumn. It then rests until Christmas
when it provides an endless source of desserts for all the winter dinner
parties. If you cannot get hold of all the varieties in the following list, it
is no matter. Add a few extra of those you can but avoid citrus fruits,
or melon which is too watery. Ideally the fruit should be quite dry so
trust the alcohol to deal with any lingering greenfly and only wash any
which might have been sprayed with insecticide. Use a large, lidded,

non-porous, earthenware jar, the bigger the better (a German *Rum-topf* is made for the purpose and holds around 5 litres or 1 gallon). Remember that every 450 g (1 lb) of fruit, plus sugar, plus alcohol will take up about 1 litre or nearly 2 pints of space.

225 g (8 oz) approx. of each of the following fruits:
sweet cherries, stemmed
strawberries, hulled
redcurrants
raspberries
apricots, halved and stoned
peaches and nectarines, skinned, stoned and sliced
plums and greengages, halved and stoned
small ripe figs
black and white grapes, seeded
equal weight in granulated sugar
1–2 litres (2–3½ pints) either eau-de-vie, vodka, brandy or white rum

Make sure the jar is clean by rinsing in boiling water and leaving to dry completely. Buy and add the fruit as available. Each time you put fruit in the pot, top with an equal weight of sugar. Don't stir. The sugar should cover the fruit and act as a weight, pushing it below the surface of the alcohol. Make sure you top up the alcohol from time to time so there is sufficient to submerge the fruit. Put the lid on the pot between whiles. Keep adding fruit over a period of weeks and remember, don't be tempted to stir. Finish by mid September, top up with alcohol. Cover tightly and leave in a dark, cool place until Christmas. It may ferment a little but this will not impair the flavour. The fruit loses its colour but the alcohol becomes rich and dark. Serve in bowls or deep glasses or, as the French do, in the coffee cups at the end of the meal.

Rosy fruit salad
Salade de fruits rouges

This salad has a special charm because it is made just at that moment when all the summer berries are available. If you can't get wild or alpine strawberries, add some loganberries or tayberries instead.

225 g (8 oz) raspberries
225 g (8 oz) strawberries
225 g (8 oz) redcurrants
225 g (8 oz) wild or alpine strawberries
3–4 tablespoons caster sugar
150 ml (¼ pint) white wine

Hull the fruit and put into a bowl, sprinkle with the caster sugar. Cover and leave in the fridge for at least an hour. Just before serving pour over the wine, sparkling if you are feeling extravagant.

Black sausage with apples
Boudin noir aux pommes

The killing of the pig in the old days was a ritual and a celebration because the pig was going to feed the family all winter. The months from December to March were nicknamed *la fête de Sent Pourquî* (the feast of Saint Pork). Nothing was wasted. Black sausage made from the blood and small pieces of pork, flavoured with spices, orange flower water and rum, was fried and shared that evening with the neighbours. The strong flavour is offset by the sweetness of apples and a dish of plainly boiled potatoes. Quite ordinary sausages are also delicious done the same way.

900 g (2 lb) sweet apples	2 tablespoons groundnut oil
25 g (1 oz) butter	2 onions, chopped
25 g (1 oz) caster sugar	450 g (1 lb) *boudin noir* or
salt	sausages
pinch of cinnamon	

Peel, core and quarter the apples, put them into a saucepan with the butter and caster sugar, put over a low heat and simmer them gently until soft; add salt and cinnamon. Meanwhile, heat the oil in a frying pan and fry the chopped onion until golden, add the sausages (cut the *boudin* into four portions and remove skin) and fry for a few minutes on a high heat, turning over and over, then lower the heat and cook gently for a further 10–12 minutes. Serve the sausages surrounded by the apples.

Roast pork with apples and celeriac
Porc aux pommes et au céleri-rave

Roast pork and apples are a familiar theme but in this recipe the apples are cooked in the oven without any added sugar or liquid. In France *reinettes* would be used – similar to Cox's orange pippins, they don't turn to a mush but the slices soften and are tipped with brown. Celeriac added to mashed potatoes turns an everyday vegetable into something special. Buy a piece of pork from the leg or loin, boned and rolled.

1–1½ kg (2¼–3½ lb) joint of pork	900 g (2 lb) celeriac
1 clove garlic	salt
freshly milled black pepper	3 tablespoons crème fraîche
olive oil	150 ml (¼ pint) red wine or
900 g (2 lb) sweet apples	water
900 g (2 lb) potatoes	

Heat oven to Gas 5/375°F/190°C. Wipe the pork with kitchen paper and pierce it at intervals with the point of a sharp knife. Cut garlic into slivers and insert these into the slits. Put the pork on a grid in the roasting tin, add pepper and pour over a little olive oil. Roast, allowing 25 minutes per 450 g (1 lb). Half an hour before the meat is done, quarter, skin and core the apples. (If you prefer to prepare them ahead, put the pieces in water with the juice of a lemon to stop them going brown.) Place the prepared apples into a heatproof dish and put into the oven. Peel the potatoes and celeriac (they too can be prepared ahead and put into a bowl of water); cut into even-sized pieces, put into a pan of water, bring to the boil, add salt, cover and simmer for about 20 minutes, until they are soft. When the meat is done (test with a skewer, the juices should run clear), turn off the heat put the meat on a dish and return to the oven to firm up and keep warm. Put the roasting tin with all the juices to one side. Drain the potatoes and celeriac and mash well. Stir in the crème fraîche and add salt and pepper to taste. Keep warm. Put the roasting tin on the stove over a medium heat. Add the wine or water, bring to the boil, stir well and pour into a gravy boat. Carve the pork, garnish with the apples and serve the celeriac purée in a separate dish.

Potato salad with walnuts
Salade de pommes de terre aux noix

This recipe from the Cévennes combines potatoes, celery and walnuts.

450 g (1 lb) potatoes	salt
2 tablespoons hot vegetable or	freshly milled black pepper
meat stock	6 tablespoons olive oil
2 tablespoons vinegar	2–3 stalks celery, chopped
1 teaspoon mustard	50 g (2 oz) shelled walnuts

Boil the potatoes in their skins until they are soft but still firm. When they are cool enough to handle, peel and cut into ½ cm (¼ in) thick slices, put into a salad bowl and sprinkle over the hot stock. As they cool, turn them over and over once or twice so that they absorb all the stock. When still warm, pour over a dressing made by beating the vinegar, mustard, salt and pepper with the olive oil. Decorate the top with the celery and the walnuts.

Greengage tart
Tarte aux reines-claudes

This is a basic fruit tart using greengages, which the French call Queen Claude, after the wife of François I, who had a passion for them. You could just as well use plums, apricots or damsons.

225 g (8 oz) sweet pastry   1 egg white
900 g (2 lb) greengages   25 g (1 oz) caster sugar
25 g (1 oz) butter

Heat oven to Gas 7/425°F/220°C. Roll out the pastry and line a 25 cm (10 in) flan tin with a removable base. Put into the fridge. Halve greengages and remove the stones. Melt the butter in a frying pan, add the greengages and cook over a medium heat for 5 minutes. Brush the pastry base with the egg white. Arrange the fruit in concentric circles over the base and bake for 20 minutes. Sprinkle with the sugar, lower the heat to Gas 5/375°F/190°C and bake for a further 15 minutes. Leave to cool.

Quince or crab apple jelly
Gelée de coing ou de pomme sauvage

The quince is a deceptive fruit. It has a mouthwatering scent of honey and pears, but bite it and it is witheringly sour. There are different varieties – some shaped like pears, others like apples. It is thought to be the legendary golden apple which Paris awarded to Aphrodite. Buy them if you ever see them, they make delicious jelly which can be spread on bread or eaten with pork or lamb. I have followed the recipe equally successfully with the yellow crab apples that litter the ground when we arrive in France in September.

900 g (2 lb) quinces or crab   700 g (1½ lb) approx. preserving
   apples   sugar

Peel and quarter the fruit and cut out the cores. Put peel and cores into a large square of muslin, bring opposite corners together and tie securely with string to form a bag. Put the fruit and the muslin bag into a wide-mouthed pan with sufficient water to cover. Bring to the boil and simmer until the fruit is quite mushy. Discard the contents of the muslin bag and put the fruit with its cooking liquid into a jelly bag (or tie in a clean square of muslin). Hang it over a basin overnight to collect all the juice – don't be tempted to hurry the process by squeezing, as this will result in a cloudy jelly.

Next day, measure the liquid and return it to the pan. Add sugar, allowing 450 g (1 lb) sugar for each 600 ml (1 pint) liquid. (Keep the fruit pulp for the following recipe.) Bring to the boil and boil hard for 20–30 minutes until the jelly reaches setting point. Test by removing pan from the heat and put a little liquid on a saucer: when it cools it should wrinkle when pushed by a finger. If it doesn't, boil a little longer and test again. Pour into dry jars warmed in the oven; when cool top with circles of greaseproof paper and seal.

Quince paste
Pâté de coing

Slabs of quince paste can be made with the residue of fruit from the previous recipe. Once set it keeps for ages. It is eaten as a sweetmeat or cut in thin slices to eat with grilled fish or pork or lamb chops or it can be used to give flavour to apple and pear pies. Weigh the fruit pulp, empty it into a saucepan and add an equal weight of preserving sugar. If the pulp is very dry, add a cup or two of water. Bring slowly to the boil, simmer gently for about 5 minutes to allow the sugar to dissolve, then raise the heat and boil, stirring constantly with a wooden spoon until the mixture thickens and deepens in colour. It bubbles very fiercely like a sort of witch's cauldron, so wrap your hand in a cloth to prevent burning. As it thickens, the more you must stir. The paste is ready when it can be lifted in one lump on the spoon. Spread it out roughly on to a baking tray lined with greaseproof or waxed paper. As it cools you can spread it more evenly with wet hands. Cover it with more paper and leave to dry for 24 hours in a warm place, or until it is firm enough to be cut. Cut into squares and put into a preserving jar with 5 or 6 tablespoons of granulated sugar. Shake the jar to coat the pieces. Store in a cool dry place.

Figs and honey

Drying figs and other fruits

Cold meat with figs

Duck with figs

Baked figs with cream

Fig jam

Dried figs with thyme

Fig and honey pie

Carrots glazed with honey

Homer's cream

Hippocras

Redcurrants with honey

Pear pie

The fig is the most ancient of fruit trees and, like the olive, it appears to live forever. Where there was a fig tree, there will always be a fig tree, pushing its branches between rock crevices and the stones of limestone walls.

In Provence and Languedoc there are two seasons, one in early summer and another in the autumn, when the crop is smaller and sweeter. Bite into a freshly picked fig and the skin splits open revealing the tiny red flowers hidden inside. Wild figs are there for the picking and when there is a glut, everyone is making jam and drying them for the winter. They make delicious sweet fritters, and an interesting golden brown and warming liqueur (follow the recipe for Fruit liqueurs).

Honey is a natural by-product of a countryside filled with sunflower and lavender fields, with wild thyme and rosemary and flowering trees such as the acacia, lime and chestnut. Each honey has a very individual flavour and is definitely something to be bought in the local markets and brought home. These special honeys are wasted if used for cooking, as the heat destroys their special aromas, so follow the recipes using any good blended honey. As honey matures, so it thickens; if it begins to crystallize, stir it to restore it, or follow the Roman rule to make bad honey good, and stir in a spoonful of good honey. I usually use runny honey for cooking – it's simply easier to measure – but thick honey will become runny when heated.

Drying figs and other fruits

Figs can be dried in a slow oven (or there's even an electric dryer, made in Switzerland, which does the job neatly and clinically), or you can use a slow cook pot, but if you have a week or two in the sun and a surfeit of figs, there is a satisfying ritual about the old method. Lay them in a single layer in wicker fruit trays so they don't touch, put them in the sun and turn them every day, bringing them indoors at night. They will be dry in about a week. Flatten them slightly between finger and thumb. Store them in paper bags or cardboard boxes with bay leaves to keep away the weevils. Eat as they are, or reconstitute them by pouring over boiling water and leaving them to soak for half an hour. This method of drying can be used for other fruits, including tomatoes, apricots and peaches; cut them in half (remove stones) and dry them cut side up first. (Store dried tomatoes in olive oil and use them to flavour soups and stews.)

Cold meat with figs
Assiette languedocienne

Allow 2 or 3 fresh figs per head, arrange them in a shallow dish on a bed of fig, vine or lettuce leaves. Serve a bowl of coarse pâté and a platter of assorted cold meats, such as raw and cured ham, two or three different sorts of dried cured sliced pork sausage – often sold in Britain under the blanket name of salami. In Languedoc this would be perhaps a *saucisson de montagne*, *saucisson de Toulouse* and the curiously named *Jésus*. Have plenty of French bread and a bowl of butter to offer round.

Duck with figs
Canard aux figues

This is an unusual and delicious way of serving duck, the sweetness of the figs nicely complementing the richness of the meat. Use a farm-reared or wild duck such as a mallard. Fresh or dried figs can be used.

1 duck	6–12 fresh figs, or use dried
2 tablespoons olive oil	3 whole cloves
2–3 tablespoons brandy	piece of lemon or Seville orange
salt	peel
freshly milled black pepper	1 egg yolk
225 g (8 oz) soft brown sugar	2 tablespoons crème fraîche
(use half this amount if using	pinch of cayenne pepper
dried figs)	juice of 1 lemon or Seville
150 ml (¼ pint) red wine	orange
150 ml (¼ pint) water	

Heat the oil in a flameproof casserole in which the duck will fit snugly. Brown it on all sides over a high flame. Put brandy into a ladle or small saucepan, heat it and set it alight, then pour over the duck. Add salt and pepper, cover and cook very gently for 45 minutes. Meanwhile, gently heat the sugar in the wine and water, and when it has dissolved add the figs, cloves and lemon or orange peel. If using fresh figs, poach them for 5 minutes; dried will take 30 minutes. They should be soft but not mushy. Add the figs to the duck and cook for a further 15 minutes. Test that the duck is cooked by inserting a skewer – the juice should run clear. If it is pink, cook a little longer. In a small bowl mix the egg yolk with the crème fraîche, cayenne pepper and the lemon or orange juice. Remove the duck to a warm serving dish, add the egg and cream mixture to the pan, stir and cook very gently without boiling for 2 or 3 minutes. Serve the duck surrounded by the fig sauce.

Baked figs with cream
Figues à la crème fraîche

In this simple dessert, the sugar slightly caramelizes and the figs are surrounded with carmine red juice. Allow 2–3 figs per head. Heat oven to Gas 5/375°F/190°C. Put the figs in an oven dish, sprinkle with 2 or 3 tablespoons of caster sugar and 1 or 2 tablespoons of water. Bake for 10 minutes. Allow to cool and eat with crème fraîche or fromage frais.

Fig jam
Confiture de figues

If you happen one day to be in France, surrounded by fig trees and want to make jam, here is how to go about it. Pick the figs when they are very firm and slightly unripe.

900 g (2 lb) figs	1 lemon
450 g (1 lb) soft brown sugar	3 cloves
300 ml (½ pint) water	

Put sugar and water into a large saucepan, bring slowly to the boil and simmer gently for 5 minutes. Add the figs, the finely pared peel of the lemon and the cloves. Poach very gently, taking care not to let the figs break up until the syrup begins to set. Meanwhile put clean jars into a cool oven to warm. After an hour, test to see if the jam has reached setting point. Remove pan from heat, put a little jam on a saucer, let it cool, then push it with your finger. It should wrinkle. If it is still runny, continue simmering and test every 5 minutes, each time removing the pan from the heat. (If you have a sugar thermometer, setting temperature is 105°C/220°F.) Skim away the froth with a slotted

spoon. Add the juice of the lemon. Pour into the warm jars, seal and
store in a cool, dark place.

Dried figs with thyme
Figues sèches au thym

Dried figs simmered with honey and thyme are delicious eaten warm
or cold with fromage frais, yoghurt or crème fraîche. Simply put 450 g
(1 lb) dried figs into a saucepan, add 150 ml (¼ pint) red wine and 300
ml (½ pint) water, 2 or 3 sprigs thyme and 3 tablespoons honey.
Simmer for an hour, turning them over from time to time. Lift out the
figs on to a serving dish, boil the liquid to reduce it by half and pour it
over the figs. (Sprigs of fennel could be used instead of thyme.)

Fig and honey pie
Croustade aux figues et au miel

This fig and honey pie is delicious eaten hot or cold. It can be made
with sweetened short pastry (see Index) or ready-made puff.

12 figs	225 g (8 oz) pastry
3 tablespoons honey	1 egg yolk, beaten

Make pastry and set aside to rest for an hour. Heat oven to Gas 6/
400°F/200°C. Put figs and honey into a saucepan and just cover with
water. Bring to the boil and poach gently for 5 minutes, 30 minutes if
using dried. Divide pastry into two, one piece a third larger than the
other. Roll out the larger piece and line a pie dish. Roll out second
piece for the lid. Put figs in the dish, top with the lid of pastry,
dampening the edges all round so the two layers stick together. Mark
all round with the prongs of a fork, and make a slit in the centre of the
lid for the steam to escape. Brush all over the top with beaten egg and
bake for 30 minutes.

Carrots glazed with honey
Carottes au miel

Honey and carrots are found in several recipes including one for jam in
which sliced, cooked carrots are boiled in their cooking liquid with
half their weight in honey, plus a sliced orange and sliced lemon, until

they reach setting point. I have yet to try it but I can vouch for this simple way of producing glazed carrots.

450 g (1 lb) carrots
salt
50 g (2 oz) butter
2 onions, chopped

1 tablespoon honey
freshly milled black pepper
handful chopped parsley

Peel and cut carrots in quarters, lengthwise, put into a pan with salt and enough boiling water just to cover. Boil for 10 minutes. Drain but reserve 150 ml (¼ pint) of the liquid. Melt the butter in the pan, add the chopped onions, stir over a medium heat for a few minutes until they begin to soften. Add the carrots, the reserved liquid, the honey, salt and pepper. Cook uncovered until nearly all the liquid has evaporated and the carrots are soft and glazed. Check to see they do not burn. Serve dusted with chopped parsley.

Homer's cream
Crème d'Homère

In Provence, any custard cream is known as *flan* and small pots glazed with caramel are an indispensable part of many menus. Caramel is sold in France in small bottles and is worth buying, although it is not difficult to make your own. This version differs from the classic *crème caramel* in that wine replaces the milk and it is sweetened with honey. It is light and delicious. Make it the day before and turn it out on to small plates just when you are ready to serve.

1 stick cinnamon
grated rind of 1 lemon
3 tablespoons thick honey

300 ml (½ pint) dry white wine
3 oz caster sugar
4 whole eggs and 6 yolks

Heat oven to Gas 4/350°F/180°C. Put cinnamon, grated lemon rind, honey and wine into a small saucepan, bring just to boiling point, take off heat, cover and leave to infuse for 10 minutes. Put sugar and a few drops of water into another pan and heat very gently. As the sugar begins to melt and crystallize, spread it about using a fork. Watch it as it begins to change colour and caramelize. Raise the heat, it will liquefy and turn from yellow to pale brown. Remove immediately from heat, otherwise it will darken too much and be bitter, and pour into 6 individual ovenproof moulds. Beat the eggs and yolks in a bowl, and strain in the wine. Ladle the mixture into the moulds. Stand them in a baking dish and pour round enough boiling water to come half-way up the moulds. Bake for 25–30 minutes. Test by inserting the blade of a pointed knife – it should come out quite clean. Leave to cool and refrigerate. Just before serving run a knife around each *flan*, invert a saucer over the top and turn it over. The *flan* will fall out of the mould and be surrounded with a caramel syrup.

Hippocras
Vin d'Hypocras

The name comes from Hippocrates, the father of medicine, and is the old French name for a mulled red wine. In this Languedoc recipe, the rules are stood on their head. The wine used is white, it is flavoured with melted honey and lemon, zipped up with a little alcohol and drunk cool – an aperitif for summer highdays and holidays. Like many old recipes it calls for alcohol at 90°. The veterans have their sources and when I ask more deeply, I am told to go the rounds of all the local pharmacies asking for a little at each for 'medicinal' purposes. It is less adventurous but easier just to add more of a lower degree spirit.

4 tablespoons honey
1 bottle dry white wine
pared rind of 1 lemon

6 tablespoons eau-de-vie, vodka
or brandy

Gently melt the honey in a small saucepan. Pour it into a 1 litre (2 lb) preserving jar with the wine, thinly pared rind of the lemon and the alcohol. Cover and leave for 3 days. Strain and put into a bottle. Serve cool.

Redcurrants with honey
Groseilles au miel

Honey is the perfect antidote to the sharpness of redcurrants. Simply remove stalks from 450 g (1 lb) of redcurrants and put them into a deep glass bowl, squeeze over the juice of an orange and add 4 tablespoons runny honey. Cover and put in the fridge for at least 6 hours. Gently mix the fruit and serve. (Or use white currants and instead of the orange juice, add 2 tablespoons redcurrant juice or cassis.)

Pear pie
Croustade aux poires

Make this honey-flavoured pear pie from small hard cooking pears and eat it with lashings of crème fraîche or fromage frais. Buy frozen puff pastry either in one piece, or use 2 sheets of ready rolled.

900 g (2 lb) pears
150 ml (¼ pint) red wine
4 tablespoons honey

1 stick cinnamon
225 g (8 oz) puff pastry
1 egg yolk

Peel and core the pears and cut in quarters. Put into a saucepan with the wine, honey and cinnamon. Cook very gently until the pears are soft and the wine has turned into a thick syrup (30–60 minutes). Heat oven to Gas 7/425°F/220°C. Divide pastry in two, one piece slightly larger than the other. Roll out and use the larger sheet to line a pie dish. Put in the pears. Dampen the edges of the pastry with water. Cover with the second piece, pressing all round to make sure it sticks, then mark all round with a fork. Make a slit in the centre of the pastry lid to allow the steam to escape. Brush with the egg yolk and bake for 30 minutes.

Grapes and wines

Wines from the must

Spiced wine

Orange wine

Red wine with raspberry syrup

Nectarine or peach wine

Lavender wine

Fruit liqueurs

Liqueurs in the window

Midsummer green walnut liqueur

Green walnut wine

Hair of the dog

Spring chicken with grapes

Partridge in vine leaves

Quail with grapes

Grape jam

Dried grapes

Grape *flan*

The *vendange*, or grape harvest, takes place in September, early or late depending on the strength of the grapes. The long year of back-breaking tasks – the winter pruning and staking, spring and summer weeding, spraying and cutting back – comes to fruition. Small groups of five or six pickers bend to the task of cutting the bunches of ripe grapes, dropping them with a dull plop into plastic buckets, which are then emptied into the trailer behind the tractor driving slowly between the rows. Along the narrow lanes, traffic builds up as the tractor, orange warning light flashing, trundles to the village cooperative, where the grapes are weighed and tested for their sugar content and then emptied into a concrete tank like a giant mincing machine to extract the juice. The skins are dumped in a heap as high as a haystack to be taken to the distillery and made into *marc*, a fiery kind of local brandy.

The hillsides are patterned with small vineyards, and in the Rhône valley and across the enormous flat Languedoc plain bordering the Mediterranean, acre upon acre of vines stretch in endless rows like rollers in enormous green seas. Much of the wine is table wine, although Government policy now is to give financial help to people who plough up the old vines and replace with those of a better quality. Village cooperatives are also being encouraged to produce finer wines than the rough kind of plonk which used to be the norm. Until recently the red and rosé wines were superior to the white, but this is rapidly changing. Look out for the Vins de Pays du Gard. The pale and delicate rosé can deceive; it looks light and harmless but is often high in alcohol.

Many small vineyards carry the *appellation d'origine contrôlée* and the *vins délimités de qualité* label and are well worth trying. The choice is wide – the light red Côtes du Rhône and the more special Côtes du Rhône Villages; reds and rosés from the Côteaux d'Ardèche, d'Aix-en-Provence, Baux-de-Provence, du Tricastin and du Languedoc; the soft rosés from Faugères, the slightly *pétillant* reds from Côtes du Ventoux, and from Lirac full reds and a dry rosé. You will often be offered a sweet, fortified aperitif wine (*vin doux*) which might be a red from Rasteau served chilled with a lump of ice, or a white from Beaumes de

Venise or Frontignan which both have a subtle but distinct flavour of muscat grapes, or the spirit-based, gentian-flavoured aperitif from Suze-la-Rousse.

There are some famous wines grown in the region, notably the dark, strong red from Châteauneuf-du-Pape, which they say goes down 'like little Jesus in velvet trousers'. Then there is the rosé from Tavel which is dry and tinged with orange; the dry white wine of Cassis; and from the slopes of the Dentelles, the sharp-toothed hills close to Mont Ventoux, come the red, white and rosé wines of Gigondas. The northern Rhône vineyards clinging precariously to the hills bordering the river produce magnificent reds from the Côte Rôtie, rich, smooth Hermitage and Crozes-Hermitage reds, the dark fruity wines of Cornas, the lighter St-Joseph and the white from Condrieu, with its flavour of apricots and peaches.

Ordinary wine is used in cooking all the time, nothing expensive unless you happen to have a little left at the end of a bottle. Most French table wine sold in Britain comes from the southern French vineyards, so will add an authentic touch to the dishes. White wine is favoured in many recipes because it is lighter than red, but use what is available and when you have no wine, add lemon juice or a tablespoon or so of wine or cider vinegar and a tablespoon of sugar.

Perhaps because there are so many grapes, everyone takes it for granted that their prime purpose is to produce wine and there are surprisingly few local dishes in which they are used. Dessert grapes are served with a soft goat's or ewe's cheese and muscat grapes are made into a liqueur (see Fruit liqueurs).

Make incisions in a joint of pork and insert slivers of garlic. Roast in the usual way, but half-way through the cooking time, take the roasting pan out of the oven, pour over a ladleful of brandy and flame, add 100 g (4 oz) grapes to the pan and return to the oven to finish roasting. Then 15 minutes before serving, crush a further 100 g (4 oz) grapes to extract their juice, and pour over the pork. Or serve grapes with roast duck. Put 100 g (4 oz) grapes into 300 ml (½ pint) of red wine with a lump of sugar and heat gently, to just below boiling point. Cook for 10 minutes. Surround the duck with the grapes and make gravy by adding the wine in which the grapes were cooked to the juices in the roasting tin. Let it reduce on top of the stove and pour into a gravy boat.

Grapes, so plentiful in the south of France, are never cheap in Britain, so only buy those that have been wrapped in bunches and have not been bruised by being thrown in heaps into boxes. You can't tell what they are like by looking at them so ask if you can taste one. Wash them in a colander under running water and stand them on kitchen paper to dry. Serve them at the end of a meal with curd or goat's cheese, and let everyone help themselves, using scissors to cut off a small bunch from the larger one. In England we pick out the pips, remembering dire childhood warnings about appendicitis, but French people think this is foolish. Pips can stick in your teeth and spoil a cooked dish or fruit salad, but pipping them is a tedious chore, so for those occasions buy pipless varieties. Unless the skins are tough, there is no need to peel them. But if you must, pour boiling water over and leave for a few minutes. Once skinned, whether white or black, all grapes have pale flesh.

Wines from the must

Once the grapes are picked and before they begin to ferment, some are put aside to be crushed and the *moût*, the cloudy grey must, is the basis of some special concoctions.

First is the *vin cuit* which is really not wine at all because the *moût* is put into a saucepan with cinnamon, dried orange peel and coriander and boiled until it reduces by half, cooled and bottled, sometimes with added eau-de-vie, left for a month to clear and bottled again to be drunk at Christmas and Twelfth Night with the dessert.

Then there is *carthagène*, known as young girl's ruin, which might be offered to a casual caller rather as we might offer a cup of tea. Preferably made from the must of white grapes, in a demi-john with half as much eau-de-vie, it is corked and shaken vigorously, then left for a week to 10 days, shaken once more and left to settle for 40 days, by which time it should have cleared and be ready to siphon into bottles. It can be drunk right away, but really should be left to age for two or three years.

Closely related to this but containing twice as much eau-de-vie is the *sauvo-crestian*, taken, as they say, to buck you up and give you a kick when feeling under the weather.

The following two recipes require a 5 litre or 1 gallon demi-john, a bung and airlock, and possibly campden tablets, all of which can be bought from wine-making counters.

Spiced wine
Vin de sautel

Even if only a few people still make *vin cuit* and *carthagène*, a great
many more make *vin de sautel*. The local *pharmacies* and *drogueries*
display the ingredients in their windows and sell the preparation of
spices in brown paper bags marked 10 or 20 litres. Cathy Pesenti, an
English wine-grower who lives over the other side of our hill, told us
how they save a few buckets of grapes during the picking. They press
them with their wellington boots, throw the skins back on the trailer
and take the juice home to make the wine. It is named after the sweet
wines which come from the Sauternes. I have made it in France from
grapes grown in our courtyard. The result is a warming, spicy wine
which can be served as an aperitif or with the dessert. In France no one
would dream of making less than 10 litres at a time, but as a mass of
ripened grapes is expensive in Britain, I have worked out a recipe for a
smaller amount. You might have a greengrocer who will get you a box,
or has throw-outs he'll save for you. The grapes need to be sweet-
tasting and well-ripened but not perfect for the table. I have also
experimented by putting the same spices into white wine and added
vodka to fortify it. It has the same spicy taste.

4 kg (9 lb) grapes *or* 2 litres (3 bottles) white wine
2 sticks cinnamon
1 vanilla pod
1 nutmeg
dried peel of 4 oranges
450 g (1 lb) caster sugar
300 ml (½ pint) vodka (if using wine)

If using grapes, crush them to extract the juice. (This amount should
yield about 2 litres or 3–4 pints of juice, but it is impossible to gauge
exactly, since so much depends on the quality of the grapes.) You can
use a mouli-légumes but the best method really is bare feet in a bowl.
Strain through a muslin in a colander and pour the juice through a
funnel into the demi-john. If using wine pour straight into the demi-
john. Add all other ingredients, only adding the vodka if using wine.
Insert the bung and airlock, fill it with water according to the maker's
instructions, and leave for 4–5 weeks. If fermentation has not ceased,
add a campden tablet and leave another week. Siphon into bottles and
cork. Leave to age for 2 or 3 months.

Orange wine
Vin d'oranges

On a summer evening you might be offered a glass of orange wine as an aperitif or with the dessert. It is heady and full of flavour and coloured a deep gold. It can be made using either white or rosé and be fortified with eau-de-vie, vodka or brandy.

2 litres (3 bottles) dry white or rosé wine
450 g (1 lb) caster sugar
dried peel of 1 orange (see Index)

300 ml (½ pint) eau-de-vie, vodka or brandy
1 lemon, chopped
2 oranges, chopped
campden tablet, if necessary

Pour the wine into the demi-john. Add the sugar, dried orange peel, eau-de-vie, and chopped lemon and oranges. (Cut them on a plate and pour the juices into the jar, too.) Put in a bung fitted with an airlock, fill this with water as per the manufacturer's instructions and leave for 6 weeks. If the wine is still fermenting add a campden tablet and leave a further week. Siphon into bottles, cork and leave for a few weeks to age.

Red wine with raspberry syrup
Communard

Kir, invented by Abbé Kir, one-time mayor and a resistance hero of Dijon, is drunk in the south of France just as much as anywhere else. Most people know it is made by putting a dash of blackcurrant liqueur (*cassis*) into a glass and topping up with chilled white wine. Less well known but just as good is *communard*, made in the same way but using raspberry liqueur and red wine. You can get much the same taste with less alcohol, if you use blackcurrant or raspberry syrup.

Nectarine or peach wine
Vin apéritif aux brugnons ou aux pêches

Another favourite aperitif wine is made with nectarines or peaches. You need 3 nectarines or peaches, plus just the stones from another 3. Peel the fruit by steeping in boiling water for a few minutes, when the skin will come away easily. Put the fruit, whole, into a 1 litre (2 lb) preserving jar. Add the 3 extra stones, a vanilla pod, 2 whole cloves and pour over a whole bottle of dry white wine. Leave for 3 days. Strain into a jug. Pour the liquid back into the jar, add 100 g (4 oz) sugar and sufficient eau-de-vie or vodka to come right to the top. Seal and leave for 3 weeks before drinking. Serve chilled.

If you have a peach tree you can even make a version by steeping the leaves, allowing 40 to a litre of white wine and adding 300 ml ($\frac{1}{2}$ pint) of eau-de-vie or vodka and 225 g (8 oz) sugar. Leave for 60 days before filtering and bottling.

Lavender wine
Vin d'aspic

The scent of lavender fills our summer. In July the lavender fields look like long lines of purple porcupines until they are cropped, when they look more like grey hedgehogs. Apart from hanging lavender to dry all round the house, buying lavender soap and little lavender bags made of bright Provençal cotton, I tried to capture its scent by making lavender wine. The wine is strong and the scent is there but the taste is peppery and bitter. I should have realized the title is a pun: it means asp as well as lavender. It is actually supposed to be a cure for colic. If you want to try it, put a large handful of lavender flowers into a bottle of red wine, leave it for 40 days, strain and re-bottle. Only a very little is needed . . .

Fruit liqueurs
Fruits à l'eau-de-vie

Fruits steeped in eau-de-vie in the months when they are cheap and plentiful provide a dazzling reminder of summer when the long winter nights begin in the middle of the afternoon. The alcohol absorbs both flavour and colour resulting in delicious and individual drinks, ranging from pale pink and yellow to deep carmine, gold and brown depending on the chosen fruit. It is normal to serve these *digestifs* after the coffee, in the still-warm cups, though you can of course use small glasses.

The fruit must be firm, ripe and clean, and if possible avoid washing it as this dilutes the alcohol. In France use eau-de-vie, in England vodka is a good substitute.

Method 1: for cherries, grapes, raspberries, strawberries, mulberries, blackberries

450 g (1 lb) fruit, approx.   600 ml (1 pint) eau-de-vie or
150 g (6 oz) caster sugar   vodka

Use one kind of fruit. If using cherries or grapes, don't remove stalks but trim with scissors leaving a tail about 1 cm ($\frac{1}{2}$ in) long. Strawberries must be hulled. Fill a 1 litre (2 lb) preserving jar right to the top with the fruit, add sugar and top with the spirit, you may need a little more or a little less than I have suggested. Seal and leave to age for 60 days, during which time the sugar will dissolve. Cherries and grapes are left in the jar, and a few served in the cup or glass to be picked up by their tails and eaten before drinking the liqueur. The berries tend to go mushy, so strain the liquid through muslin into a clean bottle with a screw top. Leave to age until Christmas if you can.

Method 2: for apricots, peaches, nectarines, plums, pears, figs and quinces

450 g (1 lb) fruit   150 ml ($\frac{1}{4}$ pint) water
600 ml (1 pint) eau-de-vie or   1 vanilla pod
  vodka   1 teaspoon cinnamon
150 g (6 oz) sugar

Use one kind of fruit. Quarter them and crack peach, apricot, nectarine and plum stones by putting them under a cloth and tapping sharply with a hammer. Put fruit (and cracked stones) into a 1 litre (2 lb) preserving jar and just cover with the spirit. Seal and leave for 2 weeks. When this time is up gently dissolve the sugar in the water with the vanilla pod and cinnamon. Let it simmer for about 5 minutes. Cool. Strain the liquid from the jar, through muslin, into a jug. Add the sugar syrup, pour through a funnel into a screw-top bottle and leave for at least 60 days to age.

Liqueurs in the window
Liqueurs de fenêtre

In the old days, women made liqueurs by standing fruit or spices steeped in alcohol on a sunny windowsill. One variation was to put 1 litre ($1\frac{3}{4}$ pints) of eau-de-vie with 450 g (1 lb) sugar into a deep glass

container with a wide opening. A large orange was threaded with
string and hung from the lid just above the level of the liquid. The
orange gradually shrank until it was quite dry and hard, the sugar
dissolved and the liqueur became lightly coloured and flavoured with
orange.

Midsummer green walnut liqueur
Liqueur de la Saint-Jean

In Britain green walnuts are usually pickled or made into ketchup. In
France they go into wines and eau-de-vie. Tradition has it that the
walnuts are at their peak on St John's day, 24th June, midsummer day.
One version tells you to gather 2 green walnuts, 4 walnut leaves, 1
sprig each of rosemary and lavender, some mint and lemon balm, a
sprig of verbena, a linden flower, a flowering stem of St John's wort,
one of hyssop and another of camomile. Crush the walnuts and put
everything into 1 litre (1¾ pints) of eau-de-vie. Leave to infuse for 50
days. Add 150 g (6 oz) sugar dissolved in 150 ml (¼ pint) water. Strain
and bottle. Below is another version which results in a golden brown
liqueur, sweet, nutty and quite heady. The walnuts must be picked in
summer before the shell has formed inside the outer skin – test by
piercing with a skewer. Cut them with a heavy, sharp knife, crushing
them under the blade. Wear gloves, as walnut juice produces an almost
indelible stain.

12 green walnuts	1 bottle (75 cl) eau-de-vie or
3 whole cloves	vodka
grated nutmeg	150 g (6 oz) caster sugar

Cut the walnuts in quarters. Put them into a 1 litre (2 lb) preserving jar
with the cloves and a generous grating of nutmeg. Add the eau-de-vie.
Leave for 30 days. Strain into a clean jar, add the sugar. Leave a further
week or so until the sugar has dissolved. Shake the jar from time to
time. Bottle and leave to age for at least 60 days.

Green walnut wine
Vin de noix

Walnuts are also made into an aperitif wine. They turn red wine to
mahogany, white to a deep green-gold and produce a drink which is

strong and full of flavour. You'll need 2 demi-johns, airlocks, bungs, campden tablets and a siphon tube bought from a wine-making counter. (Campden tablets are not included in original recipes, but they do help to stop fermentation and bacteria forming.)

25–30 green walnuts
300 ml (½ pint) eau-de-vie or
   vodka
450 g (1 lb) caster sugar
1 stick cinnamon

1 vanilla pod *or* 1 teaspoon
   vanilla essence
3½–4 litres (5–6 bottles) red or
   white wine
2 campden tablets

Cut the walnuts in quarters using a heavy knife and put them with all the other ingredients into the demi-john, making sure you fill it almost to the top with the wine. Fix bung and airlock, fill with water as per the maker's instructions. Leave for 40–50 days, add a campden tablet, reseal and leave for another week. Siphon into a clean demi-john, add the second campden tablet. Seal. Leave a further week or so until the wine looks clear. Siphon into bottles and cork. Leave to age at least until Christmas.

Hair of the dog
Liqueur d'oeufs

Egg, lemon and brandy, an old-fashioned *sauvo-vido* for that *gueule de bois*, perhaps. Whole eggs are soaked in lemon juice until the shells disintegrate then mixed with sugar and brandy and left to age. It is rich and warming on a winter's night.

6 fresh free-range eggs
juice of 10–12 lemons

225 g (8 oz) caster sugar
300 ml (½ pint) brandy, approx.

Wash and dry eggs carefully, pierce them once with a darning needle, put them into a 1 litre (2 lb) preserving jar, and add the lemon juice, which should completely cover them. Seal and leave for 2–3 days. Beat the mixture well with a fork and strain it into a jug. Add sugar, mix well and pour through a funnel into a 1 litre bottle with a screw top. Pour in sufficient brandy to fill. Seal and leave for 2 months to age.

Spring chicken with grapes
Petits poulets aux raisins

If you are having friends to dinner and want something quick and easy to prepare, try this dish of chicken delicately flavoured with grapes, brandy and crème fraîche. Serve it with rice and perhaps a green salad. A spring chicken will feed two people but if you are hungry, allow one per head.

2–4 spring chickens
2 tablespoons olive oil
4 tablespoons brandy or lemon
   juice
salt
freshly milled black pepper

sprig of thyme *or* ½ teaspoon
   dried
bay leaf
sprig of fresh parsley
225 g (8 oz) white seedless
   grapes
4 tablespoons crème fraîche

Divide each chicken into two pieces, cutting right through the breast bone. Heat the oil in a heavy-based casserole and brown the chickens all over until golden, in two batches if necessary. Add brandy or lemon juice, salt, pepper, thyme, bay leaf, parsley and the grapes. Cover and cook for 30–40 minutes, until the chickens are cooked. Test by inserting a skewer: the juice should run yellow not pink. Just before serving, remove the chickens to a warm dish and keep warm. Raise heat and reduce liquid in pan by half, lower heat, stir in the crème fraîche, pour over the chickens and serve.

Partridge in vine leaves
Perdreaux aux feuilles de vigne

Vine leaves make perfect wrappings for small game birds. If you happen to be around a vineyard in summer, pick a few and preserve them in a jar topped up with olive oil; otherwise buy packets of Greek vine leaves in brine. (Rinse however many you need and store the rest in a covered jar in the fridge still in their brine.) This recipe is for partridge but you could just as well use quail or woodcock.

4 partridges
4 vine leaves
8 rashers streaky bacon
2 tablespoons olive oil

2 onions, chopped
salt
freshly milled black pepper
4 tablespoons dry white wine

Rinse and dry vine leaves, Wrap each bird in a leaf and then in 2 rashers of bacon. Tie securely with fine string. Heat the oil in a heavy-based pan, add the chopped onion and let it soften for 5 minutes or so over a medium heat. Push to one side, add the birds and brown all over. Add salt, pepper and wine. Cover and simmer gently for 25 minutes. Test with the point of a skewer, the juice should run clear. If not, cook a little longer. Remove string before serving, perhaps with a garnish of watercress.

Quail with grapes
Cailles aux raisins

Quail are a great dinner party standby. Allow one or two per head depending on appetites and the state of your pocket.

4–8 quail	salt
8–16 rashers streaky bacon	freshly milled black pepper
2 tablespoons olive oil	pinch of nutmeg
4 tablespoons brandy	25 g (1 oz) butter
450 g (1 lb) white grapes	4–8 slices French bread

Wrap two rashers of bacon round each quail and tie securely with string. Heat oil in a heavy-based pan and fry the birds all over until they are golden. Add brandy. Cover. Put half the grapes through a mouli-légumes to extract their juice (or sieve them). Add the juice to the pan with the salt, pepper and nutmeg. Simmer gently for about 25–30 minutes until cooked. Just before serving, heat butter in a small pan, add remaining grapes, and cook them gently until they turn transparent. Fry the slices of bread to make croûtons. Serve the quail, string removed, on the croûtons, surrounded by the grapes.

Grape jam
Rasimat or Raisiné

In Languedoc they make a kind of jam which mixes grapes with all kinds of other fruit. If you are staying in France when the grapes are ripe you might like to try it. Take 2½ kg (6 lb) grapes, remove their stalks, put them into a preserving pan and bring slowly to the boil, breaking up the grapes with a wooden spoon or fork. Put them through a sieve, collecting the juice and the pulp in the bowl. Discard

skin and pips. Measure the juicy pulp and for every litre (1¾ pints) add
100 g (4 oz) preserving sugar. Return to the pan. Add 3 figs, 1 apple, 1
pear, 1 carrot and a slice of melon, all cut into small pieces; also add a
stick of cinnamon. Simmer very gently, stirring frequently, until the
mixture is thick, the fruit soft and pulpy and the jam has reached
setting point. Pour into warmed pots and seal.

Dried grapes
Raisins pendus

Dried black grapes produce raisins and currants, white grapes produce
sultanas. They can be dried in the home. You might like to try it.
Choose bunches that are ripe and firm (locally they are picked on a
sunny day and not when they are damp and swollen with moisture
after rain). Lay them in a single layer, the bunches not touching, on a
slatted fruit tray and put them in full sun for several hours. Tie a piece
of string to each bunch and hang them indoors, ideally from the ceiling
in an airy room but out of draughts, as they must hang free. By
December they will have dried and be perfect to hand round with the
famous thirteen desserts that everyone in Provence and Languedoc is
reputed to enjoy on Christmas eve. The thirteen desserts represent
Christ and the twelve apostles and they vary from place to place. A
basic choice might be raisins, dried figs, dates, walnuts, almonds,
hazelnuts, apples, pears, chestnuts, white and black nougat, clemen-
tines and *bûche de Noël* or *pompes d'huile*, special Christmas cakes
made by the baker.

Grape *flan*
Flan aux raisins

Choose ripe, seedless white grapes to make this simple *flan* which can
be eaten warm or cold.

450 g (1 lb) seedless grapes   300 ml (½ pint) water
2 eggs   300 ml (½ pint) milk
pinch of salt   1 teaspoon brandy
4 tablespoons caster sugar   25 g (1 oz) butter
2 tablespoons flour

Heat oven to Gas 5/375°F/190°C. Put the grapes into a buttered, deep ovenproof dish. Beat the eggs in a bowl with the salt and the sugar. Gradually beat in the flour, taking care that it does not form lumps, followed by the water and milk. Add the brandy and pour mixture over the grapes. Put into the oven and cook for 1 hour. Add the butter in small pieces and cook for a further 10–15 minutes, until the *flan* is cooked through to the centre. Leave to cool.

Chestnuts

Roast chestnuts

Boiled chestnuts

Peeling chestnuts

Ardèche chestnut soup

Chestnut and onion soup

Pork pie with chestnuts and apples

Chestnut sauce

Volcano

Christmas log

Pancakes with marrons glacés

Chestnut trees spread their shade in the towns and villages sheltering in the valleys of the Massif Central, the vast mountainous region of extinct volcanoes which divides France in two, and stretches westwards from the Cévennes to the old strongholds of the Cathars in Albi and Montauban, and from the flat southern vineyards of Languedoc northwards to Le Puy and the Auvergne. In the autumn their bright orange leaves turn the hills to fire and people's thoughts turn to the pleasure of being indoors and gossiping with friends over roast chestnuts and a glass of wine.

Until disease destroyed many of the trees, the starchy, sweet chestnut formed part of the staple diet of the region. They were ground into flour and made into bread, puréed and eaten like potatoes, made into soups, eaten with pork and combined with apples. Now the industry is centred almost exclusively on Privas in the Ardèche, which produces most of France's canned and puréed chestnuts as well as marrons glacés.

The Christmas turkey can be roasted with whole chestnuts in the cavity, instead of stuffing, using 900 g (2 lb) of fresh chestnuts, or half that amount of dried or canned. Put two-thirds of them inside the bird with a teaspoonful of salt and brush the turkey with olive oil. Simmer the remaining chestnuts in salted water until tender, and serve as a garnish to the roast bird. (A truffle might be inserted under the skin of the breast an hour or so before roasting.) Or you can stuff cabbage with chestnuts, following the recipe for stuffed cabbage (see Index), substituting chestnut purée in place of the meat, and making sure you season it well with salt and pepper. Or mix a purée of chestnuts with a generous dollop of butter, season with salt and pepper and add as a topping to scrambled eggs.

When buying chestnuts, choose ones which are firm, hard and shiny. It is not always easy to tell their quality just by looking at the outside shell, so ask the greengrocer to slit one open for you. Peeling chestnuts is a chore and in any case, they are often hard to find, except around Christmas, but canned unsweetened chestnut purée is a good standby and dried chestnuts are usually for sale in health shops. In both cases, allow half the weight of fresh. Dried chestnuts must be soaked for 24

hours, during which time they will swell to their original size; they may
take slightly longer to cook than fresh.

Roast chestnuts
Châtaignes sous la cendre

Use a sharp knife to score each chestnut all round. Roast them in the
embers of the fire or in a hot oven until the shells begin to char and
blacken and the flesh is soft. Eat with a little salt. (Special chestnut
roasters are used in France, like a frying pan with holes, and they are
becoming popular in Britain, too.)

Boiled chestnuts
Châtaignes à la cévenole

Score each chestnut with a sharp knife and boil for 10–20 minutes in
salted water with a sprig of fennel until they are soft. Drain them and
serve piping hot in a napkin, letting everyone cut their chestnuts in two·
and scoop out the flesh with a teaspoon.

Peeling chestnuts

Many recipes using chestnuts call for them to be peeled. This takes
time and patience. Both outer and inner husks must be removed and in
France they have a special implement known as a *déboiradour*, which
is made from two crossed pieces of wood with teeth.

First score each one on its rounded side. Throw them into a pan of
lightly salted, boiling water, cover and boil for 8–10 minutes. Take
one out to test if the outer husk comes away easily. Hold the chestnut
in a cloth and use a knife to help you. If necessary boil for a few
minutes longer. Once the chestnuts are ready, set the pan on the side of
the hotplate and deal with them one at a time. Remove outer layer
before rubbing off the inner husk. If the inner husk still won't come
away, put the chestnuts back into the pan with cold water, add a little
oil and bring to the boil, lower heat and simmer. Test one after a few
minutes: hold it in a cloth, and if the skin rubs off, remove a few at a
time, rubbing the skins off with another cloth.

Ardèche chestnut soup
Cousina

Chestnut soup is warming on a wintry day and there are many variations. Milk, often goat's, is a constant ingredient and apples or prunes contribute sweetness, or sometimes a little dark grated chocolate is added. If using prunes they must either be soaked overnight or covered with boiling water and left to plump for an hour or two.

900 g (2 lb) chestnuts, peeled *or*
    450 g (1 lb) dried chestnuts
    soaked for 24 hours *or* 450 g
    (1 lb) can chestnut purée
225 g (8 oz) sweet apples or
    prunes

1 litre (1¾ pints) cow's or goat's
    milk
salt
freshly milled black pepper
bitter chocolate (optional)
garlic bread or croûtons

Peel, core and slice the apples, if using them. Put chestnuts, apples or prunes and milk into a large pan, season with salt and pepper, bring to the boil and simmer, covered, for about 40 minutes until the chestnuts are soft and beginning to break up. (Chestnut purée will need to be broken up with a fork as you add it to the pan and cooking time reduced by half.) Purée the soup, using a mouli-légumes or food processor. Garnish with grated chocolate if desired and serve with garlic bread or croûtons.

Chestnut and onion soup
Soupe aux châtaignes et aux oignons

This recipe uses half the amount of chestnuts as the previous recipe, is made with stock instead of milk and flavoured with onions, carrots and celery.

450 g (1 lb) peeled chestnuts *or*
    225 g (8 oz) dried chestnuts,
    soaked for 24 hours *or* 225 g
    (8 oz) can chestnut purée
1 litre (1¾ pints) stock (or use
    water and stock cube)
2 tablespoons olive oil

225 g (8 oz) onions, chopped
2 carrots, chopped
stick celery, chopped
clove garlic, chopped
salt
freshly milled black pepper
croûtons

If using fresh or dried chestnuts, boil them in the stock for 20–30 minutes until soft. Remove and mash to a purée (or put through a food processor), reserving the stock. Wipe out the pan, heat the oil and fry the onions, carrots and celery over a medium heat until they are golden. Pour over the stock, add garlic, salt and pepper, bring to the boil and let it continue to bubble over a high heat for 10 minutes. Stir in chestnut purée and mix well, simmer for a further 10 minutes. Serve with croûtons of bread fried or grilled in olive oil.

Pork pie with chestnuts and apples
Tourte à la cévenole

This puff pastry pie is filled with a mixture of minced pork, apples and chestnuts, and is ideal as a dish for a buffet supper or a lunch on a sunny autumn day. It can be eaten hot but is much more delicious cold.

225 g (8 oz) chestnuts, peeled *or* 100 g (4 oz) dried, soaked 24 hours
sprig of fennel
sprig of thyme *or* ½ teaspoon dried
salt

225 g (8 oz) puff pastry
2 tablespoons olive oil
225 g (8 oz) onions, chopped
225 g (8 oz) pork, minced
225 g (8 oz) Cox's apples
freshly milled black pepper
3 eggs

Put chestnuts in a saucepan, cover with water, add fennel, thyme and salt. Bring to the boil, cover and simmer for 20 minutes until they are soft but hold their shape. Meanwhile heat oven to Gas 7/425°F/220°C. Divide the pastry into two, one piece a third larger than the other. Roll the pieces out, the larger to fit the base of a 20 cm (8 in) pie dish, the smaller as a lid. Heat oil in a frying pan and fry the chopped onions until they are soft and golden. Take off the heat, mix in the pork. Peel, core and slice the apples finely and add to the mixture. Drain the cooked chestnuts, saving the cooking liquid. Chop them roughly and add to the pork and apples. Stir in 3 or 4 tablespoons of the chestnut liquid. Season with salt and pepper and mix in two of the eggs. Line the pie dish with pastry, fill it with the mixture, top with the pastry lid, dampening it all round the edge so that the two pieces stick well together. Mark all round with the prongs of a fork. Make a slit in the centre of the lid, and decorate if you wish with pastry leaves made from the offcuts. Brush with the third egg, beaten, using a brush or your fingers. Bake for 40 minutes until puffed and golden.

Chestnut sauce
Sauce aux châtaignes

This sauce goes beautifully with turkey or wild boar, or provides a
pleasant alternative to the usual apple sauce when eaten with pork.

25 g (1 oz) butter	salt
450 g (1 lb) can chestnut purée	freshly milled black pepper
150 ml (¼ pint) milk	

Melt the butter in a saucepan and gradually mix in the chestnut purée
breaking it up with a wooden spoon. Stir in the milk a tablespoon at a
time. Heat gently, continuing to stir, and season to taste with salt and
pepper. When the meat is ready to serve, add 2 or 3 tablespoons of the
cooking juices, until the purée is much the same consistency as apple
sauce. Serve in a bowl.

Volcano
Volcan

From the war memorial in the tiny village of Issirac, high in the
wooded hills between the rivers Cèze and Ardèche, you can watch the
sun go down behind the prehistoric landscape of the Cévennes – layer
upon layer of domed, volcanic mountains receding through blues and
purples to a sky ablaze with red. From there comes this chestnut
dessert topped with meringue, a flambéed variation of the well-known
Mont Blanc.

450 g (1 lb) can chestnut purée	175 g (7 oz) caster sugar
4 tablespoons rum or brandy	3 egg whites
4 tablespoons crème fraîche	juice of ½ lemon
100 g (4 oz) almonds, chopped	salt

Empty the purée into a bowl and mash with a potato masher. Beat in
half the rum or brandy, the crème fraîche, half the almonds and 100 g
(4 oz) sugar. Pile the mixture into an oven dish and shape it into the
form of a tall dome. Cover and put in the fridge. Half an hour or so
before you are ready to eat the volcano, heat oven to Gas 6/400°F/
200°C. Fifteen minutes before eating, beat the egg whites with the
lemon juice and a pinch of salt until very stiff and beat in the remaining
sugar, a spoonful at a time. Cover the chestnut dome with this
meringue mixture and sprinkle over remaining almonds. Put into the

oven for about 10 minutes, until meringue is golden. Warm remaining
2 tablespoons of rum or brandy in a soup ladle, flame it, pour over the
pudding and bring immediately to the table.

(Beaten egg whites collapse very quickly unless heat or cold is
instantly applied, so if you want to prepare this dessert ahead of time,
use a dish or tin that can be brought from freezer to oven. Add the
meringue topping an hour or two before you are ready to eat, and put
the volcano into the freezer until it is ready to go into the hot oven.)

Christmas log
Bûche de Noël

This sumptuous Christmas log is vastly superior to the Swiss roll
variety and if you use canned chestnut purée is much easier to make.
Apart from melting chocolate and butter it needs no cooking. Before
the topping is added the log must be firmed for several hours in the
fridge. It freezes well so can be made a week ahead; don't leave it
longer or the flavour will be spoilt. If you don't fancy a log make it in a
loose-bottomed cake tin, lining the base with a circle of greaseproof
paper, pile in the chestnut mixture, smooth the top, put in the fridge to
firm, unmould and cover with the chocolate topping.

200 g (8 oz) bitter chocolate	100 g (4 oz) caster sugar
125 g (5 oz) butter	3 tablespoons brandy or rum
450 g (1 lb) can chestnut purée	4 tablespoons crème fraîche

Break up 50 g (2 oz) chocolate and melt it with the butter over a basin
of hot water or in a warm oven. (Or use the microwave, a minute at a
time, turning and stirring the mixture until the butter and chocolate
are soft.) Beat well with a fork. Empty the can of chestnut purée into a
bowl, mash it and add the sugar, stirring well before mixing in the
melted butter and chocolate. Beat well together until light and creamy
and stir in the brandy or rum. Use a loaf tin or other oblong receptacle
to form the log. Line it with a sheet of greaseproof paper big enough to
wrap the long sides right over into a parcel. Fill with the chestnut
cream. Fold the ends of the paper over the top, completely enclosing
the log. Put it into the fridge to firm for at least 5 hours or into the
freezer for 1 hour. Make the topping by breaking up and melting the
remaining chocolate. Stir in the cream and beat until it is shiny and
smooth. Lift the log in its wrapping out of the tin and roll it gently on

to a plate. Cover with the topping, and mark it with the prongs of a fork to simulate the roughness of bark. Decorate it if you like with a piece of holly and then put into the fridge for an hour or two for the topping to set.

Pancakes with marrons glacés
Crêpes à la cévenole

Chestnuts in French are called *châtaignes* or *marrons*, and the difference between the two is that the first are smaller, often two in a shell. It is the superior *marrons* which are used to make the famous chestnut sweetmeats. The whole process must be done by hand and entails many different stages, which is why they are so expensive. If you are ever given any as a present, try this recipe for pancakes.

4 marrons glacés	8 pancakes (see Index)
1 tablespoon brandy or rum	icing sugar
1 tablespoon crème fraîche	

Crush the *marrons*, and mix with the brandy or rum and crème fraîche. Make the pancakes, put a little of the chestnut mixture on to each, roll up and keep warm. Dust with the icing sugar and serve at once.

Autumn and Winter Matters

Beneath the forest of the Valbonne stands Carsan, a hamlet of cream buildings pale against the tapestried blue of three domed hills. Hidden in the woods is the village water tower where they are practising *ball-trap*, clay-pigeon shooting, in preparation for the winter's hunting that is about to begin. All day we hear the monotonous double-barrel of the guns but as the sun goes down, the shooting stops and there is nothing but the sound of male voices and drunken laughter floating down the hill.

We see a solitary pheasant strolling between the vines and a sudden flurry of a flock of red-tailed partridges rising above the fields. We begin to fear for the safety of the black rabbit which has lived at the back of the house since the spring, sleeping under the cars parked next to the crab apple and being fed by all the summer visitors.

The clocks go back at the end of September, cutting the evenings short. The weather breaks and for days it does nothing but rain. The whole valley is blotted out in a gauze of grey and everyone feels depressed. Then overnight the wind changes, the sky is blue and the sun appears, but with the *mistral* blowing it is freezing in the shade. Vineyards and woods blaze with all the colours of autumn until at last the leaves are on the ground and everything is stark and skeletal.

Now is the time for mushrooms and pumpkins. The new season's olives appear in the market and in November the first truffles arrive. By December shops and stalls are bulging with food for the two winter feasts, Christmas and New Year. The menu at Le Mas at Trescouvieux reads like a medieval banquet, with its *pâté de foie gras*, snails, giant prawns, frogs' legs, *confit de canard*, turkey with chestnuts, wild boar and pheasant. In the market, they are selling *santons*, brightly painted clay figures representing the Nativity and all the villagers and country people. Exiled in England, I arrange mine on the mantelpiece.

The winter pruning begins. Each vine must be cut back. Gradually, as the farmer goes up and down each line, the vineyards turn into regimental rows studded with stakes and resemble the war cemeteries of northern France. The mountains are defined against the clear sky and the wind is merciless. The water freezes in the chicken house and the air feels thin and cold enough for snow. People's thoughts turn to warm and filling casseroles, marinated game, wild mushrooms, soups, cabbages and beans.

The olive

Green olives pickled and in oil

Marinated black olives

Sandwiches with olive oil

Provençal caviar

Sausages with green olives

Stuffed mussels with olive oil

Venison with green olives

Guinea fowl stuffed with olives

Squid or cuttlefish with black olives

Madame Lacour's rabbit with olives

Madame Boeuf's larks without heads

Quail with green olives

Roast duck with olives

The Greeks brought the olive, with its silver leaves and gnarled and twisted trunk, to France 2500 years ago. It has a reputation for immortality because when a tree is cut down, four new trunks appear in the base, and even when apparently destroyed by frost, within a few years, it renews itself. You need faith to plant olives, as they don't produce for at least six years and then only every other year. The fruit which is at first hard and green ripens to black, sometimes with a purple sheen.

The word 'oil' stems from 'olive', and the oil it produces is at the very heart of the cooking of southern France. Use it whenever you can to give a rich, fruity flavour to the recipes. The choice can be bewildering. How good it is will depend on where the olives are grown, who by and how they are pressed. Local people will sometimes drive miles to buy what they consider to be the best. When staying in France, it is an interesting experience to visit an olive mill, still to be found in many places such as La Lucques in Languedoc or Les Barronnies at Nyons, Beaumes-de-Venise or Mouriès in Provence. If offered the chance to sample some, test the flavour by treating the oil like perfume. Put a little in the palm of your hand, rub well and sniff to discover how the aromas vary.

A low acid content means a better quality oil and the oil of Provence is lower than most. There it is graded according to its acidity. Ripe olives are first given a cold pressing and the oil that is produced has an acidity below 1 per cent. Sold as *vierge extra*, it is the best and most expensive. Cold water is then added to the mash which is pressed again under heat and produces oils of a higher acidity, all carrying the word *vierge* but qualified by words like *fine*, *extra fine*, *courante* or *semi-fine*. Their acidity varies from around 1–3 per cent. Olive oils which don't carry the word *vierge* are refined from virgin oils which don't come up to standard in terms of taste or acidity or may be a mixture of virgin and refined oils from different countries.

Good quality olive oil from Provence is very expensive in this country, so it is a definite must to bring home after a visit. Fortunately, most supermarkets now sell virgin oils, often under their own label. These are probably not from Provence, but still have a good flavour.

Cheaper blended or refined olive oils are worth using in cooked dishes especially when the flavour of the oil is likely to be swamped by other powerful ingredients. When you just can't afford any sort of olive oil, use one of the other oils which are used in southern France, notably *arachide*, groundnut oil, which is tasteless but excellent for deep-frying, or the lightly flavoured *tournesol*, sunflower, and grape oils, both of which are cheaper alternatives for salad dressings. Store oils in a dark place; light affects their colour and taste.

There is a stall in the Saturday market at Pont St Esprit which sells gherkins and capers, pulpy jujubes, pistachios and peanuts, anchovies and salt cod and wonderful olive oil. But mostly it is devoted to olives. There are at least a dozen varieties to choose from, displayed glistening in tubs, and nobody objects to the customer tasting a few before buying. There are black and green olives pickled in brine, the early *olives d'été* or bitter *olives amères*, the wrinkled black *à la grecque* and *olives piquées*, grey-green ones stuffed with pimiento or anchovy, the violet *olives taillées* and green *picholines*. There are tiny, shiny black olives from Nyons and a tub of brilliant green ones mixed with anchovy, then another of black in a fiery mixture of hot red chillies and garlic next to one of green mixed with Provençal herbs. Early in October the first *olives cassées* appear. These were picked during August and September, when their bright green colouring begins to turn to yellow and violet, and have been flavoured with fennel and herbs.

All these olives make wonderful drinktime eats or they can be used to add their own special flavours to poultry, fish, game and meat. When roasting lamb or chicken try adding a handful of stoned black olives to the roasting tin 15 minutes before the joint is cooked. Then transfer the lamb to a dish and keep warm, pour away most of the fat from the roasting tin, add a glass of white wine and stir until boiling over a medium heat, pour the sauce with the olives into a gravy boat and serve separately. When cooking with olives, remember they are already quite salty, so make sure you taste before adding extra salt.

All olives, whether picked when green and unripe or left to ripen and blacken, are bitter and inedible straight from the tree and must go through stages of soaking and pickling.

Green olives pickled and in oil
Olives vertes cassées and *à l'huile*

If you are in France in autumn when the fresh green olives are on sale buy a kilo and bring them home to pickle. Put a handful at a time on a board and crack them with the base of a heavy glass, or you can use a wooden mallet if you prefer. The skins must split but the olives remain intact. Put them into a bowl, cover with water, and change the water every day for 9 days. Drain them and put them into preserving jars with 100 g (4 oz) salt, 2 sprigs of fennel, the finely peeled rind of an orange, 3 or 4 bay leaves and 6 coriander seeds. Cover completely with water, seal and shake the jar to dissolve the salt and leave for at least a week before eating. They will keep for about a month in the fridge, but remember to take them out an hour or so before eating as they are not so good when they are very cold.

You can improve ordinary canned or bottled olives by steeping them in olive oil and flavouring them with the same herbs. Use a large, lidded jar and keep replenishing olives and oil as you go, adding more flavourings from time to time. You can thus always be sure of having a supply on hand.

225 g (8 oz) green olives
3 bay leaves
1–2 sprigs of fennel, fresh or dried

1 teaspoon fennel seeds
1 teaspoon coriander seeds
piece of dried orange peel
olive oil

Drain the olives and put them into the jar with all the other ingredients, making sure they are completely covered with the oil. Leave at least a week before eating. Remove olives from the jar with a slotted spoon.

Marinated black olives
Olives noires marinées

The black, ripened olives appear in the market from January to March and are also delicious steeped in olive oil. Use the same herbs and spices as in the above recipe, or if you like a fiery taste try the version below.

Bottled or canned black olives can be put in the oil right away but if the olives are fresh they must be pricked all over first. Use a sharp-pronged fork or cut a cork in half lengthwise and stick five or six

needles into it. Put olives into a preserving jar and add 225 g (8 oz) salt
per 1 kg (2¼ lb) of olives. Shake them well. Leave for a week, shaking
them two or three times a day and pouring off the liquid they will
exude. Finally drain them, wash out and dry the jar and return the
olives to it, and proceed with the recipe.

450 g (1 lb) black olives
1 bay leaf
6 dried red chillies
2 tablespoons dried thyme
freshly milled black pepper

2–3 sprigs of fennel *or* 1
   tablespoon fennel seeds
4 cloves garlic, chopped
3–4 spring onions *or* 2 shallots
   or 1 small onion, chopped
olive oil

Put all the ingredients into a jar, make sure the olives are completely
covered in the oil. Keep at least a week before eating. Remove olives
from the jar with a slotted spoon. Replenish olives, oil and flavourings
from time to time.

Sandwiches with olive oil
Pan bagnat

These Provençal sandwiches make wonderful picnic fare; wrapped in
foil they can be made the night before and kept in the fridge. The name
means soaked bread, and the first and most important ingredient is
olive oil. Cut a round loaf or *baguette* in half, remove some of the soft
centre to make a hollow. Rub each half with the cut side of a clove of
garlic and sprinkle with a very little vinegar and a generous amount of
olive oil. It is now ready for the filling which might consist of sliced
tomatoes, crushed anchovy fillets or tuna, a sliced hard-boiled egg,
some finely sliced spring onions and a few chopped basil leaves. Press
the two sides together, wrap in foil and set the whole thing aside for at
least an hour for the oil and flavour of the other ingredients to saturate
the bread. Cut into individual portions.

Provençal caviar
Tapenado

It seems likely that this shiny mud-grey paste flecked with black came
to France with the Greeks. The name derives from the Provençal word
for caper, *tapeno*, which is the pickled bud of the caper bush which

grows wild on walls and in stony places, but it owes its flavour and texture just as much to its other main ingredients, anchovies and olives. It makes the most delicious midday snack with a quite different flavour from the other olive-based 'caviar' given in the Aubergine section. It can be spread on buttered toast or on French bread brushed with olive oil which has been very lightly browned either under a grill or at the top of a hot oven. Serve it as an *amuse-gueule*, spread on little canapés to accompany an aperitif, or use it as filling for hard-boiled eggs, mashing it with the yolks and piling the mixture back into the whites. Or simply spread a layer at the base of a simple tomato salad. No two versions are exactly alike, every household having their particular recipe. Below is one version; you can vary it by adding tuna, more or fewer olives, and experiment with different herbs and spices.

225 g (8 oz) black olives, stoned
1 clove garlic
50 g (2 oz) can anchovy fillets
2 tablespoons capers
1 teaspoon mild Dijon mustard

4 tablespoons olive oil
pepper
pinch each of thyme and nutmeg
1 teaspoon brandy or lemon
 juice

Crush the olives, garlic, anchovies and capers (rinse capers under running water before using) to a pulp in a mortar with a pestle, or use a food processor. Add the mustard and beat in the oil a little at a time as if you were making a mayonnaise. Season with freshly milled pepper, add thyme and nutmeg. Finally add the brandy, or lemon juice. Store in small jars topped with a thin layer of olive oil and put on lids or cover with cling film. Keep cool.

Sausages with green olives
Saucisses aux olives vertes

In France you can buy thin, pink sausages speckled with white which are much tastier and spicier than the run-of-the mill English equivalent. Look out for Toulouse or Cumberland sausages in delicatessens or go for spiced or herby ones. Whatever you use they are much enhanced by the flavour of the green olives and the sticky tomato sauce.

1–2 tablespoons olive oil
450 g (1 lb) sausages
4 cloves garlic

1 can chopped Italian tomatoes
12 green olives
handful of chopped parsley

aucepan, add the sausages and brown them all over. Add
cloves and the tomatoes. Bring to the boil, cover, lower
and simmer for about 15 minutes. Take off the lid, raise the heat
and cook briskly to reduce the liquid in the sauce. Add the olives and
allow them a couple of minutes to heat through. Serve the sausages
topped with the sauce and sprinkled with parsley.

Stuffed mussels with olive oil
Moules à la provençale

Instead of stuffing mussels with the usual garlic butter, try this recipe
which uses olive oil. It is quick and easy to prepare and the flavour of
the oil adds to the pleasures of the dish. The mussels can be stuffed in
their half-shells, or you might prefer to use those special individual
dishes with six or twelve hollows which are meant for serving snails.

450 g (1 lb/1 pint) mussels	4 tablespoons chopped parsley
freshly milled black pepper	4 tablespoons breadcrumbs
2–3 cloves garlic, chopped	olive oil

Scrub and clean mussels (see Index). When they are clean, put them in
a large saucepan and stand it over a high heat for several minutes. As
soon as the shells open, remove from the heat and empty into a
colander. When they are cool enough to handle, discard one half of the
shell and lay the mussels in their half-shells in the base of one or more
ovenproof dishes. (Or put mussels into the hollows of snail dishes.)
Add a sprinkling of freshly milled black pepper. Mix together the
garlic, parsley, and breadcrumbs and add a little of the mixture to each
mussel. Sprinkle liberally with olive oil. Heat oven to Gas 7/425°F/
220°C and bake for about 10 minutes, until piping hot. Serve with
plenty of bread to mop up the juices.

Venison with green olives
Epaule de chevreuil aux olives vertes

Chevreuil is the meat of the tiny roe deer which live wild in the forests
of France. Roe deer also live in Britain but so do the much bigger and
tougher fallow and red deer and if you buy venison meat over the
counter, you are not likely to know from which animal it comes.

However, the long marinade and slow cooking of this recipe will result
in a delicious stew flavoured with onions, juniper and olives. Serve it
with a chestnut purée or bitter-sweet sauce (see Index).

700–900 g (1½–2 lb) boned
  shoulder of venison
3 onions, chopped
2 carrots, chopped
2 cloves garlic, chopped
bay leaf
12 juniper berries
salt
8 whole peppercorns

sprigs of thyme and rosemary
3 tablespoons olive oil
2 tablespoons white wine
  vinegar
300 ml (½ pint) approx. white
  wine
20 green olives
6 rashers streaky bacon
salt, pepper

Cut the meat into chunks and put it in a china or glass dish with one of
the onions, the carrots, garlic, bay leaf, juniper berries, salt, peppercorns, thyme, rosemary, olive oil, vinegar and wine – there should be
sufficient just to cover. Leave for 3–6 days covered in the fridge,
turning the meat over once or twice each day. When you are ready to
cook it, heat oven to Gas 2/300°F/150°C. Dry the meat and put it in an
earthenware pot into which it fits snugly. Add remaining onions and
olives and lay the bacon on top. Strain in the liquid from the marinade.
Cover with foil and the lid and cook in the oven until it is tender, about
4 hours.

Guinea fowl stuffed with olives
Pintade aux olives

Guinea fowl can be dry, but in this recipe it is gently simmered in wine
and flavoured with a simple stuffing made with olives and ham. Failing
a guinea fowl, use a maize-fed or free-range chicken.

50 g (2 oz) butter, softened
100 g (4 oz) stoned black olives,
  chopped
100 g (4 oz) ham, chopped
4 cloves garlic, chopped
fresh thyme and parsley,
  chopped

salt
freshly milled black pepper
1 guinea fowl
4 tablespoons olive oil
150 ml (¼ pint) dry white wine
watercress

Mash the butter and mix with the olives, ham, garlic and herbs. Season
with salt and pepper. Fill the cavity of the guinea fowl. Heat the oil in a

heavy-based pan in which the bird will sit comfortably and brown it all over on a medium heat, pour in the wine, cover and lower the heat. Simmer gently for 45–60 minutes until the bird is cooked. Test with the point of a skewer: the juice should run yellow not pink. Remove bird to a serving dish, garnish with watercress. Reduce liquid by boiling hard and serve separately.

Squid or cuttlefish with black olives
Calmars ou seiches aux olives noires

This dish can be made with either squid or cuttlefish. The latter are not easily found in Britain but you will see them in the markets in France. You may be able to buy squid already emptied and cleaned. If not, they are easy to do. First, cut off the tentacles just above the eyes. Hold the squid in one hand and with the other carefully pull off and discard the head which will come away with most of the innards. Pull out the long, central, transparent quill. Use scissors to slit the pouch in half and wash away any remaining innards and rub off the purplish membrane under running cold water.

750 g (1½ lb) squid
2 tablespoons olive oil
1 tablespoon brandy (optional)
12 shallots or 2 onions
2 cloves garlic, chopped
2 tablespoons chopped parsley
1 can drained Italian tomatoes

salt, pepper
3–4 medium-sized potatoes
  (optional)
2 dried red chillies
150 ml (¼ pint) white wine
20 black olives

Cut each squid into 3 or 4 pieces, leaving the tentacles whole. Heat the oil in a saucepan and fry the squid for a few minutes, turning over and over and continue to cook over a high heat to evaporate as much of the liquid as possible. Pour the brandy into a ladle or small saucepan, heat it and set it alight, pour it over the squid and shake until the flames subside. Peel the shallots (pour boiling water over them to loosen the skins) or chop the onions. Add to pan, followed by garlic and parsley and cook for a few minutes longer over a medium heat, stirring from time to time. Add tomatoes, salt, pepper, quartered potatoes, if using, and the chillies. Pour over the wine, bring to the boil, then lower the heat and simmer, covered, for about 30 minutes. Add the olives. Check the seasoning and cook for a further 5 minutes. Serve with rice.

Madame Lacour's rabbit with olives
Lapin aux olives

Emile and Henri were coming to lunch and naturally wanted to know
what they were going to have. Rabbit, I said, so they gave me their
mother's recipe which has no garlic because Emile detests it. Instead, I
simmered a handful of garlic cloves in a little white wine and served
them separately.

3 tablespoons olive oil
100 g (4 oz) streaky bacon,
  chopped
1 rabbit, cut into 8 pieces, plus
  the liver
1 onion, chopped
450 g (1 lb) tomatoes, peeled *or*
  1 can chopped Italian
  tomatoes

150 ml (¼ pint) dry white wine
sprigs of thyme and rosemary
bay leaf
salt
freshly milled black pepper
12 green olives
juice of ½ lemon

Heat the olive oil in a heavy-based pan and brown the pieces of bacon.
Remove and keep warm while you brown the rabbit pieces (except the
liver) all over, in two batches if necessary. When they are golden,
remove and put aside with the bacon. Add onion to the pan and cook
over a medium heat until it is soft but not brown. Return the rabbit
and bacon to the pan and add tomatoes, wine, thyme and rosemary,
bay leaf, salt and pepper. Bring to the boil, cover and simmer for 1½
hours. Remove lid and cook for 15 minutes more to reduce the sauce.
Add the olives. Crush the liver with 2 tablespoons of the cooking
liquid and add to the pan. Squeeze over the lemon juice. Remove from
the heat, cover and set aside for 5 minutes before serving.

Madame Boeuf's larks without heads
Alouettes sans têtes

Madame Boeuf had come to look after her grandson Jean-Pierre while
his family stayed at the seaside and this is what she cooked us for lunch
one day. She was at great pains to assure us it had nothing to do with
larks, headless or otherwise, but was thin slices of beef rolled round a
stuffing. She wrote down the recipe. They serve it too at the Oustelet
Maïanen, in Mistral's home village of Maillane, where you can sit
under a canopy of vines helping yourself from the casserole brought to
the table.

8 very thin slices of beefsteak
100 g (4 oz) cooked ham,
  chopped
handful finely chopped parsley
2 cloves garlic, finely chopped
freshly milled black pepper
2 tablespoons olive oil

1 small onion, finely chopped
1 tablespoon tomato purée
1 can chopped Italian tomatoes
1 glass dry white wine
1 chilli
handful black olives
salt, if necessary

Flatten the pieces of beef with a rolling pin. In the centre of each put a little of the ham, some chopped parsley and garlic, and season with a little pepper. Roll the meat up and tie it securely with string or thread. Heat the oil in a flameproof casserole and brown the pieces of meat all over. Add the onion, tomato purée and the tomatoes and pour over the wine. The pieces should be covered; if they are not top up with water. Add the chilli. Simmer, covered, for about 1–1½ hours, until the meat is tender. Add the olives and cook for a further 10–15 minutes. Check the seasoning and if necessary add a little salt and more pepper.

Quail with green olives
Cailles aux olives vertes

Wrap a piece of bacon round each quail, secure with string and brown them all over in a tablespoon of olive oil, using a heavy-based casserole in which they sit comfortably. Add a chopped onion, a can of chopped Italian tomatoes, 2 crushed cloves of garlic, a sprig of fennel and some parsley and a handful of stoned green olives. Season with salt and pepper and simmer gently, covered, for 30 minutes.

Roast duck with olives
Canard aux olives

A small French Barbary duck makes a lovely dinner for two, first roasted and then simmered for 10 minutes in a casserole with wine and green olives.

1–1¼ kg (2¼–3 lb) duck
2 sprigs of thyme *or* 1 teaspoon
  dried
1 onion, chopped
salt
freshly milled black pepper

1 carrot, chopped
2 tablespoons olive oil
150 ml (¼ pint) dry white wine
225 g (8 oz) green olives, stoned
watercress

Heat oven to Gas 7/425°F/220°C. Put thyme and half the onion into the cavity of the duck and season with salt and pepper. Lay the duck, breast uppermost, in a roasting tin, surround with remaining onion and the carrot and sprinkle over the olive oil. Roast, allowing 20 minutes per 450 g (1 lb) and 20 minutes over. After the first 15 minutes lower the heat to Gas 5/375°F/190°C and turn the bird on its side. After a further 20 minutes, turn to its other side and, 20 minutes later, turn it breast up. Strain a little of the cooking juices into a heavy-based casserole in which the bird will sit, stir in the wine, bring to the boil, add duck and olives and simmer for 10 minutes. Serve on a dish surrounded by the sauce and olives and garnished with watercress.

Mushrooms and a black truffle

Dried mushrooms

Mushrooms with bacon

Fried mushrooms

Mushrooms with cream

Baked garlic mushrooms

Stuffed mushrooms with chicken livers

Mushrooms with anchovies

Mushroom and leek tart

Little carrot pots with mushroom sauce

Betty's mushrooms with artichokes and peas

Guinea fowl stuffed with mushrooms

Beef stewed with mushrooms

Hunter's pheasant

A black truffle

After rain in autumn, those in the know go in search of mushrooms and soon they are on sale in the market. Not your common, cultivated mushroom, but great, shaggy heaps of wild fungi with strange country names. Local *pharmacies* carry notices offering advice on identification; everyone knows that few are deadly but it is vital to be sure. You can choose from small thin-stalked fairy ring mushrooms or bright yellow chanterelles, speckled parasols or the soft-spined wood hedgehogs. Sometimes there are green russula or a pile of giant white puffballs in stark contrast to another of trumpets of death. The exotic sounding *lactaire délicieux* are tempting but they turn out to be not quite as delicious as the name suggests. Or there might be tawny grisettes and *coucoumelles* and occasionally you may see the most highly prized of all – the Caesar's mushrooms with their yellow caps. If you don't know how to cook them ask the stall keeper who whatever the variety almost invariably advises you to fry them in butter with lots of garlic and fresh herbs.

Buy mushrooms when they are firm and fresh-looking, and avoid those which look damp and limp. Don't store them in plastic bags or they will go soggy. Cultivated mushrooms only need to be wiped over with kitchen paper and don't need peeling. Some wild mushrooms can be maggoty or gritty so need to be washed by dipping them in and out of several changes of water with a tablespoon or so of vinegar. Discard any that are infected. Then drain and dry well in between sheets of kitchen paper.

Most of the wild mushrooms detailed below can be found in Britain. If you are interested in hunting them out, find a local expert to teach you where and what to look for, and buy a well-illustrated book to help you in your search. All the following recipes can be made with the kind of mushrooms readily available in Britain. As well as button and flat field mushrooms look out for oyster and chestnut varieties. Bring back packets of dried mushrooms from France and look out for some interesting alternatives in Chinese and oriental supermarkets.

Mushrooms can be eaten as a starter or vegetable course or even as a simple meal on their own. A few fried mushrooms, seasoned with garlic and herbs make a delicious filler for an omelette and one of the nicest meals I can remember is pancakes filled with wild mushrooms baked in a creamy sauce and topped with cheese, prepared by a farmer's wife in her *cave* restaurant in the foothills of the Cévennes. They are also delicious sliced raw, mixed with garlic, parsley, lemon juice and plenty of olive oil, and seasoned with salt and black pepper. You can eat them on their own or try mixing them with prawns and squid which has been cut in rings and gently poached until tender.

Below are a few notes regarding some of the mushrooms you might see on a market stall in France.

BOLET or CÈPE (*Boletus* family). Several varieties with flat, bun-like tops. They have a wonderful flavour. Those found in pinewoods nicknamed *champignons de pin*. No gills but thin tubes which look like holes in a pin cushion. The tubes are edible but if damp and discoloured, peel them off. Can be maggoty, so wash well. Slice stalks. Young bolets can be eaten raw in salads, otherwise use in any manner for cooking mushrooms. Sold in France in great quantities dried, after soaking can be used to flavour any recipe which calls for mushrooms.

CHANTERELLE or GIROLLE (*Cantharellus cibarius*). Also known as *chevrette, crête de coq, gallinace, jaunette, oreille de Jésuite, oreillette* and *roussotte*. A common woodland mushroom varying from a bright to dark egg yellow. Has firm, dense flesh with apricot-like perfume and is free of parasites. Very expensive. Often used just as a garnish or to flavour an omelette, pancakes and sauces. Needs thorough cooking. Can be sliced and softened in boiling water before being stewed with butter etc. Dries well.

COULEMELLE (*Lepiota procera*) – parasol mushroom. Also known as *baguette de tambour, champignon à la bague, nez de chat, parasol, potiron* and *St Michel*. The stalks are inedible but many people consider the heads the most delicious of all mushrooms. Best simmered gently in a generous amount of butter for about 30 minutes and lightly seasoned with a little salt and pepper. No other flavouring is needed; just serve with a green salad.

LACTAIRE DÉLICIEUX (*Lactarius deliciosus*). Also known as *barigoule, catalan, marseillais, orangé, pignen, pinet, roussillon, vache rouge* or *vachotte*. Red-orange with orange-yellow gills; old ones have greenish spots on stems. Very common. Good with a dense, brittle flesh. Produces an orange milk. There are several related species, including the more highly esteemed *lactaire sanguin*, also known as *pinin* or *sang de Christ*. Can be very maggoty so need careful washing. Need long cooking, so good baked or stewed.

MOREL (*Morchella vulgaris*) – honeycomb-capped morel. Not very common. Expensive. Can be bought canned, in jars or dried. Use sparingly to flavour omelettes, fish or chicken dishes, and stews. Soak dried morels for an hour, then trim, split and rinse and use as for fresh. Need to be well cooked. The caps are hollow, fleshy, slightly brittle, ideal for stuffing. To prepare: Remove base of stalk and cut the morels in half lengthwise. Soak them for 5–10 minutes in salted water to evacuate any insect life, rinse under the tap to make sure you remove all sand and grit. Dry gently with kitchen paper. Can be threaded on strings to dry. Found spring to autumn.

MOUSSERON (*Marasmius oreades*) – fairy ring mushroom. Can be as large as 5 cm (2 in) across but are often a quarter of this size. The stringy, tough stalks must be discarded – a thumb nail will sever them at their heads. Wash in water to which a tablespoon of vinegar has been added. Drain and dry between sheets of kitchen paper. Need long, slow cooking, good in soups, stews, tarts, omelettes and scrambled eggs. Often dried or pickled. Found late spring to autumn.

ORONGE (*Amanita caesara*) – Caesar's mushroom. Also known as *amanite des césars* or *roumanel*. Not found in Britain. Most prized in France. Yellow orange cap. Good fried, grilled or baked. Related to the highly dangerous Fly Agaric toadstool (*Amanita muscaria*) and also to the delicate, edible *vineuse* or *oronge vineuse* (*Amanita fulva* – tawny grisette) and the *coucoumelle* or grisette (*amanita vaginata*).

PETIT GRIS D'AUTOMNE and JAUNET (*Tricholoma* family) – related to St George's mushroom. Stew with ham or bacon or slice and fry in olive oil with thyme or savory.

PIED DE MOUTON (*Hydnum repandum*) – wood hedgehog. Also known as *barbe de chèvre*, *chevrette*, *langue de chat* and *oursin*. Very common in Languedoc. Bitter flavour if eaten raw but excellent cooked in most recipes.

PSALLIOTE CHAMPÊTRE (*Psalliota campestris*) – field mushroom. Also known as *rose des prés*, *vinou* and *vineux*, related to cultivated mushrooms.

RUSSULES (*Russula* family). Huge family of brightly coloured fungi; some are distinctly unpleasant, hot and burning to eat while others, like the green-capped, are very edible, with firm, white flesh scented with hazelnuts. Use in any mushroom recipe.

TROMPETTE DE LA MORT (*Craterellus cornucopioides*) – trumpet of death or horn of plenty. Also known as *champignon noir, corne d'abondance, trompette des Maures* and *truffe du pauvre*. No gills, dark brown to blackish. Good to dry for winter, when it can be powdered and used sparingly to flavour rice, soups, stews, omelettes etc. It blackens whatever it is cooked with. It has a very faint whiff of truffles and is often used in pâtés as a substitute. Needs long, slow cooking. Best stewed with bacon or ham.

VESSE DE LOUP (*Lycoperdon*). Several species of this puffball family. Good to eat when white and young, either in fritters flavoured with thyme, or thinly sliced, fried and eaten with a salad.

Dried mushrooms

Dried mushrooms are a useful addition to the kitchen, as they often have a much more pronounced flavour than the fresh cultivated variety. If you are in France and are presented with a mass of mushrooms you might like to dry your own. Line slatted wooden greengrocer's trays with newspaper and tissue paper, spread the mushrooms on top and cover with another sheet of tissue. Put them outdoors in the shade and turn them occasionally until they are completely dry, which can take several days, according to the temperature. Bring them indoors at night. They can be dried indoors in an airing cupboard or any other warm, ventilated place, (never over 50°C (120°F)). Some varieties, like the fairy ring mushroom, can be threaded on string and hung up to dry. To use dried mushrooms, cover them with tepid water and soak them for up to 24 hours.

Mushrooms with bacon
Champignons au lard

Bacon and mushrooms have an affinity. You can vary the recipe by leaving out the tomatoes and, instead of thyme, sprinkle liberally with parsley right at the very end of the cooking.

4 tablespoons olive oil
225 g (8 oz) lean bacon,
  chopped
450 g (1 lb) mushrooms, sliced
2 tomatoes, chopped
1 small onion, chopped

2 sprigs of thyme *or* 1 teaspoon
  dried
2 cloves garlic, chopped
salt
freshly milled black pepper

Heat the oil, add bacon and fry briskly for 3 or 4 minutes. Add the mushrooms, tomatoes, onion and thyme. Stir over a high heat until all the liquid from the mushrooms has evaporated. Lower the heat, add garlic, salt and pepper. Continue to cook gently for 5–10 minutes, turning occasionally. Serve very hot with toast or croûtons of fried bread.

Fried mushrooms
Champignons sautés à la poêle

Most mushrooms are delicious sliced and fried.

450 g (1 lb) mushrooms
4 tablespoons olive oil
sprig of fresh thyme *or* 1
  teaspoon dried
2 shallots *or* 1 small onion,
  finely chopped

1 clove garlic, crushed
salt
freshly milled black pepper
handful chopped parsley.

Slice the mushrooms finely. Heat the oil in a frying pan and cook them with the thyme over a medium heat until golden, turning often until they are soft and their liquid has evaporated. Add the shallots and the garlic and stir briskly – don't let them burn. As soon as the shallots are cooked, add salt and pepper and sprinkle over the chopped parsley. Serve at once.

Mushrooms with cream
Champignons à la crème

Follow the above recipe but use butter instead of oil. As soon as the shallots are cooked, remove from the heat and stir in 3 or 4 tablespoons of crème fraîche (or use double cream and squeeze over the juice of half a lemon), sprinkle with the parsley and serve on their own or with freshly cooked pasta.

Baked garlic mushrooms
Champignons au gratin

This is a quick-to-prepare starter that is a favourite of all garlic lovers.

700 g (1½ lb) flat, medium-sized mushrooms	2–3 cloves garlic, chopped
	handful chopped parsley
salt	3–4 tablespoons breadcrumbs
freshly milled black pepper	olive oil

Heat oven to Gas 7/425°F/220°C. Remove and finely chop the mushroom stalks. Lay the mushroom caps in a single layer in a buttered gratin dish. Spoon the chopped stalks into the cavities, season with salt and pepper, and sprinkle over the garlic and parsley. Cover with the breadcrumbs and moisten generously with the oil. Bake for about 10 minutes.

Stuffed mushrooms with chicken livers
Champignons farcis aux foies de volaille

Most large mushrooms are good stuffed. For a simple starter or snack, the filling could be nothing more elaborate than a combination of the chopped stalks mixed with onion, ham, garlic, thyme and bread-crumbs, sprinkled with oil and baked for 30–40 minutes in a moderate oven, basting with water or wine half-way through the cooking time. For something a little more filling try the recipe below.

4–8 flat mushrooms	freshly milled black pepper
100 g (4 oz) chestnut or button mushrooms	½ teaspoon dried thyme
	300 ml (½ pint) stock
2 tablespoons olive oil	1 heaped tablespoon flour
1 small onion, chopped	25 g (1 oz) butter
225 g (8 oz) chicken livers	3–4 tablespoons breadcrumbs
1 tablespoon tomato purée	olive oil
salt	

Remove stalks from the large mushrooms, butter a gratin dish and arrange them in a single layer. Chop stalks and the smaller mushrooms finely. Heat oil in a frying pan, add the onion and cook over a medium heat for 3–4 minutes. Add the chicken livers, cut in small pieces, and fry quickly over a high heat to seal in the juices. Remove from heat, add finely chopped mushrooms and tomato purée, season with salt, pepper and thyme. Spoon the mixture into the large mushrooms. Heat oven to Gas 5/375°F/190°C. Make a sauce by putting stock, flour and butter into a small saucepan. Bring to boiling point on a medium heat, beating all the time. As it thickens, lower heat and continue to cook for a couple of minutes; season to taste and carefully spoon sauce over the mushrooms. Sprinkle with the breadcrumbs and a little olive oil, put into the oven and bake for 25–30 minutes.

Mushrooms with anchovies
Champignons aux anchois

Anchovies make even the blandest button mushrooms taste exciting. Serve them on croûtons of bread fried in oil until golden.

100 g (4 oz) butter
2 tablespoons olive oil
6 anchovy fillets
2 cloves garlic, chopped
450 g (1 lb) mushrooms, sliced

4 tablespoons dry white wine
freshly milled black pepper
salt to taste
handful chopped parsley and
    mint

Heat butter and oil in a frying pan, add anchovy fillets and garlic. Crush the fillets with a wooden spoon before adding mushrooms, toss for a few minutes over a medium heat, add wine and season with pepper. Cover and cook gently for 10–15 minutes. Remove lid, raise heat and cook until most of the liquid has evaporated. The anchovies are salty, so taste and only if necessary add a little salt. Serve garnished with the parsley and mint.

Mushroom and leek tart
Tarte aux champignons et aux poireaux

Leeks and mushrooms combine to make this creamy tart which can be served as a starter or as a main course for a light supper or lunch. Use this same basic recipe for other vegetable tarts, such as onion, spinach or just plain leeks or mushrooms. You can use shortcrust pastry but if you do, bake it blind for 15–20 minutes (cover pastry with foil and a layer of dried beans or rice to prevent it collapsing) before adding the filling. I prefer puff because it needs no preliminary cooking and I do as the French do and buy it ready-made, suffering as little guilt as they do.

225 g (8 oz) puff pastry
2 tablespoons olive oil
350 g (12 oz) leeks, sliced
50 g (2 oz) butter
150 g (6 oz) mushrooms, sliced
2 heaped tablespoons flour

300 ml (½ pint) milk
salt, pepper
nutmeg
2 eggs
100 g (4 oz) streaky bacon,
    chopped

Heat oven to Gas 6/400°F/200°C. Roll out pastry and line a 20 cm (8 in) flan dish or tin. Heat oil in a heavy-based saucepan, add sliced leeks and cook gently until soft (about 10 minutes), turning them over from time to time. To make the sauce, add the butter to the pan and as soon as it has melted, raise the heat and add the mushrooms. Toss them for 2 or 3 minutes until they begin to soften, lower the heat and sprinkle in the flour. Mix it and cook it stirring for a couple of minutes before gradually adding the milk. Continue to cook and stir until the sauce thickens and begins to bubble. Season with salt, pepper and nutmeg. Off the heat, stir in the eggs, one at a time. Pour the sauce into the pastry shell, arrange pieces of bacon all round the edge. Put into the oven and bake for 30–35 minutes.

Little carrot pots with mushroom sauce
Petits pots de carottes aux champignons

These vivid orange pots turned out and surrounded by a creamy mushroom sauce make a pretty starter, or if you prefer you can bake the mixture in a loaf tin and serve it as a main vegetarian course.

700 g (1½ lb) carrots
sprig of parsley
50 g (2 oz) flour
3 eggs, beaten
4 tablespoons crème fraîche
pinch of nutmeg
1 clove garlic, chopped

salt
freshly milled black pepper
50 g (2 oz) butter
150 g (6 oz) mushrooms,
    chopped
300 ml (½ pint) milk

Peel and slice carrots and cook them in boiling salted water with the sprig of parsley until soft (about 20 minutes). When they are cooked heat oven to Gas 6/400°F/200°C. Drain and mash the carrots, stir in 25 g (1 oz) flour, the beaten eggs, crème fraîche, nutmeg, garlic and season to taste with salt and pepper. Butter 6 individual cocotte pots, line each with a circle of greaseproof paper (or use a greased and papered loaf tin). Fill with the mixture. Stand the pots or loaf tin in a baking tin half-filled with boiling water and bake for 20–25 minutes (40–45 minutes if using a loaf tin).

Meanwhile, make a sauce by melting the butter in a small pan. Add the chopped mushrooms and stir over a medium heat until they are soft. Lower the heat, sprinkle over the remaining 25 g (1 oz) flour and stir for about 2 minutes until well mixed. Gradually stir in the milk, raise heat and continue to stir as the sauce comes to the boil. Lower the heat, add salt and pepper. Let the sauce cook very gently – it should barely simmer so if necessary set it to one side of the hotplate. It will thicken and reduce. Stir it from time to time, taking care it does not stick to the bottom of the pan. When the carrot mixture is set and firm (test by piercing with a skewer, which should come out clean), run a knife around each pot (or loaf tin) and turn out on to individual plates or a serving platter. Serve sauce separately.

Betty's mushrooms with artichokes and peas
Champignons aux artichauts et aux petits pois

When I'm in a real hurry but want something a bit special for a starter that old and young alike will enjoy, I make this dish which uses canned mushrooms mixed with those tiny peas the French and Belgians put in tins, and artichoke hearts. Betty first came across it in a restaurant in Tullins and when she tried it out on us, we all agreed it was delicious.

1 tablespoon olive oil
100 g (4 oz) streaky bacon, chopped
1 small onion, chopped
150 g (6 oz) can button mushrooms
450 g (1 lb) can petits pois
450 g (1 lb) can artichoke hearts
salt, pepper
thyme
150 ml (¼ pint) stock or water
1 clove garlic, chopped
handful chopped parsley

Heat a heavy-based casserole, add oil, bacon and onion and let them brown lightly over a medium heat. Add drained mushrooms, peas and artichokes, salt, pepper, thyme and stock or water. Bring to the boil, lower heat, cover and simmer for 5–10 minutes until everything is heated through. Turn on to a shallow serving dish and sprinkle over the chopped garlic and parsley.

Guinea fowl stuffed with mushrooms
Pintade farcie aux champignons

_a fowl may look small but it is very meaty and one is usually
su___ ent for four, unless you are very hungry. This recipe works just
as well with a free-range or maize-fed chicken.

6–7 tablespoons olive oil	2 tablespoons red wine
100 g (4 oz) mushrooms,	salt
chopped	freshly milled black pepper
50 g (2 oz) ham, chopped	1 guinea fowl
4 tablespoons breadcrumbs	100 g (4 oz) streaky bacon

Heat oven to Gas 6/400°F/200°C. Make the stuffing by heating 2
tablespoons of oil in a frying pan. Add the mushrooms, cook over a
medium heat until they are soft, then stir in the chopped ham,
breadcrumbs, wine, salt and pepper. Spoon the mixture into the cavity
of the bird and put it in a roasting tin. Cover the breast with rashers of
streaky bacon and sprinkle over 4 or 5 tablespoons of oil. Roast,
allowing 20 minutes per 450 g (1 lb) and 20 minutes over, weighed
when stuffed. Turn and baste the bird every 15 minutes.

Beef stewed with mushrooms
Estouffade de boeuf aux champignons

This slow-cooked casserole of beef in a dark, mushroomy sauce is very
quick to prepare. It is traditionally eaten with *milhas* or a dish of
haricot beans flavoured with parsley and garlic (see Index).

2 tablespoons flour	2 carrots, sliced in rings
700 g (1½ lb) stewing beef, cut	sprigs of thyme and parsley
in cubes	bay leaf
225 g (8 oz) streaky bacon, cut	salt
in pieces	freshly milled black pepper
2 tablespoons olive oil	300 ml (½ pint) dry white wine
3 onions, chopped	225 g (8 oz) mushrooms
3 cloves garlic, chopped	

Put the flour into a bowl and turn the cubes of meat over and over until
they are all well coated. Heat a heavy-based frying pan, add the bacon
pieces, and fry until they release their fat. Remove to a flameproof
casserole set over a low heat. Heat the oil in the frying pan and fry the

line each with a circle of greaseproof paper (or use a greased and
papered loaf tin). Fill with the mixture. Stand the pots or loaf tin in a
baking tin half-filled with boiling water and bake for 20–25 minutes
(40–45 minutes if using a loaf tin).

Meanwhile, make a sauce by melting the butter in a small pan. Add
the chopped mushrooms and stir over a medium heat until they are
soft. Lower the heat, sprinkle over the remaining 25 g (1 oz) flour and
stir for about 2 minutes until well mixed. Gradually stir in the milk,
raise heat and continue to stir as the sauce comes to the boil. Lower the
heat, add salt and pepper. Let the sauce cook very gently – it should
barely simmer so if necessary set it to one side of the hotplate. It will
thicken and reduce. Stir it from time to time, taking care it does not
stick to the bottom of the pan. When the carrot mixture is set and firm
(test by piercing with a skewer, which should come out clean), run a
knife around each pot (or loaf tin) and turn out on to individual plates
or a serving platter. Serve sauce separately.

Betty's mushrooms with artichokes and peas
Champignons aux artichauts et aux petits pois

When I'm in a real hurry but want something a bit special for a starter
that old and young alike will enjoy, I make this dish which uses canned
mushrooms mixed with those tiny peas the French and Belgians put in
tins, and artichoke hearts. Betty first came across it in a restaurant in
Tullins and when she tried it out on us, we all agreed it was delicious.

1 tablespoon olive oil
100 g (4 oz) streaky bacon, chopped
1 small onion, chopped
150 g (6 oz) can button mushrooms
450 g (1 lb) can petits pois

450 g (1 lb) can artichoke hearts
salt, pepper
thyme
150 ml (¼ pint) stock or water
1 clove garlic, chopped
handful chopped parsley

Heat a heavy-based casserole, add oil, bacon and onion and let them
brown lightly over a medium heat. Add drained mushrooms, peas and
artichokes, salt, pepper, thyme and stock or water. Bring to the boil,
lower heat, cover and simmer for 5–10 minutes until everything is
heated through. Turn on to a shallow serving dish and sprinkle over
the chopped garlic and parsley.

Guinea fowl stuffed with mushrooms
Pintade farcie aux champignons

A guinea fowl may look small but it is very meaty and one is usually sufficient for four, unless you are very hungry. This recipe works just as well with a free-range or maize-fed chicken.

6–7 tablespoons olive oil
100 g (4 oz) mushrooms,
  chopped
50 g (2 oz) ham, chopped
4 tablespoons breadcrumbs

2 tablespoons red wine
salt
freshly milled black pepper
1 guinea fowl
100 g (4 oz) streaky bacon

Heat oven to Gas 6/400°F/200°C. Make the stuffing by heating 2 tablespoons of oil in a frying pan. Add the mushrooms, cook over a medium heat until they are soft, then stir in the chopped ham, breadcrumbs, wine, salt and pepper. Spoon the mixture into the cavity of the bird and put it in a roasting tin. Cover the breast with rashers of streaky bacon and sprinkle over 4 or 5 tablespoons of oil. Roast, allowing 20 minutes per 450 g (1 lb) and 20 minutes over, weighed when stuffed. Turn and baste the bird every 15 minutes.

Beef stewed with mushrooms
Estouffade de boeuf aux champignons

This slow-cooked casserole of beef in a dark, mushroomy sauce is very quick to prepare. It is traditionally eaten with *milhas* or a dish of haricot beans flavoured with parsley and garlic (see Index).

2 tablespoons flour
700 g (1½ lb) stewing beef, cut
  in cubes
225 g (8 oz) streaky bacon, cut
  in pieces
2 tablespoons olive oil
3 onions, chopped
3 cloves garlic, chopped

2 carrots, sliced in rings
sprigs of thyme and parsley
bay leaf
salt
freshly milled black pepper
300 ml (½ pint) dry white wine
225 g (8 oz) mushrooms

Put the flour into a bowl and turn the cubes of meat over and over until they are all well coated. Heat a heavy-based frying pan, add the bacon pieces, and fry until they release their fat. Remove to a flameproof casserole set over a low heat. Heat the oil in the frying pan and fry the

meat all over, in two or three batches as necessary, transferring the
pieces to the casserole as you go. Add the onions, garlic, carrots,
thyme, parsley, bay leaf, salt and pepper and mix. Pour in the wine,
bring to the boil, cover and simmer gently for 2–2½ hours. Add the
mushrooms and cook for a further hour until the meat is tender.

Hunter's pheasant
Faisan chasseur

Mushrooms and game birds go together. The hunter returned with
whatever he had shot and an assortment of wild mushrooms found in
the woods. The following recipe can be adapted to suit whatever bird
you fancy. Leave small birds like quail whole, but partridges or
woodcock can be cut in half. In France you could use pigeons which
are specially reared for the table. The wood pigeons sold in Britain
would need to be cooked for considerably longer as they tend to be
very tough and need slow stewing. Failing a game bird, use a guinea
fowl or a free-range or maize-fed chicken. The livers are a delicacy
added right at the end; if none is available you could use chicken livers
instead.

50 g (2 oz) butter
1 tablespoon olive oil
2 pheasants, quartered, plus
   their livers
2 shallots *or* 1 small onion,
   chopped
4 tomatoes, halved

1 tablespoon tomato purée
225 g (8 oz) mushrooms,
   quartered
150 ml (¼ pint) dry white wine
2 sprigs of thyme
salt
freshly milled black pepper

Melt butter with the oil in a heavy-based casserole and brown the
pheasant pieces all over, in two batches if necessary. Remove and keep
warm. Put shallots and tomatoes into the pan with the tomato purée,
cover and let them sweat over a low heat for 5–10 minutes. Add
mushrooms, mix and cover, cook for a further 5–10 minutes. Return
the pheasant pieces to the casserole, add wine, thyme, salt and pepper.
Simmer for 30–40 minutes. Add livers and cook for 5 minutes more.

A black truffle
La truffe

Black diamonds may mean coal to the English, but it was the French
gourmet-philosopher, Brillat-Savarin, who gave the name to the truffle
(*Tuber melanosporum*) which at that time was found in enormous
numbers all round the region of the Massif Central, from Périgord in
the west, eastwards to the Rhône valley and as far north as Burgundy.
Nowadays they are scarce and have been elevated from peasants' food
to a luxury in the caviar class.

From November to March, small groups of truffle sellers gather in
the market. At the sound of a bell they unwrap the rags which hide
their treasures and the bargaining begins. In the winter of 1989 they
were changing hands for £300–£400 a kilo. The season builds to a
peak just before Christmas but it is later, after the New Year frosts,
that they are at their best and cheapest. Though never cheap, so be
wary of a truffle bargain.

Warty, strongly scented and as black as coal – or, as the peasants
say, as the love of a woman, *negro coumo l'âmo d'un domna*, truffles
grow about 30 cm (12 in) below ground around the roots of the holm
oak, the white oak, the leaves of which have a whitish down on the
underside. It is everyone's dream to grow a truffle plantation for their
old age but as the spores lie dormant for up to seven years, and in the
roots of only some trees, it is a risky undertaking. So the truffle hunter
must go into the forest and search them out, walking into the sun so
the light shines on the transparent wings of a swarm of tiny flies who
lay their eggs where the truffles lie. He has his dog, specially trained
since a puppy to recognize that smelling out a truffle will bring a
reward. Once pigs were used, but their interest was for the truffles
themselves, and their efforts to eat them had to be constantly foiled.
The hunters guard their patch jealously and if you come across one in
the woods, he will saunter nonchalantly by, swinging his stick and
pretending he is looking for firewood.

Most truffles go to restaurants and hotels and find their way to the
very rich but you might, just might, have a friend who is or who knows
a truffle hunter, or be given one as a love-token by an admirer who has
heard of their aphrodisiac promise, so it is as well to know what to do
with it. However you acquire it, it is unlikely to be more than the size
of a nugget but do insist it is a fresh one, as when they are canned they
lose their flavour and are still very expensive. If you can't cook it

straight away keep it in the fridge, or in a jar of rice (the Romans kept theirs fresh in sawdust) or wrap it in foil and freeze it, when it will keep for ages. Defrost it rapidly in warm olive oil.

Brush all the dirt from the truffle and simmer it for 10–15 minutes in sweet white wine with a little salt and serve it on a dazzling white napkin; or slice it finely and add it raw to a salad of fresh young spinach and lamb's lettuce, dressed with lemon juice, olive oil, salt and pepper; or casually sprinkle slivers over a dish of plainly boiled potatoes.

Use it to flavour scrambled eggs or an omelette. Put the truffle overnight in a covered container with the eggs still in their shells. Next day, break the eggs, mix in the finely sliced or grated truffle, add salt, pepper and a teaspoon of olive oil and leave for a further hour so that the perfume develops. Cook scrambled eggs or omelette in the usual way.

Juniper and la chasse

Rabbit with juniper

Marinade for wild rabbit

Little pots of pâté

Chicken and pork liver terrine

Quail with juniper

Jugging hare, rabbit or pork

Languedoc piquant sauce

Duck with turnips

Angel's casserole of wild boar

False boar

Boar's head brawn

Roast leg of boar

Boar or pork chops with bitter-sweet sauce

The juniper berries are ready to be picked in the autumn. Their sweet, aromatic perfume is used to flavour many game dishes. In southern France, juniper grows wild on the hillsides and if you are there in the autumn, it is well worth gathering some of the berries to bring home. Pick only the ripe ones, which are a dark blue. Each bush produces fresh berries every year and they take two to three years to mature, so you will find they all have a mixture of unripe green berries as well as ripe ones. Wear gardening gloves to avoid nasty scratches from the needle-sharp thorns.

You can grow juniper berries in Britain though the flavour will never be as intense as those ripened in the heat of the Mediterranean sun, but they will be better than the ones you buy. They only produce berries on the female bush, so you will need two, one of each sex, for cross-pollination. Make sure you plant *Juniperus communis*, because there are many other species whose berries are inedible.

When buying dried juniper berries be wary, because not all the dried berries that are sold have that wonderful pine flavour of the true Mediterranean juniper, so go to a reputable herbalist. Or better still buy them from a market in the south of France.

Crushed juniper berries are used to flavour marinades and wild game as well as pâtés and terrines. Try rubbing a handful into a leg of lamb you are going to roast. Crush them using a pestle and mortar or in a garlic press, or with the base of a bottle.

The game season, *la chasse*, begins in Provence and Languedoc on the second Sunday in September and goes through to March. There are certain rules which must be followed (it is hard to find out quite what they are) but, unlike England, the landowner does not have a right to prohibit the hunters. They can go anywhere, although the vineyards are out of bounds whilst the wine harvest is in progress. The game varies from rabbits and hares, to pheasant, partridge and other game birds. The greatest prize of all is the wild boar, which live in great numbers in the forests and which are hunted by as many as twenty or thirty hunters at a time. If they don't catch anything no one seems to mind – it's really an excuse for the men to have a day out.

Rabbit with juniper
Lapin au genièvre

In a hurry and friends coming to dinner? Make this simple dish of
rabbit marinated overnight in olive oil and juniper then simply baked
the next day with thyme, bacon and tomatoes.

1 rabbit, cut into 8 pieces	2 cloves garlic, chopped
4 tablespoons olive oil	freshly milled black pepper
12 juniper berries, crushed	8 rashers bacon
8 sprigs of thyme	1 can chopped Italian tomatoes

Put rabbit, olive oil and juniper berries into a glass or china dish and
leave overnight. Next day, heat oven to Gas 6/400°F/200°C. On each
piece of rabbit put a sprig of thyme, a sprinkling of garlic and black
pepper, and wrap in bacon. Empty the contents of the can of tomatoes
into a shallow ovenproof dish, pack the rabbit on top in a single layer,
pour over oil and juniper berries from the marinade and roast in the
oven for 45–60 minutes, basting once or twice during this time.

Marinade for wild rabbit

A wild rabbit (lapin de garenne) has much more flavour than tame
rabbit but, like most game, it can be tough and benefits from being
marinated for a day or two. It can then be used in any of the recipes,
the marinade itself can be strained and used as part of the cooking
liquid.

Divide the rabbit into pieces and put them into a glass or china bowl
with sprigs of thyme and parsley, a bay leaf, 8 crushed juniper berries,
a sliced onion, crushed clove of garlic, 1 tablespoon each of wine
vinegar and olive oil, 150 ml (¼ pint) dry white or red wine and
perhaps a tablespoon of brandy.

Little pots of pâté
Petits pots de pâté

There was a time when we ate thrush pâté served in little pots with a lid
like a bird at l'Auberge des Gorges, sitting under a willow on ground
which sloped gently towards the river. As the light faded and the wind
dropped, mayflies and moths began to dance under the hanging lamps

to the song of the crickets, and although we felt guilty we had to agree with Dominique that it tasted very good. Nowadays thrush are protected and the pâté is no longer served; in any case it was very fiddly to make. Quick to prepare is this mixture of pork and chicken livers flavoured with juniper. Make it in individual pots, one for each guest.

225 g (8 oz) pork liver
225 g (8 oz) chicken livers
1 tablespoon brandy
4 tablespoons white wine
4–5 sprigs of thyme *or* 1
  teaspoon dried
bay leaf
pinch each of ground nutmeg,
  cinnamon and ginger

2 whole cloves
freshly milled black pepper
6 juniper berries, crushed
250 g (8 oz) streaky bacon,
  chopped
100 g (4 oz) butter
salt
freshly milled black pepper
garnish of bay leaves or parsley

Put livers, brandy, wine, thyme, bay leaf, nutmeg, cinnamon, ginger, cloves, pepper and juniper berries into a glass or china bowl. Cover and marinate overnight or for at least 6 hours. At the end of this time, fry the bacon gently in the butter until soft. Drain the livers, add them to the pan and let them cook for 5–10 minutes over a low heat without browning, turning them over from time to time. When the meat is cooked through and no longer pink, put the contents of the pan into a processor or blender (or use a mortar and pestle). Mix or pound until you have a smooth paste. Taste and add salt and pepper as necessary. Fill individual pots. Garnish each with a bay leaf or a sprig of parsley. Serve cold with toast. If you want to keep the pâté for a few days, cover each pot with a layer of melted butter and refrigerate.

Chicken and pork liver terrine
Terrine

A *terrine* is a lidded earthenware dish which is used to cook pork pâté and the name is given to the cooked dish itself. This one, flavoured with juniper and brandy, includes chicken livers too. It is a bit messy to make but the result is infinitely better than most bought varieties. It can be made even more interesting by adding 100 g (4 oz) chopped chestnuts to the mixture, or sandwiching some chopped cooked spinach in between layers of the meats.

50 g (2 oz) end crust of French
  bread
150 ml (¼ pint) milk
450 g (1 lb) chicken livers
225 g (8 oz) pork liver
225 g (8 oz) belly of pork
2 eggs, beaten
3 tablespoons brandy
salt
freshly milled black pepper

10 juniper berries, crushed
½ teaspoon each of nutmeg,
  cinnamon and ground ginger
2 whole cloves
1 teaspoon dried thyme
1 tablespoon chopped parsley
1 clove garlic, chopped
225 g (8 oz) streaky bacon
bay leaf

Soak bread in the milk. Mince livers and pork twice, once through a
medium blade and once through a fine (or persuade your butcher to do
this for you). Put into a large bowl and add the beaten eggs. Squeeze
out the bread and add, followed by the brandy. Season generously.
Crush the juniper berries, add to the mixture with the spices, herbs and
chopped garlic. Line a *terrine* with the bacon, draping each piece over
the edge. Pour in the mixture. Top with the bay leaf and fold bacon
over the top. Put into a baking tin half-filled with boiling water, and
put in the oven Gas 3/325°F/160°C to bake for 2–3 hours. It is done
when the sides begin to shrink and the juices are clear. Remove from
the oven, cover with a piece of foil, put a heavy weight on top (use a
can or a flat iron) and leave to cool completely. Keep two days before
eating.

Quail with juniper
Cailles au genièvre

These tiny birds sold oven-ready, often in pairs, are bred specially for
the table. They may look puny but are surprisingly meaty and one is
sufficient for most appetites. Serve them on a long dish surrounded by
watercress.

4 quail
8 rashers streaky bacon
2 tablespoons olive oil
salt
freshly milled black pepper

12 juniper berries
2 cloves garlic, chopped
25 g (1 oz) butter
4 slices French bread about 1 cm
  (½ in) thick

Wrap each bird in 2 rashers of bacon, stretching it slightly to make it
cling snugly. Secure with string or cotton. Heat the olive oil in a heavy-

based pan, add birds and brown them quickly all over. Add a pinch of salt and a generous amount of freshly milled pepper. Cover and cook on a low heat for 15 minutes. Meanwhile crush the juniper berries with the garlic with a pestle and mortar. Add the butter in pieces and gradually mix everything to a paste. Spread this mixture on to the slices of bread. Take the quail out of the pot, add the bread, butter side down, and put a quail on to each piece. Cover and cook for a further few minutes to brown the bread; take care it does not burn.

Jugging hare, rabbit or pork
Civet de lièvre ou de lapin ou de porcelet

A *civet* is a method of stewing a small animal in red wine thickened at the end with the blood, just as in our method of jugging. Nowadays *beurre manié* is often used instead. (This is butter mixed with flour; for recipe see Etceteras.) The animal might be a hare, a rabbit or a young sucking pig, *porcelet* (but you can use stewing pork instead). If using hare insist on a young one that has been hung for at least 3 days; old hare can take hours to become tender. Ask your supplier to joint it for you and to save the liver and the blood.

1 hare or rabbit, jointed into 8 pieces, plus liver and blood *or* 700 g (1½ lb) lean stewing pork, cut in cubes
4 onions, chopped
2 cloves
2 cloves garlic, peeled
1 carrot, sliced
sprigs of parsley, thyme and rosemary

bay leaf
12 juniper berries, crushed
1 bottle red wine
1 tablespoon vinegar
2 tablespoons olive oil
100 g (4 oz) streaky bacon, chopped
3 tablespoons brandy
salt, pepper

Wipe the pieces of meat and put them in a large china or glass bowl. Add 2 of the onions, the cloves, garlic, carrot, parsley, thyme and rosemary, bay leaf and juniper berries, and pour the wine over. Cover and leave to marinate for 48 hours in a cool place. Turn the pieces over twice each day. (During this time keep the liver and blood in a covered bowl with a tablespoon of vinegar which will prevent the blood from coagulating.)

When you are ready to cook, remove the pieces of meat from the marinade and dry them on kitchen paper. Heat the oil in a heavy-based

casserole and soften the bacon and 2 remaining onions until they begin
to brown. Remove with a slotted spoon to a plate and keep warm.
Turn up the heat and brown the pieces of meat all over, two or three at
a time, transferring them to the plate as they are done. Return onion,
bacon and meat to the casserole. Heat the brandy in a metal ladle or
small saucepan, light it and pour it, while still flaming, over the meat.
Shake the pan until all the flames die down. Strain over the liquid from
the marinade, add sprigs of fresh herbs, salt and pepper and bring just
to the boil. Cover the pan and simmer very slowly until the meat is
tender, usually 1½–2 hours (an old hare can take up to 4 hours). Test
with the point of a knife, the meat should feel soft but not be so soft
that it is breaking up. Crush the liver in a mortar, gradually beat in the
blood to make a sort of paste, and off the heat stir into the stew just
before serving. Don't let the sauce boil or it will curdle. Alternatively,
thicken with *beurre manié*.

Languedoc piquant sauce
Saupiquet du Languedoc

After a successful day, the rabbit or hare shot by the hunters would be
put to roast over the fire while the men made the *saupiquet*, a fairly
savage sort of mayonnaise made by pounding the liver with plenty of
garlic and beating in vinegar and olive oil, and finally seasoning with
salt and pepper. For more tender stomachs, the liver might first be
lightly cooked.

Duck with turnips
Canard aux navets

Duck pieces are now quite widely sold in supermarkets and are
delicious cooked in this way with juniper berries and turnips.

2 tablespoons olive oil
4 duck pieces
salt
freshly milled black pepper
6 juniper berries, crushed

4 tablespoons brandy or white
   wine
450 g (1 lb) turnips
handful chopped parsley

Heat oil in a heavy-based casserole, add the pieces of duck and brown
them all over. Season with salt and pepper, add the juniper berries and

the brandy. Cover and leave to cook gently while you peel and quarter the turnips and blanch them for 5 minutes in boiling, salted water. Drain well and add to the duck. Cover and cook for a further 30–35 minutes. The duck is done when the juices run yellow when the bird is pricked with a skewer. Serve the duck surrounded by the turnips and sprinkled with the chopped parsley.

Angel's casserole of wild boar
Daube de sanglier

From late autumn through to the end of the hunting season in March, huge, tusked carcases hang in the butcher's shops. These are the wild boar, the hunters' literal and metaphorical *bête noire*, which live in the forests and leave pronged hoofmarks in the soft earth around the vineyards. Angel Garcia gave us our first taste, arriving with a huge chunk of the dark meat and instructions on how to cook it, brushing aside Emile's and Henri's warnings about swine fever (trichinosis). He assured us it had been stored for over three weeks at −15°C (5°F) which is enough to kill the parasitic worm. Boar is now being reared in Britain and sold in upmarket shops, and has a clean bill of health. It won't have that savage gamey flavour of nuts and berries, oak and mushroom that makes the wild boar so distinctive, but is nevertheless good. A long marinade is the key to successful preparation – leave for at least a week.

900 g (2 lb) boar meat, cut in
  pieces
2 onions, chopped
2 carrots, sliced
2 cloves garlic, chopped
8 peppercorns
2 bay leaves
sprigs of thyme and rosemary
8 juniper berries, crushed
2 tablespoons wine vinegar
300 ml (½ pint) red wine

3–4 tablespoons olive oil
100 g (4 oz) unsmoked streaky
  bacon, chopped
2 tablespoons brandy
sprigs of fresh rosemary, thyme
  and parsley
6 cloves garlic, left whole
salt
freshly milled black pepper
beurre manié (see Index)

Put the meat into a china or glass bowl with the onions, carrots, chopped garlic, peppercorns, bay leaves, thyme and rosemary, juniper berries, vinegar and the wine. Cover and leave in a cool place for at least a week, turning the meat over once or twice each day.

When you are ready to cook, remove meat, onion and carrot from the marinade, strain it and reserve the liquid. Dry the meat with kitchen paper. Heat oil in a heavy-based casserole and brown the meat in several batches, putting it on to a warm plate as it is done. Add the bacon pieces to the pan together with the onion and carrot from the marinade and cook for a few minutes. Return the meat to the pan. Heat the brandy in a metal ladle or small pan, set it alight and pour it while still flaming over the contents of the casserole. Shake the pan well and when the flames die down, pour in the marinade liquid. Bring to the boil, add fresh herbs, whole garlic cloves, salt and pepper. Cover and simmer for 2–3 hours until the meat is tender. Thicken the sauce by stirring in small pieces of the *beurre manié*.

False boar
Faux sanglier

Failing boar, which is expensive, you can use pork for the previous recipe. It won't of course acquire the same flavour but will have all the fragrance of the herbs and spices. Plan it a week ahead, because it is essential that the meat has a long marinade, but the cooking period can be reduced to 1–1½ hours.

Boar's head brawn
Fromage ou hure de sanglier

In Issirac, an isolated village in the hills bordering the rivers Cèze and Ardèche, is a restaurant hidden behind a high stone wall, called Au Vieux Fusil. It is at the heart of wild boar country and on Sundays during the season, the huntsmen search for their quarry in ancient Deux Chevaux. In the restaurant, they make brawn with the head – if you see it on a menu, don't expect cheese. *Fromage* comes from the word *fourme* which means mould, and this is the deep dish in which the brawn is packed. The head is simmered for several hours with calf's feet and vegetables in white wine, flavoured with thyme, bay leaves and cloves and finally packed without the bones into the mould. It is sliced and served cold surrounded by a rich and tasty jelly.

Roast leg of boar
Jambon de sanglier

To roast a leg of boar, marinate it for a week using the same marinade
as the *daube* (page 209) but there must be sufficient wine to cover it
completely. It is best pot-roasted. First brown it all over in olive oil in a
heavy pan in which it sits comfortably. Chop up an onion and carrot
and add to the pan with a little salt and no more than 150 ml (¼ pint) of
liquid from the marinade. Simmer very slowly, covered, for about 3
hours, checking from time to time and adding more liquid as
necessary. Traditionally it is accompanied by a chestnut sauce (see
Index).

Boar or pork chops with bitter-sweet sauce
Côtelettes de marcassin à la sauce aigre-douce

Young boar, up to six months old, is called *marcassin*. The name
appears often on menus, though it may not always be accurate. A boar
has several ages. From six months to a year it is called a *bête rousse*; up
to two years, a *bête de compagnie*; up to three a *ragot* and so on, until
in old age it is a *solitaire* or *hermite*. Old boars are very tough and
gourmets won't look at anything except a *marcassin* or a *bête rousse*.
Chops of young boar are marinated in olive oil with thyme and
rosemary, before being grilled and served with a bitter-sweet sauce.
Use pork if you prefer, or serve the same sauce with other game such as
venison.

4 young boar or pork chops	white wine or water
3 tablespoons olive oil	2 tablespoons caster sugar
sprigs of thyme and rosemary	1 tablespoon white wine vinegar
freshly milled black pepper	salt
2 cloves garlic, chopped	freshly milled black pepper
225 g (8 oz) large prunes	2 tablespoons pine nuts

Marinate the chops for 24 hours in the olive oil, with the thyme,
rosemary, pepper and garlic. Turn them over several times. Soak the
prunes overnight in sufficient white wine or water to cover.

Next day, gently heat the sugar in a small saucepan with the vinegar.
When the sugar has dissolved, raise the heat and cook until it begins to
turn from yellow to brown. Add the prunes and 2 or 3 tablespoons of
the soaking liquid. Season with salt and pepper, cover and simmer

gently for about 30 minutes until the prunes are soft. Check from time to time and if necessary add a little more liquid. Meanwhile heat the grill and when it is very hot, grill the chops, allowing 5–10 minutes on each side – they are done when the juice runs yellow when the meat is pricked with a skewer. Sieve the sauce in a mouli-légumes to remove the stones. Stir in the pine nuts. Pour sauce into a bowl and hand round separately.

Pumpkin to beans

Pumpkin soup

Sweet pumpkin pie

Pumpkin au gratin

Monique's cous-cous

Preserved duck

Using *confit*

Cassoulet

Maize meal

Chick pea soup

Haricot beans with bacon, garlic and parsley

Stuffed cabbage

Lentil salad

Pumpkins (*potirons*) bigger than footballs and the related rugby-shaped *courges*, mean autumn. They have bright orange flesh surrounded by a rough, tough outer skin and are sold whole or sliced by weight. In the markets they sell pumpkin and *courge* bread or brioches which are delicious spread with butter and honey.

In Britain, pumpkins are most plentiful around Hallowe'en and then tend to disappear from the shops but they can be stored for up to three months if suspended in a net. If you search out ethnic shops or markets, you will find them right through the autumn and winter. You won't find *courges* in England, but pumpkin can be used instead in any recipe. They are very hard and usually need to be softened by either boiling or frying before being transformed into the finished dish. If you have more pumpkin than you know what to do with, peel and de-seed it, chop the flesh and cook it in boiling water until just soft (about 10 minutes), then freeze it in batches of about 450 g (1 lb), to be used later in whatever way you fancy. Uncooked pumpkin weighed before skinning and seeding will yield about half its weight in flesh.

The seeds can be washed, dried and toasted in a frying pan with a little oil, when they will swell and crackle. Turn them on to grease-proof paper and sprinkle with salt. Delicious as a snack or appetizer.

Pumpkin soup
Soupe au potiron

This is a warm and satisfying soup for those misty days full of the hint of winter.

450 g (1 lb) pumpkin	pepper
2 tablespoons olive oil	nutmeg
2–3 medium potatoes, sliced	stock or water to cover
2 leeks, sliced	knob of butter
2 sprigs of celery or parsley	2 tablespoons milk or crème
1 teaspoon salt	fraîche

Skin the pumpkin, scoop out the seeds with a spoon and cut the flesh into dice. Heat oil in a large pan and add pumpkin, potatoes, leeks and celery or parsley. Cover and let the vegetables sweat over a medium heat for 10 minutes. Add salt, pepper and nutmeg. Pour in the stock or water, bring to the boil and simmer, covered, for 20 minutes. Liquidize or put through a mouli-légumes. Return to the heat, add butter and stir in the milk or crème fraîche. Taste and if necessary add more seasoning. Bring just to the boil and serve.

Sweet pumpkin pie
Tarte de potiron

Pumpkins came to France from the New World and perhaps this sweet pumpkin pie did too. It is light and creamy with a rich, spicy flavour.

900 g (2 lb) pumpkin	4 tablespoons crème fraîche
225 g (8 oz) puff pastry	½ teaspoon cinnamon
2 eggs, beaten	½ teaspoon grated nutmeg
75 g (3 oz) caster sugar	juice of ½ lemon

Peel the pumpkin, de-seed and chop the flesh. Cook it for 10–15 minutes in boiling, salted water. Drain well in a colander. Heat oven to Gas 7/425°F/220°C. Roll out the pastry and line a round tart tin or dish about 20 cm (8 in) in diameter. Mash the pumpkin flesh and mix it with the eggs, sugar, crème fraîche, cinnamon, nutmeg and lemon juice. Spoon the mixture into the pastry shell, spreading it evenly. Bake for 25–30 minutes until the pastry is cooked and the top is golden.

Pumpkin au gratin
Potiron au gratin

This gratin, so familiar in the south of France, is sufficiently unusual to astonish English friends. I might top it with a hard mature cheese like Cantal or Cheddar but I like it best with goat's cheese.

900 g (2 lb) pumpkin	pepper
2 tablespoons oil	pinch of nutmeg
2 onions, chopped	50–75 g (2–3 oz) cheese
1 clove garlic, chopped	2 eggs, beaten
4 tablespoons cooked rice	4 tablespoons crème fraîche
(optional)	4 tablespoons milk
salt	breadcrumbs

Peel and de-seed the pumpkin and cut into small pieces. Heat oil in a frying pan and add the pumpkin pieces, cook very gently on a low heat for about 30 minutes, turning them over from time to time. Add the onions and garlic and continue cooking until pumpkin and onions are soft. Drain well through a colander, pressing a plate or saucer on top to extract as much moisture as possible. Heat oven to Gas 5/375°F/ 190°C. Put the mixture into a gratin dish, add rice (if using), salt, pepper, nutmeg, cheese (either grated or cut in thin slices), eggs, crème fraîche and milk. Mix well. Sprinkle over the breadcrumbs and a little oil. Bake for 25–30 minutes until the top is golden.

Monique's cous-cous

Cous-cous came to the Midi via North Africa. It is a complete meal in a pot, quick and easy to prepare. *Merguez* are spicy sausages which you might find in some delicatessens, otherwise use the spiciest you can find. *Harissa* is sold in Indian or ethnic shops; failing this buy a good chilli sauce. Cous-cous grain is to be found in health shops and large supermarkets. Ideally, use a special *couscousier* which has its own steamer sitting on top through which the grain absorbs the flavours; a saucepan with a colander is a suitable substitute.

700 g (1½ lb) boned lamb neck fillets	1½ litres (2½ pints) water salt
2 courgettes, sliced	freshly milled black pepper
1 can chopped Italian tomatoes	450 g (1 lb) cous-cous
2 onions, chopped	450 g (1 lb) can chick peas
1 green pepper, chopped	100 g (4 oz) raisins
3 cloves garlic, crushed	50 g (2 oz) butter, cut in small
2 carrots, sliced	pieces
2 leeks, sliced	350 g (12 oz) *merguez* or spicy
1 aubergine, chopped	sausages
3 medium potatoes, quartered	2–3 tablespoons *harissa* or hot
2 dried red chillies	chilli sauce

Put meat, courgettes, tomatoes, onions, pepper, garlic, carrots, leeks, aubergine, potatoes and chillies into the saucepan with 1 litre (1¾ pints) water; add salt and pepper. Bring to the boil, cover and simmer. Soak cous-cous in a bowl with remaining water for 15 minutes. Empty

it into the steamer or colander, season with salt and set it over the pan
of meat and vegetables. Cover, and cook for 45 minutes. Soak raisins
in a little boiling water. Then add the chick peas to the stew and, at the
same time, add butter and drained raisins to the grain, stirring gently
with a fork. Continue to cook for a further 15 minutes, add sausages to
the stew and cook for another 15 minutes. Put the *harissa* into a bowl
and stir in some of the liquid from the pan. Serve stew and cous-cous in
separate dishes. Everyone helps themselves to the chilli sauce, stirring
in as much or as little as they like.

Preserved duck
Confit de canard

South-western France on the other side of the Massif Central is the
true home of *confit*. There geese and ducks are raised and fattened for
their livers which are made into *pâté de foie gras*. The birds themselves
are preserved in their own fat to feed the family during the winter. But
duck *confit* appears on menus in the Cévennes, Ardèche and Auvergne,
either on its own or as part of the famous *cassoulet*. If you've never
eaten *confit* or *cassoulet* you may wonder what all the fuss is about,
but once tried, chances are you will want to know how to reproduce
them. I give the recipe for duck, which is readily available and not too
expensive. If you are rich, you can substitute a goose which has so
much fat you won't need any extra lard. Pork, chicken and rabbit can
all be preserved in the same way. Use two 1 litre (1¾ pint) glass or
stoneware preserving jars – earthenware is not suitable because it is
porous. *Confit* will keep for six months to a year in a cool place. If you
buy the duck from a poulterer rather than a supermarket, ask to have it
divided for you. Otherwise use a sharp knife and kitchen shears. Cut
the bird right down the breast bone, open it out and cut along the
spine. Cut each half into four.

2–2½ kg (4½–5½ lb) duck,   1 teaspoon dried thyme
  divided into 8   bay leaf
25 g (1 oz) coarse salt for each   225 g (8 oz) lard for each 450 g
  450 g (1 lb) duck   (1 lb) duck

Dry duck pieces with kitchen paper, cut away all excess fat and save.
Put the duck pieces in a china or glass dish and rub each well with the
salt. Add thyme and bay leaf, cover and put in the fridge for 36 hours.

Meanwhile, cut the fat into small pieces, put into a saucepan with 150 ml (¼ pint) water and heat very gently until it just reaches boiling point. Simmer for 30 minutes or so to melt the fat. Pour through a sieve into a bowl, allow to cool and put in the fridge. The fat will rise to the surface and solidify.

After 36 hours take out the duck pieces, shake them well and wipe off excess salt. Remove bowl of fat from fridge and lift off the layer of fat which will have formed on top of the water. Put the fat into a heavy-based saucepan with all the lard and heat until it melts. Add the duck pieces and simmer them, covered, on top of the stove for 1¼ hours. Test by piercing with a skewer, the juice should run yellow. If not, cook for a further 10 or 15 minutes but don't overcook. Strain a ladleful of fat from the pan into each jar. Pack in pieces of the duck to about 5 cm (2 in) below the top, fill completely with more strained fat. As the fat cools it will shrink, so if necessary add a little more. Cover with a ring of greaseproof paper and seal. Store in a cool place, the fridge if you like, and leave at least three or four weeks before using.

Using *confit*

Pieces of the duck are removed from the fat as and when needed. To do this, put the pot on a warm stove so that the fat begins to melt, it is then easy to lift out as much as you want. Make sure the remaining pieces are well covered in their protective layer of fat, reseal and return to a cool place. Pieces are fried until golden on both sides, drained on kitchen paper or greaseproof, and served either dusted with parsley accompanied by a potato *galette* or allowed to cool and served with a green salad. Pieces of *confit* are often added to soups, vegetables and stews to give extra flavour and richness. One of these is the famous *cassoulet*.

Cassoulet

There is as much mystique surrounding the *cassoulet* as there is around the *bouillabaisse*. Both are homely dishes with as many variations as there are cooks. Three towns, Carcassonne, Castelnaudary and Toulouse, all lay special claim to this dish, cooked in a large, wide-mouthed, earthenware pot called a *cassou*, and each version is

different. Basically it is haricot beans stewed with different meats and
sausages, usually but not always flavoured with goose or duck *confit*.
Some versions include tomatoes and this is the one that appeals most
to the people who live closer to Provence. In some versions, the pot
must be stirred up to seven times during the cooking so that the
breadcrumbs on top form a thick golden crust. Or you can remove the
lid half an hour before the end of the cooking time, sprinkle the crumbs
with a little oil and leave them to brown. The following is my version.
Before you begin make sure you have a deep, wide-mouthed earthenware casserole with a lid. *Cassoulet* is very filling and only needs to be
served with a green vegetable, nothing starchy like rice or potatoes.
Any left over can be re-heated the next day; give it a good 2 hours at
Gas 3/325°F/160°C.

450 g (1 lb) haricot beans	450 g (1 lb) lamb neck fillets
olive oil	225 g (8 oz) Toulouse or herb
2 onions, chopped	sausages
parsley, thyme and bay leaf	1 can chopped Italian tomatoes
2 cloves garlic, chopped	150 ml (¼ pint) red wine
1½ litres (2½ pints) water	(optional)
225 g (8 oz) ring smoked pork	freshly milled black pepper
boiling sausage	generous handful of
2–3 pieces duck *confit* (optional)	breadcrumbs
450 g (1 lb) pork spare ribs	salt

Soak the haricot beans overnight in cold water or put them in a
saucepan, cover with water, bring to the boil, simmer for 5 minutes
and set aside for an hour. Heat 1 tablespoon olive oil in a large
saucepan, add the chopped onions and fry over a medium heat until
golden. Add soaked and drained beans, a sprig of parsley, 1 teaspoon
dried thyme, a bay leaf, the garlic and water, bring to the boil. Cover
and simmer for 1 hour. Add the boiling sausage, chopped into several
large pieces, and continue to simmer.

Heat oven to Gas 3/325°F/160°C. Heat the pieces of duck *confit* in a
heavy-based pan. As soon as the fat surrounding them has melted,
remove duck to a large, warm bowl. Brown the pieces of pork in the fat
(or if omitting duck, brown the pork in 2 tablespoons olive oil), then
lay them at the base of the casserole in which you plan to cook the
cassoulet. Brown the pieces of lamb, put them in the bowl with the

duck and brown the Toulouse or herb sausages all over. Pour off
excess fat and return duck and lamb to the pan with the sausages.
Empty in the canned tomatoes and wine (if using), bring to the boil,
season with pepper, thyme, parsley and bay leaf. Drain the beans but
keep the liquid. Put half the beans in the casserole, add the contents of
the pan, top with the rest of the beans and add sufficient bean liquid
just to cover. Taste and if necessary add a little salt. Cover with the
breadcrumbs and sprinkle with olive oil. Put on the lid and put in the
oven for 2½ hours. Check once or twice and if necessary top up with a
little more liquid. Remove lid, sprinkle top with olive oil and cook for
a further 30 minutes to allow breadcrumbs to brown.

Maize meal
Milhas

With the pumpkin from the New World came maize, or dent corn. In
southern France, millet, le mil, was the daily cereal (bread made from
wheat was only for high days and holidays) and the newcomer became
known as le gros mil and eventually milhas or millas. It is simply boiled
and either eaten as it is or formed into a ball, left to get cold, then sliced
and fried in hot oil until golden on both sides. Either way, it can be
eaten salted or sugared. Coarse cornmeal is fine for the first method,
but if it is to be fried, use fine meal. As the maize absorbs the water it
must be constantly stirred; in the old days a special three-pronged fork
called a toudeillo was used but a wire whisk will do.

1 litre (1¾ pints) water   2 tablespoons olive oil
salt   225 g (8 oz) cornmeal

Put the water, salt and oil into a saucepan and bring to the boil. Add
the cornmeal in a gentle stream, stirring all the time. Bring to the boil,
stirring constantly until the meal absorbs all the water and begins to
come clean from the side of the pan. Remove from the heat. Either eat
at once or form mixture into a cylindrical shape, wrap it in foil, leave
to cool and put in the fridge. Next day slice and fry pieces until golden
in hot olive oil. Eat sprinkled with salt to accompany soup or a stew, or
with sugar as a pudding or teatime treat.

Chick pea soup
Soupe aux pois chiches

Chick peas marry with tomatoes to make this warming winter soup. If you baulk at the time taken to soak and cook chick peas, use canned.

225 g (8 oz) chick peas *or* 450 g (1 lb) can chick peas
3 tablespoons olive oil
1 onion, chopped
2 leeks, sliced
salt

freshly milled black pepper
1 tablespoon tomato purée
1 can chopped Italian tomatoes
4 slices French bread sprinkled with olive oil

If using dried chick peas soak them by putting them into a bowl of cold water and leaving overnight. Or put them in a pan of cold water, bring them to the boil, boil for 5 minutes and set aside off the heat for 1 hour. Drain them, put them into a pan with fresh water (don't add salt, which will prevent them from softening), bring to the boil and simmer, covered, for 1 hour. Drain but save the cooking liquid. Wipe out the pan and heat the oil. Add onion and leeks, cover and let them soften for about 10 minutes over a medium heat. Add the chick peas and 1½ litres (2½ pints) of the cooking liquid, topped up if necessary with water. Simmer for about 30 minutes until the vegetables are soft. Season with salt and pepper. Add tomato purée and tomatoes, and cook for a further 10–15 minutes. Liquidize or put through a mouli-légumes. Grill the bread sprinkled with oil until golden. Put a slice in each bowl and pour over the soup.

Haricot beans with bacon, garlic and parsley
Haricots secs au hachis

Beans cooked like this go well with a stew of beef, or roast lamb or pork. The beans need to be soaked overnight or brought to the boil in a pan of water and then left to steep for an hour before cooking. Salt inhibits dried beans from softening, so add it only at the end. You can of course use a can of haricot beans instead.

225 g (8 oz) dried haricot beans, soaked
1 onion
2 cloves garlic, chopped
1–2 tablespoons parsley, chopped

50 g (2 oz) streaky bacon, chopped
salt
freshly milled black pepper

Drain the soaked beans, put them in a saucepan with the whole onion, cover with water, bring to the boil and cook for 1 hour. Add the garlic, parsley and bacon and cook for a further hour. The beans should be soft but not mushy. If using canned beans, drain them, cover them with water, bring to the boil and add garlic, parsley and bacon, and simmer for 15–30 minutes. Add salt and pepper to taste before bringing to the table.

Stuffed cabbage
Sou-fassum or poule verte

When it is cold and damp and winter is at its worst, this hearty and economical dish makes a warm and satisfying meal. In shape and size it resembles a green chicken, hence its second name. The whole cabbage is stuffed and held together in a net or string bag – you could use one of those mesh bags in which citrus fruit is often sold, or tie it in a square of muslin. It is prepared the day before and left overnight to absorb the flavours. It is the man of the house who traditionally serves the *sou-fassum* – no one wants to be referred to as the one who doesn't cut the *farce (ce n'est pas lui qui coupe le farce)*, which labels him as the one who doesn't wear the trousers. This recipe can be made using chestnut purée instead of meat.

1 savoy cabbage	½ teaspoon nutmeg
3 tablespoons olive or peanut oil	½ teaspoon cinnamon
2 onions, chopped	4 cloves
100 g (4 oz) streaky bacon, chopped	salt
	freshly milled black pepper
225 g (8 oz) minced pork or beef, or a mixture of the two	2 eggs, beaten
	1 tablespoon brandy
handful breadcrumbs	1 carrot, chopped
2 cloves garlic, crushed	1 medium can chopped Italian
sprigs of parsley and thyme	tomatoes

Wash the cabbage under running cold water, keeping it intact. Boil some water in a big saucepan, add salt and blanch the cabbage for 10 minutes. Drain well. Heat 2 tablespoons of the oil in a frying pan and add 1 onion and half the bacon. Fry them for several minutes over a medium heat. Add the meat and let it brown, turning it over and over with a spatula. Remove from the heat and stir in breadcrumbs, garlic, herbs and spices. (Break off the heads of the cloves and crush them in your fingers, discarding the stalks.) Season generously with salt and pepper. Mix well and add the beaten eggs. Cut two pieces of string long enough to tie round the cabbage and lay them crosswise in a colander, their ends hanging over the side. Put the string bag or muslin on top, opening it wide. Carefully put in the cabbage and gradually unfurl the leaves, one by one, draping their edges over the side of the colander. Cut out the heart, chop and add to the stuffing mixture. Stuff the cavity with half this mixture and then reform the cabbage, putting a little stuffing between the leaves. Sprinkle with brandy. Close over the outside leaves and the top of the string bag or muslin. Tie the string to secure the parcel. Put the stuffed cabbage into a glass or china bowl and leave in a cool place, covered, until the next day.

Choose a heavy-based casserole, heat the remaining oil, add the second onion and the carrot and let them sweat for a few minutes. Add half the tomatoes, carefully put in the cabbage and pour over the remaining tomatoes. Bring to the boil. Season well with salt and pepper. Cover with a piece of greaseproof paper and the lid of the pot. Simmer very slowly for 3–4 hours. Remove the string and bag in the kitchen and bring to the table on a dish surrounded by rice.

Lentil salad
Salade aux lentilles

Lentil salad is often offered as an accompaniment to *crudités*. This recipe uses small brown lentils, not the red split lentils used in English cooking – you will find them in ethnic or health shops. Wash 225 g (8 oz) lentils and put them in a pan with 1 litre (1¾ pints) water, 1 onion and 2 carrots, both finely chopped, and 3 whole, peeled cloves of garlic. Bring to the boil and simmer for 25–30 minutes until lentils and vegetables are soft. Drain well. Add 1 tablespoon of vinegar, 4 tablespoons olive oil, and salt and pepper. Allow to cool.

Cheese

Grilled goat's cheese

Goat's or curd cheese with herbs

Fried goat's cheese

Goat cheese omelette

Fried potato cake

Drunkard's soup

Goat's cheese in oil

Preserved goat's cheeses

Blue cheese with vinaigrette

Baked potato cakes with cheese

Roquefort turnovers

Braised chicory with Roquefort

Cheese tart with prunes

Strong cheese

This region has a host of small, dusky, farm-produced goat's cheeses, *tomme de chèvre*, each weighing around 100 g (4 oz) and known collectively as *picodon* in the Rhône, *pélardon* or *rogeret* in the Cévennes, and elsewhere as *cabécou*, the Occitan word for little goat. Each variety has its individual flavour, some pungent, others delicately flavoured with *herbes des prés*, wild herbs. Some people find their flavour overwhelming but once the taste is acquired their pungency spells part of their charm.

From Arles and the Camargue come cheeses made from ewe's milk flavoured with thyme and bay leaves. These are soft, mild and creamy, and sold by a small local dairy, Lou Gardian, as Tomme de Camargue or Arlésienne.

Provence produces Banon, a mild and nutty ewe's milk cheese flavoured with *marc* and wrapped in chestnut leaves, and goat's cheeses called *poivre-d'âne*, or *pèbre d'ai*, after the savory (donkey's pepper) which lines the baskets in which these mild aromatic cheeses are displayed. From the slopes of Mont Ventoux come the *cachat*, a fresh, salted, farm-made cheese which is sweet and creamy, and the unsalted *caillé* or *brousse* (Provençal for vigorous stirring). This is a curd cheese, or fromage frais, once simply a farm cheese but now produced commercially, which is made by heating goat or sheep milk until it forms soft curds.

From further afield come the cheeses produced in the mountainous regions of the Massif Central, such as the garlic-flavoured Gaperon and the pungent Bleu d'Auvergne and the gentler Bleu des Causses. Both these cheeses are dried in humid cellars like their more famous cousin, Roquefort, but are made using cow's rather than sheep's milk. Roquefort itself is the sole product of a tiny village, Roquefort-sur-Soulzon, perched against a cliff face high in the Cévennes, where the cheese ferments in the constant temperature of natural caves. Then there is Cantal or Fourme de Cantal, not unlike Cheddar, which is matured for 3–6 months and is marvellous in cooking and has a mild and nutty flavour. Don't confuse this with Tomme de Cantal or Tomme d'Aligot, a soft unfermented cheese which is used in an Auvergne potato dish called *aligot* and is basically mashed potato

flavoured with garlic, salt and pepper and beaten with lashings of
butter and an equal amount of cheese until the cheese begins to form
threads. It takes a strong arm and usually the man of the house is given
the job.

Grilled goat's cheese
Fromage chaud

They serve grilled goat's cheese as a first course at L'Escarbille in St
Martin d'Ardèche where, if it is spring, you will hear what sounds like
a flock of ducks gone mad, but is in fact the mating chorus of frogs in
the river. The cheese they use is St Marcellin, creamy and rich, but any
pungent goat's cheese will do.

1 clove garlic
4 slices French bread 2 cm (1 in)
   thick
olive oil

225 g (8 oz) goat's cheese,
   thickly sliced
freshly milled black pepper

Heat the grill for 5 minutes. Cut the garlic in half and rub the cut sides
all over the slices of bread. Lay them in the grill pan, sprinkle each with
olive oil. Put under the grill just until they begin to turn golden. Cover
the bread with slices of goat's cheese, put back under the grill until the
cheese has melted, is bubbling and beginning to change colour. Season
generously with black pepper.

Goat's or curd cheese with herbs
Fromage de chèvre aux herbes

Cylindrical soft goat's cheeses are delicious sliced and dipped in olive
oil and herbs. A bland curd cheese can be given a lift with the same
ingredients, only in this case mash everything together and put the
curd cheese in a small jar or pot and leave until the next day to absorb
the flavours.

1 clove garlic, chopped
2 spring onions *or* 1 shallot,
   chopped
2–3 tablespoons chopped mixed
   herbs, such as chives, basil
   and thyme

2–3 tablespoons olive oil
paprika
salt
freshly milled black pepper
225 g (8 oz) cylindrical soft
   goat's cheese

Mix chopped garlic, onions and herbs on a plate and, on another, the olive oil seasoned with paprika, salt and pepper. Cut the goat's cheese into 3 or 4 slices and dip each one first in the oil then into the herb mixture, coating both sides. Serve as a starter on lettuce leaves, surrounded by olives and gherkins.

Fried goat's cheese
Chèvre frite

Goat's cheese can also be fried. Cut cylindrical cheese in half to form two rounds. Heat 2 or 3 tablespoons olive oil in a frying pan and when it is hot, add the cheese rings, pressing them with a spatula to flatten them slightly. When they are golden on one side, turn them over and cook until that side too is golden. Serve them, very hot, on a bed of lettuce, and let everyone add their own freshly milled black pepper.

Goat cheese omelette
Omelette au chèvre

Try this simple omelette made for us by Dominique Feijoo and his poet wife, Rosaline Roche, in their house in Malateverne high above the gorge of the Ardèche. Beat 2 eggs lightly, add a few drops of water, salt, pepper and some thyme. Heat olive oil with a little butter in a frying pan and when it sizzles pour in the egg mixture. Stir it around and, as soon as it begins to set, add a few slices of soft goat's cheese. As the cheese melts, flip the omelette in half and slide on to a warm plate.

Fried potato cake
Criquette

There are many versions of potato cake with names like *truffado*, or the evocative *criquette* or *cantermerlou*, so called because the sizzling pan sounds like chirping crickets or blackbirds singing. Below is a simple version, but you can ring the changes by adding pieces of fried bacon, chopped onion and garlic.

Most recipes suggest grating the potatoes but I find they turn grey and watery, so I cut them into very thin strips. Don't soak them but cook right away, because the starch is needed to make the cake hold together. Add salt right at the end – added too soon it makes the cake stick to the pan. Use a small, heavy-based frying pan and allow sufficient time to cook the cake over a slow heat. High heat will burn the base and leave the potatoes raw. In this recipe the cake is sprinkled at the last minute with a *persillade*.

olive or groundnut oil	salt
1 large onion, chopped	freshly milled black pepper
450 g (1 lb) potatoes	1 tablespoon parsley, chopped
1 goat's cheese, sliced	1 clove garlic, chopped

Heat sufficient oil to cover the base of the frying pan, add the chopped onion and fry over a medium heat while you peel and cut the potatoes into very thin strips. Stir the potatoes into the onion as you go. Finally press them down with a spatula, lower the heat and cover, either with a lid or foil weighted down with a plate. Cook for 15–20 minutes, then turn the cake over. If you are clever you can do this using an upturned plate held over the pan – a quick flip and the cake rests on the plate to be slid back into the pan – but it's a tricky operation. It doesn't really matter if the cake breaks up at this stage, simply press it back into the pan. Add cheese slices, raise the heat slightly and cook for a further 10 minutes or so until the underside is crisp and golden and the cheese has melted. Season with salt and pepper, sprinkle over the parsley and garlic and bring to the table in the pan.

Drunkard's soup
Soupe à l'ivrogne

This is a splendid soup lavishly flavoured with white wine. If it seems too extravagant use dry cider instead or, if you are broke, skip the wine, substitute stock or water and you will have a perfectly acceptable *soupe au fromage*, cheese soup.

2 tablespoons olive oil	300 ml (½ pint) stock *or* 1 can
450 g (1 lb) onions, chopped	of consommé
8 slices French bread	300 ml (½ pint) dry white wine
225 g (8 oz) cheese such as	salt
Cantal or Cheddar	freshly milled black pepper

Heat oven to Gas 7/425°F/220°C. Heat the oil in a frying pan, add the onions and brown over a medium heat. Put layers of bread and cheese into a deep, preferably earthenware, casserole, finishing with a cheese layer. Put onions on top, pour over the stock or consommé and the wine. Season with salt and pepper. Put into the oven for 20 minutes until everything is heated through and the cheese has melted.

Goat's cheese in oil
Chèvre à l'huile

Goat's cheese softened in olive oil, flavoured with spices, herbs and garlic is delicious with hunks of French bread and a tomato salad for a midday snack or a first course for a summer dinner party. The oil can later be used to give a wonderful flavour to salads. I have suggested using *marc* as this fiery spirit is what is usually used locally, but any cheap brandy will do perfectly well.

225 g (8 oz) goat's cheese
sprigs of fresh thyme and
   rosemary
bay leaf
1 whole red chilli

1 clove garlic, chopped
8 whole black peppercorns
olive oil
brandy or *marc* (optional)

Cut cheese into slices about 1 cm ($\frac{1}{2}$ in) thick and put them in a small, deepish bowl or jar. Add herbs, chilli, garlic and peppercorns. Pour over sufficient oil to immerse the cheese. Cover and leave – not in the fridge – for 24 hours. Serve sprinkled with a little brandy or *marc* if you like. Vary the flavour by adding whole coriander seeds or juniper berries instead of the chilli.

Preserved goat's cheeses
Foudjou and *Sarrassou*

Goat's cheeses are at their best and most plentiful between May and November. Preserving them is so easy that anyone on holiday might consider bringing some home as a souvenir of summer. Basically the cheeses are preserved with flavourings in alcohol or vinegar and will keep several months.

Foudjou

1 soft and 1 hard goat's cheese	1 tablespoon brandy, vodka or
2 cloves garlic, crushed	eau-de-vie
1 tablespoon chopped fresh	pinch of salt
thyme	freshly milled black pepper
1 tablespoon olive oil	

Put the soft cheese into a bowl and mash it well. Grate the hard cheese and add with the crushed garlic and the thyme. Mix well and gradually stir in olive oil and spirit. Season with salt and a generous amount of pepper. Put into a glass or stoneware preserving jar, seal and leave in a cool place for at least a month.

Sarrassou

2 fresh goat's cheeses	salt
1 teaspoon mustard	freshly milled black pepper
½ teaspoon vinegar	

Put the cheese into a bowl, crush it with a fork and add mustard, vinegar, salt and pepper. Mix well and put into a glass or stoneware preserving jar. Seal and leave in a cool place for at least a month.

Blue cheese with vinaigrette
Fourme en vinaigrette

The word *fourme* in Occitan means mould and is used as a prefix for many of the semi-hard cheeses, cylindrical in shape, which are moulded and left to mature for several months. Many of these are blue-veined and this recipe may be made with Roquefort, Bleu d'Auvergne or an English cheese such as Stilton or blue-veined Cheshire. It makes a robust filling for jacket potatoes.

100 g (4 oz) blue-veined cheese	freshly milled black pepper
4 tablespoons olive oil	pinch of cayenne pepper
1 teaspoon white wine vinegar	salt
2 cloves garlic, chopped	

Remove any rind from the cheese. Mash it with a fork and gradually add all the other ingredients one at a time, except the salt. Taste first and only add salt if necessary. Put cheese into a small pot, cover and keep in a cool place.

Baked potato cakes with cheese
Galettes de fourme

These potato cakes can be made with any blue-veined cheese or, if you prefer something milder, use a plain English cheese such as Cheddar.

450 g (1 lb) potatoes	2 tablespoons crème fraîche
100 g (4 oz) grated cheese	salt, pepper
25 g (1 oz) butter	

Boil the potatoes in their skins in salted water until they are soft. Drain them. Heat oven to Gas 4/350°F/180°C. Peel the potatoes when they are cool enough to handle and mash with a fork, adding the cheese and butter and enough crème fraîche to form a thick paste. Season with pepper and taste before adding any salt. Put heaped tablespoons of the mixture on to a buttered baking sheet. Bake for 30 minutes until golden.

Roquefort turnovers
Chaussons au roquefort

They offer these blue cheese turnovers as a first course at La Beaugravière outside the village of Mondragon in the Drôme. They melt in the mouth and if you use bought puff pastry, they take only a few minutes to prepare. If the pastry is frozen, let it thaw at room temperature before using.

225 g (8 oz) puff pastry	1 tablespoon crème fraîche
50 g (2 oz) Roquefort or other	1 egg yolk, beaten
blue cheese	

Roll puff pastry very thinly and cut out 4 strips measuring approximately 20×10 cm (8×4 in) (or use two sheets ready rolled and cut each in half). Mash the cheese and mix it with the crème fraîche. Put a spoonful on one half of each strip. Dampen the edges of the strips with water, fold in half over the cheese mixture and press the two layers of pastry together, making sure they are completely sealed. Mark the edges with the prongs of a fork, cut a small slit on top of each and brush all over with egg yolk. Heat oven to Gas 7/425°F/220°C. Put turnovers on to a baking sheet and bake in the oven for 15 minutes until they are piping hot and golden.

Braised chicory with Roquefort
Endives braisées au roquefort

For reasons a trifle obscure, what the British call chicory is known as
endive in France and the name *chicorée* is given to the salad leaves that
we know as endive. Whatever the name, it is the furled, white heads,
tinged with gold that are called for in this recipe. The blue cheese
added at the last moment becomes a melting and tasty sauce.

4 heads chicory	freshly milled black pepper
salt	50 g (2 oz) Roquefort or other
2 tablespoons olive oil	soft blue cheese

Wipe the chicory with kitchen paper, remove woody base. Blanch for
10 minutes in boiling, salted water. Drain well. Heat the oil in a
saucepan and add the chicory. Cook over a high flame, turning the
heads over and over until they just begin to brown. Lower the heat,
add pepper (no salt because the cheese is salty), cover and cook gently
for 15 minutes. At this point, add the cheese in small pieces and cook
for a further 5–10 minutes.

Cheese tart with prunes
Tarte au fromage frais aux pruneaux

We are prejudiced about prunes, those dried and wrinkled plums. It
seems as if we all associate them with some nasty childhood memory.
But this dessert tart with its light creamy filling contrasting dramati-
cally with the blackness of the fruit is guaranteed to convert all but the
most reactionary diehards. (If you have to cater for one of these make
it with dried apricots instead.) Use a 20 cm (8 in) flan tin with a
removable base.

12 large prunes	2 eggs
225 g (8 oz) puff pastry	3 tablespoons caster sugar
225 g (8 oz) fromage frais or	few drops vanilla essence
soft curd cheese	

Two hours ahead of time, put the prunes in a bowl, pour over boiling
water and leave them to swell. Roll the pastry into a circle, line the flan
tin, prick the base all over with a fork and put it covered into the fridge
until you are ready to use it. Heat the oven to Gas 6/400°F/200°C. Put
the fromage frais into a bowl, beat in the eggs one at a time, stir in the

sugar and vanilla essence. Strain the prunes and stone them, using a knife to slit them open. Pour the cheese mixture into the tin lined with pastry, scatter the prunes on top and bake for 30–35 minutes. Serve hot or warm.

Strong cheese
Fromage fort or *le cachat*

Ends of cheeses are given a boost by beating in herbs, seasonings, *marc* or brandy (or failing the last, a little vinegar). Grate three or four different sorts of cheeses into a bowl and, using a fork, mix in 2–3 tablespoons of crème fraîche and plenty of freshly milled black pepper. Add a tablespoon of brandy and put into a small jar.

Etceteras

from breadcrumbs to a chocolate mousse . . . by way of a hedgehog.

Dried breadcrumbs

Dried orange peel

Thickened butter

Crème fraîche

Shortcrust pastry

Omelette

Béchamel sauce with olive oil

Pancakes

Scrambled eggs

Fritters

Hedgehog in clay

Little pigs' ears

Elixir of long life

Chocolate mousse

Dried breadcrumbs
Chapelure

Put slices of breadcrust in a low oven, Gas 3/325°F/160°C for 30 minutes. Crush with a rolling pin and either sieve or put through a food processor. Keep in an airtight jar.

Dried orange peel

Dried orange peel is used in some of the recipes for wines, as well as to flavour fish and meat stews. It can be dried in a warm oven but this method tends to evaporate the essential oils. It is better to remove the peel in one piece in a coil from the stem to the base of the orange and hang it from a hook in a warm part of the kitchen. Leave for several days to curl and harden and become brittle enough to break off small pieces. Use the peel from sweet or Seville oranges; the latter will add a sharper flavour. Store in an airtight jar.

Thickened butter
Beurre manié

It is a well-known trick of French cooking to thicken sauces by stirring in small pieces of a paste made by mixing equal amounts of butter with flour. This is done right at the end of the cooking time and is often used to thicken slow-cooked stews which might burn if they were thickened too soon. It doesn't take long to mash a tablespoon or so of butter with one of flour but it is useful to have a supply on hand to be used as and when necessary. Mash together 100 g (4 oz) softened butter with 100 g (4 oz) flour, form into a roll, wrap in greaseproof paper and store in the fridge. Slice off what you need.

Crème fraîche

I recommend crème fraîche throughout the book because, apart from its pleasant nutty flavour, it does not curdle even when it is boiled. This gives it an advantage over other forms of cream. It is produced in much the same way as soured cream, has the same fat content as double cream and is as firm and thick as clotted cream. It will keep for up to 10 days in a fridge and apart from its uses in cooking it is delicious with all sorts of desserts and fruit. It is now quite widely available but if you cannot buy it, you can approximate your own. It is rather simpler to make than home-made yoghurt. Some recipes specify heating the cream to blood temperature but I find this process unnecessary.

300 ml (½ pint) double cream   150 ml (¼ pint) soured cream

Mix the two creams together in a bowl. Cover and leave in a warm place overnight or for 8–12 hours. Stir well and transfer to the fridge.

Subsequent batches can be made by stirring 2–3 tablespoons of this mixture into double cream before following the same process.

Shortcrust pastry
Pâte brisée

Most people have their own basic pastry recipe and method, so this is just a reminder. If you want a sweetened version, simply add 1–2 tablespoons sugar and an egg and sufficient water just to bind.

250 g (8 oz) flour   pinch salt
125 g (4 oz) softened butter   2–3 tablespoons cold water

Put the flour into a wide bowl, add the butter cut in pieces and rub with your fingers until the mixture looks like breadcrumbs. Add salt. Make a well in the centre and add 2 tablespoons of water. Mix to a dough using a knife, adding more water as needed. Flour your hands and the table, knead dough into a ball and put in a plastic bag in the fridge to rest for an hour or two. (If you omit this last procedure, the pastry will shrink when it is cooked.)

Omelette

This is a basic plain omelette. All sorts of flavours can be added (see Index). It is cooked in olive oil and not the butter of classic French cooking. Allow 2 eggs per person, beat them lightly and add a few drops of milk or water, season with salt and pepper. Heat 1–2 tablespoons of oil in a small frying pan and when it is very hot, pour in the egg mixture. Stir it quickly round and around, then let it set, lifting the sides to let the uncooked mixture run under. When the centre is cooked but still wet and glistening, fold the omelette in half and slide on to a warm plate.

Béchamel sauce with olive oil
Sauce béchamel à l'huile

A basic white sauce is usually made with butter, flour and milk. It is just as good with olive oil. You can make it in the conventional way by heating oil, stirring in flour, cooking for a couple of minutes before stirring in the milk and cooking until thick – or you can use the quicker method below. This will give a reasonably thick, pouring sauce; if you want a thicker sauce, add a little more oil and flour. If you want a cheese sauce, simply add a pinch of nutmeg and stir in 50–100 g (2–4 oz) grated cheese off the heat.

300 ml (½ pint) milk   salt
2 tablespoons olive oil   pepper
2 tablespoons flour

Put milk, oil and flour into a small saucepan and beat over a medium heat using a wire whisk. As the sauce begins to thicken, lower the heat, bring to the boil and continue to beat for 2 minutes. Season to taste with salt and pepper.

Pancakes
Crêpes

Candlemas, 2nd February, is pancake day in France. The batter may be made with plain flour, buckwheat (*farine de sarrasin*) flour or a mixture, two to one, of chestnut and plain flour. The method is the same.

225 g (8 oz) flour   1 tablespoon olive oil
pinch of salt   450 ml (¾ pint) milk
4 eggs

Put flour and salt into a bowl, make a well in the centre and break in the eggs, mix with a wooden spoon. Add the oil and gradually beat in the milk. Leave for a hour for the batter to rest. Use a small, heavy frying pan, heat it and grease the base with a little butter. Pour in just enough batter to cover the base and tip the pan from side to side. Turn the pancake over as soon as it is cooked on the underside and cook for 30 seconds more. Slide on to a plate, interleaving the pancakes as you go with greaseproof or kitchen paper.

Scrambled eggs

Unlike omelettes, scrambled eggs are cooked slowly. Allow 2 eggs per person, beat them with a few drops of milk and season with salt and pepper. Heat 25 g (1 oz) butter in a small heavy-based pan and when it is hot pour in the eggs and cook over a low heat, stirring constantly with a wooden spoon, until they thicken and form soft curds. Remove from heat and stir in a very little butter or crème fraîche.

Fritters
Beignets

Fritters are made at the slightest excuse. Anything goes. Sliced aubergines, courgettes, onions or green tomatoes; asparagus tips or tiny, violet artichokes; wild mushrooms, apples and figs, not to mention *animelles* (testicles) – those of the bull are known as *criadillas*. Flowers of the acacia or locust tree are also frittered, and you might see courgette flowers for sale on market stalls, although you are unlikely to find them in Britain unless you grow your own. Choose a fine, dry day and make the batter before you pick the flowers as they quickly wilt. Remove the stems and calyx before cooking. Even pieces of stale bread are made into a kind of fritter, *pain perdu*, after first being soaked in milk flavoured with rum or brandy. Use your own favourite fritter batter or try the one below.

100 g (4 oz) flour
salt
freshly milled black pepper
1 tablespoon oil
2 eggs

150 ml (¼ pint) milk or tepid
     water, or a mixture of milk
     and water
oil for deep frying

Put the flour in a bowl, make a well in the centre and add salt, pepper and the tablespoon of oil. Separate the eggs, add the yolks to the well and keep the whites in a separate bowl. Mix ingredients into the flour and gradually beat in the liquid. Set aside to rest for an hour. Beat the egg whites until stiff and fold into the batter. Heat oil in a deep pan, or in a wok. Dip whatever you are using for the fritters into the batter and plunge, a few at a time, into the hot oil. As soon as they are puffed and golden, take them out, drain them on greaseproof or kitchen paper. Sprinkle savoury fritters with salt and eat with a squeeze of lemon or a home-made tomato sauce; sweet ones are sprinkled with sugar and lemon juice.

To finish, some odds and ends that wouldn't be left out but couldn't find a place in any of the chapters.

Hedgehog in clay
Hérisson à la terre

I have always wondered just how the gypsies went about cooking their hedgehogs and when I came across a recipe for baking partridge and other small game in clay in André Bonnaure's *La cuisine en Langue-doc*, I thought I might have found the answer. You take a large lump of clay and sprinkle it with a little eau-de-vie. Knead it well and wrap it, gingerly, around the hedgehog. The coating must be about 1–2 cm (½–1 in) thick. Make a hole in the ground 30–40 cm (12–16 in) deep. Line it with flat stones and make a wood fire which must burn briskly for half an hour. Push the hedgehog into the hot ash and keep the fire at a cracking pace for a further half an hour. Break away the hard shell of baked clay which will come away with the sharp spines. Please don't write and protest . . . I don't intend to try it.

Little pigs' ears
Oreillettes

Not pigs' ears at all, of course, although shaped like them. These are a cross between a fritter and a biscuit, a treat for high days and holidays which children especially love. If you prefer you can make the dough in a food processor. These amounts make about 30.

100 g (4 oz) plain flour	1 teaspoon orange flower water
50 g (2 oz) caster sugar	groundnut oil for frying
1 tablespoon melted butter	icing sugar
1 egg, beaten	

Sieve the flour into a bowl, stir in the sugar. Make a well in the centre and pour in the butter, beaten egg and orange flower water. Mix to a firm, pliant dough, adding a very little water if necessary. Flour your hands and the work surface and knead the dough into a ball. Put it into a plastic bag and leave for an hour in the fridge to firm up. Roll the chilled dough into a rectangle on a floured board – it should be quite thin, not more than 3 mm (⅛ in) thick. Using a pastry or pasta cutter, or a knife, cut out oblongs about 4 cm (1½ in) wide and 8 cm (3 in) long. Divide these diagonally into triangles. Heat the oil in a deep fryer or wok and fry the *oreillettes* three or four at a time. As they puff and rise, turn them over, leave for a moment or two more then remove with a slotted spoon and drain them on a plate lined with greaseproof or kitchen paper. Put 2–3 tablespoons of icing sugar into a bag and add a handful of the *oreillettes* at a time. Shake well to coat all over. Store in an airtight jar or tin.

Elixir of long life
Elixir de longue-vie

This ancient recipe is attributed to a Genoese doctor who lived in Marseille and died at the age of 104 in a riding accident. It is recommended as a cure for stomach and toothache, gout, plague, cholera, smallpox, heartburn, fever, as an emetic and for the aged who are advised to take a spoonful once a week to keep them bright and cheerful. It is difficult to work out exact quantities but the gist of it is that you must mix 1 litre of eau-de-vie at 90° and 1 litre of white wine, add bitter aloes, zedoary, agaric votane, gentian, saffron, rhubarb, quinine, senna, veronica root and extract of juniper, leave to infuse for a fortnight, then strain and bottle. Leave to age.

Chocolate mousse
Mousse au chocolat

France would not be France without a chocolate mousse to end it all. Not a particularly southern French recipe but it is there on all the menus and is a family favourite. It is so easy, it seems every French child, boy or girl, is taught how to make it. You can make it more luxurious by stirring in a tablespoon of brandy, rum or cointreau or simply the juice of an orange.

225 g (8 oz) bitter chocolate   4 eggs
25 g (1 oz) butter, cut in pieces

Break the chocolate into a bowl and put it into a warm oven to melt (or
in a microwave for a minute or two). Separate the eggs. When the
chocolate has melted beat in the pieces of butter, followed by the egg
yolks. Whip the whites until stiff and fold gently into the chocolate
mixture. Ladle into small cocotte pots or deep glasses. Put in the fridge
for a couple of hours to set.

Bibliography

Alibert, Louis, *Dictionnaire Occitan–Français*, Institut d'Etudes Occitanes, 1966

Andreis, Florence de, *La cuisine provençale d'aujourd'hui*, Rivages, 1980

Bailley, Jean-Claude and Naddeo, Jean-Paul, *Manuel pratique de cuisine provençale*, Pierre Belfond, 1980

Besson, Joséphine, *La Mère Besson: 'Ma cuisine provençale'*, Albin Michel, 1977

Binding, G. J., *FRHS About Garlic*, Thorsons, 1977

Binns, Richard, *French Leave 3*, Chiltern House, 1983

Blaumac, Yvonne de, *Cuisine d'Ardèche*, Simone Sudre, 1984

Bonnaure, André, *La cuisine en Languedoc*, Collot, 1971

Brillat-Savarin, Jean-Anthelme, trans. Anne Drayton, *The Philosopher in the Kitchen*, Penguin, 1970

Brown, Michael and Sybil, *Food and Wine of France*, Exeter Books, 1983

Castignac, Huguette, *La cuisine occitane*, Solar, 1973

Chanot-Bullier, C., *Vieilles recettes de cuisine provençale*, Tacussel, 1983

Child, Julia, *From Julia Child's Kitchen*, Penguin, 1981

Christian, Glynn, *Edible France*, Ebury Press, 1986

Clayton, Gerald, *Looking and Cooking in Provence*, Gerald Clayton, 1974

Clifton, Claire, *Edible Flowers*, Bodley Head, 1983

David, Elizabeth, *French Provincial Cooking*, Penguin, 1977

Davidson, Alan and Jane, *Dumas on Food*, Oxford University Press, 1987

Fisher, M. F. K., *The Art of Eating*, Faber and Faber, 1963

Fisher, M. F. K., *Two Towns in Provence*, The Hogarth Press, 1985

Flower, Barbara and Rosenbaum, Elisabeth, *The Roman Cookery Book*, Harrap, 1958 (a critical translation of *The Art of Cooking* by Apicius)

Fuller, John G., *The Day of St Anthony's Fire*, Hutchinson, 1969

Githens, John, *Encyclopedia of Cheeses*, Omnibus Press, 1976

Gray, Patience, *Honey from a Weed*, Papermac, 1987

Green Guide: Provence, Michelin
Green Guide: Vallée du Rhône, Michelin
Grigson, Jane, *Charcuterie and French Pork Cookery*, Penguin, 1970
Grigson, Jane, *Fruit Book*, Penguin, 1985
Grigson, Jane, *The Mushroom Feast*, Penguin, 1981
Grigson, Jane, *Vegetable Book*, Penguin, 1980
Headlam, Cecil, *Provence and Languedoc*, Methuen & Co. Ltd, 1912
Hemphill, Rosemary, *Herbs for all Seasons*, Penguin, 1975
Holland, Philip, *Living in France Today*, Robert Hale, 1985
Holt, Geraldine, *French Country Kitchen*, Penguin, 1987
Hume, Rosemary and Downes, Muriel, *The Cordon Bleu Book of Jams, Preserves and Pickles*, Pan Books, 1976
Johnson, Hugh, *Pocket Wine Book*, Mitchell Beazley, 1977
Lheureux, Simone, *La cuisine du soleil entre Provence et Languedoc*, Lacour, 1986
Luard, Elisabeth, *European Peasant Cookery*, Bantam Press, 1986
Lyon, Ninette, *Le Tour de France gourmand des spécialités régionales*, Marabout, 1985
Mathiot, Ginette, *La cuisine pour tous*, Albin Michel, 1955
Mayle, Peter, *A Year in Provence*, Hamish Hamilton, 1989
Mazille, La, *La bonne cuisine du Périgord*, Flammarion, 1929
Médicin, Jacques, *Cuisine niçoise*, translated and edited by Peter Graham, Penguin, 1983
Min. of Ag. and Fish, *Edible and Poisonous Fungi*, Bulletin No. 23, HMSO, 1940
Mistral, Frédéric, *Mireille* (Bilingual edition), Garnier-Flammarion, 1978
Montagné, Prosper, *Larousse gastronomique* (English translation), Paul Hamlyn, 1961
Olney, Richard, *Simple French Food*, Penguin, 1983
Parker, Audrey, *A Country Recipe Notebook*, Faber and Faber, 1979
Philippon, Henri, *Cuisine de Provence*, Albin Michel, 1966
Philips, Roger, *The Photographic Guide to Identify Common and Important Mushrooms*, Elm Tree Books, 1986
Polunin, Oleg and Huxley, Anthony, *Flowers of the Mediterranean*, The Hogarth Press, 1987
Pomiane de, Edouard, *Cooking with Pomiane*, Faber and Faber, 1976
Reboul, J. B., *La cuisinière provençale*, Tacussel, 1895
Richardson, Capt. Leslie, *Things Seen in Provence*, Seeley, Service & Co. Ltd, 1928

Roden, Claudia, *Mediterranean Cookery*, BBC Books, 1987
Sharman, Fay, *The Taste of France*, Macmillan, 1984
Stobart, Tom, *The Cook's Encyclopaedia*, Papermac, 1982
Stobart, Tom, *Herbs, Spices and Flavourings*, Penguin, 1977
Stodola, Jiří and Volák, Jan, *The Illustrated Book of Herbs*, Octopus
   Books, 1985
Tannahill, Reay, *Food in History*, Penguin, 1988
Vassas, Janine, *La cuisine occitane d'aujourd'hui*, Rivages, 1983
Wathelet, Jean-Marc, *Dictons des bêtes, des plantes et des saisons*,
   Belin, 1985

Index

All the entries and page numbers in bold type are for the main ingredients and recipes. Other entries, such as ideas for dishes, names of people, places etc. are in lighter type.

acacia flower, fritters, 242
aïado, 20
aigo bouido, 10, 43
Aiguèze, 30
ail, aulx, 13, *and see garlic*
aillade languedocienne, 15
aïoli, 10, 20
garni, 21
with monkfish stew, 21
salt cod with, 21
Albi, 159
aligot, 227
almond spread with mint and anchovies, 53
alouettes sans têtes, 181
amanita
caesara, fulva, muscaria, vaginata, 189
amanite des césars, 189
amuse-gueule, 177
anchoïade, 68
anchois frais, 75
anchovy(ies), 65
almond spread with mint, 53
in beef stew, with capers and gherkins, 73
beetroot with, 65
butter, 65
cabbage with, 65
cardoons with, 69
courgettes with, 69
Easter salad, 65
en escabèche, 75
on French bread, 66
with egg, 66
fresh, 75
gratin of with artichoke hearts, 70
guinea fowl with, 74
mushrooms with, 193
pastry, 70
rabbit in a piquant sauce, 72
rice salad, 66
stuffed
eggs, 67
vegetables, 71
salad
ideas, 65
dressings, 65, 68
sauce, hot with celery, 68
sweet peppers with, 72
Swiss chard stalks with, 106
Angel's casserole of wild boar, 209
anise, 47
Nectar of the Gods, 50
animelles, 242

Aphrodite, 128
apple(s)
black sausage with, 126
fritters, 242
in pork pie with chestnuts, 162
roast pork and celeriac with, 126
apple mint, 47
and honey sauce with melon, 53
tea, 47
apricot(s)
bread, 123
dried, in cheese tart, 234
liqueur, 149
Arabia, 95
arachide, 174
Ardèche, 3, 5, 30, 33, 42, 108, 163, 210, 218, 229
chestnut soup, 161
Arles, 227
Arlésienne, 227
artichauts en barigoule, 30
artichokes
ways of eating, 30
artichoke hearts, gratin with anchovies, 70
fritters, 242
with mushrooms and peas, 195
with thyme, 30
asparagus
ways of eating, 112
with lemon sauce, 112
soup with spinach or sorrel, 113
tip, fritters, 242
asperges à la sauce au citron, 112
assiette languedocienne, 134
Auberge des Gorges, 204
aubergine(s), 95
preliminary preparation, 95
barbecued, 96
caviar, 96
fried, 96
fritters, 242
gratin
with béchamel and cheese, 95
with tomatoes and courgettes, 99
grilled, 96
with onions and tomatoes, 98
the Pope's, 97
with pork and rosemary, 40
ratatouille
Avignon's with tomato, 100
the gypsies', 98
stuffed, 71
Auvergne, 159, 218, 227

Avignon('s), 18, 97, 100
    aubergine and tomato *ratatouille*, 100
    casserole of lamb, 18

bacon
    and croûtons in mixed green salad, 112
    with haricot beans and garlic, 222
    mushrooms with, 190
baguette de tambour, 188
baked
    figs with cream, 135
    or fried tomatoes, 85
    garlic mushrooms, 192
    potato(es)
        cakes with cheese, 233
        with garlic, 17
ball-trap, 169
Banon, 58, 227
Barbary duck, 182
barbecued aubergines, 96
barbe de chèvre, 189
barigoule, 31, 188
Barronnies, Les, 173
basil, 57
    chicken with, 61
    courgette salad with, 57
    lamb chops with, 61
    preserved, 57
    salade niçoise, 60
    sauce (*pistou*), 58
        soup with, 59
    tomato salad with, 58
    with warm potato salad, 60
    wine, pick-you-up, 62
baudroie, 21
beans, *see* separate headings
Beaugravière, La, 233
Beaumes-de-Venise, 143, 173
bécasses de mer à la marseillaise, 91
béchamel sauce with olive oil, 241
beef
    daube, 18
    stewed
        with capers, gherkins and anchovies, 73
        with fennel, 52
        with mushrooms, 196
beetroot with anchovies, 65
beignets, 242
berlingueto, la, 67
bête
    de compagnie, 211; *noire*, 209; *rousse*, 211
bette, 103
Betty's mushrooms with artichokes and peas, 195
beurre
    d'ail, 16
    d'anchois, 65
    manié, 239
bigarreau, 121
bitter-sweet
    cherries, 122

sauce with prunes, 211
Blache, la, 117
black
    diamonds, 198
    olives, *see* olives
    sausage with apples, 126
    a truffle, 198
blackberry liqueur, 149
bléa, blète, blette, 103
Bleu
    d'Auvergne, 227, 232
    des Causses, 227
blue cheese, *see* cheese
boar, *see* wild boar
bohémienne, 98
boiled chestnuts, 160
bolet, 188
boletus family, 188
bombine, 33
Bonnard, André, 243
boops, en escabèche, 75
boudin noir aux pommes, 126
boui-abaisso, 10
bouillabaisse, 21, 24, 35, 51, 105, 219
    d'épinards ou de blettes, 105
bouquet garni, 29, 52
bourride, 21
braised chicory with roquefort, 234
brawn, boar's head, 210
bread
    anchovies on French, 66
        with egg, 66
    apricot, 123
    crumbs, dried, 239
    garlic, 14
Brillat-Savarin, 198
broad bean(s), 107
    raw with gros sel or butter, 107
    salad, 111
    with savory, 35
    with sorrel, 107
broth, spinach or Swiss chard with eggs, 105
broufado, la, 10, 73
brousse, 227
broutard, 34
brugnons, 124
bûche de Noël, 154, 164
buckwheat flour, 241
Burgundy, 198
butter
    anchovy, 65
    garlic, 16
    golden of Provence, 20
    thickened, 239

cabbage
    with anchovies, 65
    stuffed, 223
        with chestnuts, 159
cabécou, 227
cabri, 34
cachat, le, 227, 235

Caesar's mushroom, 187, 189
caillé(s), 227, and see quail
  à la cévenole, 42
  au genièvre, 206
  aux olives vertes, 182
  aux raisins, 153
caillettes, 109
calmars ou seiches aux olives noires, 180
Camargue, 5, 9, 24, 52, 66, 227
camomile tea, 41
canard, and see duck
  aux figues, 134
  aux navets, 208
  aux olives, 182
  confit de, 218
Candlemas, 241
Cantal, 216, 227
cantermerlou, 229
cantharellus cibarius, 188
capers, 176
  in beef stew, with anchovies and
    gherkins, 73
  guinea fowl with, 74
Carcassone, 219
cardes, 103, and see Swiss chard
  à l'anchoïade, 106
cardons de Noël, 69
cardoons with anchovies, 69
carottes au miel, 136
Carpentras, 117
carrot(s)
  glazed with honey, 136
  and honey jam, 136
  little pots with mushroom sauce, 194
Carsan, 169
carthagène, 145
casserole
  of lamb from Avignon, 18
  of wild boar, 209
Cassis, 144
cassis, 147
cassou, 219
cassoulet, 218
Castelnaudary, 219
Cathars, 159
catigot d'anguilles, 24
catalan, 188
caul, 109
cauliflower, rosy, 89
caviar
  d'aubergines, 96
  provençal, 176
céleri à l'anchoïade, 68
celeriac, roast pork and apples, with, 126
celery with hot anchovy sauce, 68
cèpe, 188
cerises, and see cherries
  à l'aigre-douce, 122
  au sirop, 121
Cévennes, 5, 127, 159, 163, 188, 218, 227
Cèze, 163, 210
champignon(s), and see mushrooms
  aux anchois, 193

aux artichauts et aux petits pois, 195
  à la bague, 188
  à la crème, 191
  farcis aux foies de volaille, 192
  au gratin, 192
  au lard, 190
  noir, 190
  de pin, 188
  sautés à la poêle, 191
chanterelle, 187, 188
chapelure, 239
chasse, la, 203
châtaignes, 165, and see chestnuts
  à la cévenole, 160
  sous la cendre, 160
Châteauneuf-du-Pape, 144
chatons, 96
chaussons au roquefort, 233
Cheddar, 23, 58, 85, 95, 216, 233
cheese, 227
  blue
    in baked potato cakes, 233
    chicory braised with Roquefort, 234
    Roquefort turnovers, 233
    with vinaigrette, 232
  curd with herbs, 228
  in fried potato cake, 229
  goat's
    fried, 229
    grilled, 228
    with herbs, 228
    in oil, 231
    omelette, 229
    preserved, 231
  in sauce, 241
  in soup, drunkard's, 230
  strong, 235
  tart with prunes, 234
cherry(ies), 121
  bitter-sweet, 122
  custard cream, 121
  liqueur, 149
  in sugar syrup, 121
Cheshire cheese, 232
chestnut(s), 159
  boiled, 160
  Christmas log, 164
  flour, 241
  marrons glacés in pancakes, 165
  peeling, 160
  in pork pie with apples, 162
  roast, 160
  sauce, 163
  soup
    Ardèche, 161
    and onion, 161
  Volcano, 163
chestnut mushroom, 187
chèvre, and see cheese, goat's
  frite, 229
  à l'huile, 231
chevreau rôti, 34
chevrette, 188, 189

chevreuil, *see* venison
chichoumeille, 98
chick pea soup, 222
chicken
    with basil, 61
    with forty cloves of garlic, 19
    garlic croûton with, 14–15
    with mushrooms, 197
    roasted with olives, 174
    spring
        with grapes, 152
        grilled with rosemary, 41
    stuffed
        with mushrooms, 196
        with olives, 179
        with thyme and garlic, 30
chicken liver(s)
    mousse with fresh tomato sauce, 90
    mushrooms stuffed with, 192
    and pork terrine, 205
    salad with thyme and garlic, 33
chicorée, 234
chicory braised with Roquefort, 234
chocolate mousse, 244
choufleur d'églantine, 89
Christmas, 69, 103, 108, 124, 145, 154,
        159, 164, 169, 198
    log, 164
civet de lièvre ou de lapin ou de porcelet,
        207
clafoutis, 121
Clive, Lord, 48
cod, salt with aïoli, 21
cold meat with figs, 134
communard, 147
Condrieu, 144
confit
    de canard, 218
    using, 219
confiture
    de figues, 135
    de vieux garçon, 124
Cornas, 144
corne d'abondance, 190
Côte Rôtie, 144
Coteaux
    d'Aix-en-Provence, Baux-de-Provence,
        du Languedoc, du Tricastin, 143
côtelettes
    d'agneau au basilic, 61
    de marcassin à la sauce aigre-douce, 211
Côtes
    du Rhône, du Rhône Villages, du
        Ventoux, 143
côtes de poirée, 103
coucoumelle, 189
coulemelles, 188
coulis de tomates, 89
courges, 215
courgette(s)
    à l'anchoïade, 69
    with anchovy, 69
    aubergine and tomato gratin, 99

au basilic en salade, 57
flower fritters, 242
fritters, 242
    with rosemary, 40
    salad with basil, 57
    stuffed, 71
    and tomatoes with fennel, 50
cous-cous, Monique's, 217
couscousier, 217
cousina, 161
Cox's orange pippins, 126
crab apple, or quince, jelly, 128
craterellus cornucopioides, 190
cream
    with baked figs, 135
    cherry custard, 121
    golden of Languedoc, 20
    Homer's, 137
    mushrooms with, 191
crème fraîche, 239
crème
    d'or, 20
    d'Homère, 137
crèpes, 241
    à la cévenole, 165
crépine, 109
crête de coq, 188
criadillas, 242
criquette, 10, 229
croustade
    aux figues et au miel, 136
    aux poires, 139
croûtons
    à l'ail (with garlic), 14
    ways with, 15
    with mixed green salad and bacon, 112
Crozes-Hermitage, 144
crudités, 16, 224
cuisine en Languedoc, La, 243
Cumberland sausages, 177
curd cheese, *see* cheese, 228
custard cream, cherry, 121
cuttlefish
    with black olives, 180
    to clean, 91, 180
    with *rouille*, 24
    salad with fennel, 49

daube
    avignonnaise, 18
    de sanglier, 209
déboiradour, 160
Dentelles, 144
digestif, 35, 39
Dijon, 147
Dominique's lamb on the fire, 19
dried
    breadcrumbs, 239
    figs with thyme, 136
    grapes, 154
    mushrooms, 187, 190
    orange peel, 239

Drôme, 233
drunkard's soup, 230
drying
    figs and other fruit, 133
    fennel, 47, garlic, 13, thyme and savory,
        29, sage, 39
duck
    with figs, 134
    with grapes, 144
    preserved, 218
    roast (Barbary) with olives, 182
    with turnips, 208

Easter salad, 65
Edam, 58, 95
egg(s) and see omelette and scrambled egg
    and anchovies on French bread, 66
    fried with tomatoes, 83
    hair of the dog, 151
    with spinach or Swiss chard broth, 105
    stuffed, 67
eel stew, 24
eiderdown soup, 86
Elisabeth of Poland, 39
elixir de longue-vie, 244
elixir of long life, 244
endive(s), 234
    braisées au roquefort, 234
en escabèche, 75
ensalado de favo, 111
épaule de chevreuil aux olives vertes, 178
Escarbille, 90, 228
escargots à la suçarelle, 87
estouffade de bœuf aux champignons, 196

Fabre
    Charles, 59, 68; Jean-Pierre, 4, 181;
        Monique, 4, 23, 217
fagòt, 109
faggots, Languedoc, 109
fairy ring mushroom, 187, 189, 190
faisan chasseur, 197
false boar, 210
farigoule, 29
farigouleto, la, 35
farine de sarrisin, 241
Faugères, 143
faux sanglier, 210
Feijoo
    Dominique, 4, 19, 205, 229; Roseline, 4,
        229
fennel, 47
    beef stewed with, 52
    courgettes and tomatoes with, 50
    cuttlefish (or squid) salad with, 49
    fish stew with, 51
    mackerel with, 49
    seed tea, 41
fennel, Florentine, 47
fête de Sent Pourqui, 126
fèves, and see broad beans
    fraîches à la sarriette, 35
    à l'oseille, 107

field mushroom, 189
fig(s), 133
    baked with cream, 135
    cold meat with, 134
    dried with thyme, 136
    drying, 133
    duck with, 134
    fritters, 242
    and honey pie, 136
    jam, 135
    liqueur, 149
figues
    à la crème fraîche, 135
    sèches au thym, 136
filets de poivron aux anchois, 72
fish, and see separate headings
    stew with fennel, 51
flan, 40, 97, 137
    aubergine, 97
    aux cerises, 121
    de courgettes au romarin, 40
    aux raisins, 154
    grape, 154
fly agaric toadstool, 189
foudjou, 232
fougasse aux anchois, 70
fourme, 210, 232
    de Cantal, 227
    en vinaigrette, 232
fraises au vin, 122
François I, 128
fresh
    anchovies, 75
    tomato sauce, 89
fried
    aubergines, 96
    eggs with tomatoes, 83
    goat's cheese, 229
    potato cake, 229
    mushrooms, 191
    (or baked) tomatoes, 85
fritters, 242
frogs' legs, 90
fromage, and see cheese
    chaud, 228
    de chèvre aux herbes, 228
    fort, 235
    ou hure de sanglier, 210
Frontignan, 144
fruit, and see separate headings
    drying, 133
    liqueurs, 148
    old has been's dessert, 124
    rosy fruit salad, 125
    tart, 128
fruits à l'eau-de-vie, 148

galettes de fourme, 233
gallinace, 188
Gaperon, 227
Garcia, Angel, 209
Gard, 30
Gardian, Lou, 227

Gardiane, la, 52
gardians, 52
garlic, 13
  aïoli, 20
    monkfish stew with, 21
    salt cod with, 21
  bread, 14
  croûtons, with, 14
  toasts, 15
  butter, 16
  chicken
    with forty cloves of, 19
    with thyme and, 33
  eel stew, 24
  golden cream of Languedoc, 20
  haricot beans, bacon and parsley with,
    222
  lamb
    casserole, 18
    on the fire, 19
    roast with garlic sauce, 20
  mushrooms baked with, 192
  omelette, 16
  potatoes baked with, 17
  rouille, 22
    fish soup with, 23
    squid with, 24
  sausages with, 17
  soup, 15, 43
Garn, le, 42
garrigue, 9, 10
gâteau aux foies de volaille au coulis de
    tomates, 90
gelée de coing ou de pomme sauvage, 128
gherkins, in beef stew with capers and
    anchovies, 73
Gigondas, 144
girolle, 188
glass snails, 87, 88
goat cheese, *see* cheese
golden
  cream of Languedoc, 20
  butter of Provence, 20
graillons, 70
grape(s)
  dried, 154
  flan, 154
  jam, 153
  liqueur, 149
  quail with, 153
  spring chicken with, 152
  oil, 174
gratin
  of artichoke hearts with anchovies, 70
  aubergine, tomato and courgette, 99
  languedocien, 99
  aux pommes de terre au thym (potato
    with thyme), 32
  pumpkin, 216
  of Swiss chard or spinach, 103
gratons, gratterons, 70
green
  -capped russule, 187, 190

olives, *see* olives
  tomato, fritters, 242
  walnuts, *see* walnuts
greengage tart, 128
grenouilles à la provençale, 90
grilled
  aubergines, 96
  goat's cheese, 228
grisette, 189
groseilles au miel, 138
groundnut oil, 174
growing basil, 57; juniper, 203; rosemary,
    38; thyme and savory, 29;
    tomatoes, 83
Gruyère, 58, 85
guinea fowl
  with anchovies and capers, 74
  with mushrooms, 197
  stuffed
    with mushrooms, 196
    with olives, 179
gypsies' *ratatouille,* 98

hair of the dog, 151
hare, jugging, 207
haricot beans with bacon, garlic and
    parsley, 222
haricots secs au hachis, 222
harissa, 217
hedgehog in clay, 243
herb(s) *and see separate headings*
  with goat or curd cheese, 228
  teas, 41
herbes des prés, 227
hérisson à la terre, 243
Hermitage, 144
hermite, 211
Hippocras, 138
Hippocrates, 138
Homer's cream, 137
honey, 133
  and apple mint with melon, 53
  and carrot jam, 136
  carrots glazed with, 136
  and fig pie, 136
  with figs (dried) and thyme, 136
  Hippocras, 138
  Homer's Cream, 137
  pear pie, 139
  redcurrants with, 138
hop shoot salad, 111
horn of plenty, 190
hunter's pheasant, 197
hure de sanglier, 210
hydnum repandum, 189

iced tomato soup, 86
India, 57
Issirac, 163, 210

jam
  fig, 135
  grape, 153

honey and carrot, 136
jambon de sanglier, 211
jelly, quince or crab apple, 128
jaunet, 189
jaunette, 188
Jésus, 134
jugging hare, rabbit or pork, 207
juniper berries, 203
  in chicken and pork liver terrine, 205
  with duck and turnips, 208
  with false boar, 210
  with jugged hare, rabbit or pork, 207
  in little pots of pâté, 204
  in marinade for wild rabbit, 204
  with quail, 206
  with rabbit, 204
  with wild boar
    in Angel's casserole, 209
    with roast leg of, 211
juniperus communis, 203

kid, roast, 34
King of Hungary, 39
kir, 147
Kir, Abbé, 147
kitchen utensils, 6

Lacour, Emile and Henri, 4, 30, 80, 88,
    181, 209
lactaire
  délicieux, 31, 187, 188
  sanguin, 189
lactarius deliciosus, 188
lamb
  casserole, from Avignon, 18
  chops
    with basil, 61
    and thyme, 33
  roast
    Dominique's lamb on the fire, 19
    with garlic sauce, 20
    with olives, 174
langue de chat, 189
Languedoc, 4, 9, 10, 17, 20, 22, 33, 34, 83,
    95, 99, 103, 133, 138, 143, 153,
    154, 159, 173, 189, 203
  faggots, 109
  piquant sauce, 208
lapin, and see rabbit
  au genièvre, 204
  de garenne, 204
  aux olives, 181
  au pèbre d'ai, 36
  en saupiquet, 72
larks without heads, 181
lavender
  tea, 41
  wine, 148
leek
  and mushroom tart, 193
  and potato soup with thyme, 31
légumes farcis, 71
lemon sauce with asparagus, 112

lentil salad, 224
lepiota procera, 188
life-saving soup with sage, 43
lime flower tea, 41
liqueur(s)
  de fenêtre, 149
  fruit, 148
  hair of the dog, 151
  midsummer green walnut, 150
  d'œufs, 151
  de la Saint-Jean, 150
  thyme (and other herbs), 35
  in the window, 149
Lirac, 143
little
  carrot pots with mushroom sauce, 194
  pig's ears, 243
  pots of pâté, 204
liver, chicken,
  in little pots of pâté, with pork liver, 204
  mushrooms stuffed with, 192
  mousse with fresh tomato sauce, 90
  salad with thyme, 30
  and pork liver terrine, 205
loaf, spinach or Swiss chard, 104
locust flower, fritters, 242
log, Christmas, 164
Lord Clive's original mincemeat pies, 48
lotte, 21
Louis XIV, 39
Lucques, la, 173
lycoperdon, 190

mackerel with fennel, 49
macquereaux au fenouil, 49
Madam Boeuf's
  larks without heads, 181
  thyme liqueur, 35
Madam Lacour's rabbit with olives, 181
Maillane, 181
maize meal, 221
Mallard duck, 134
marasmius oreades, 189
marc, 143, 227, 231, 235
marcassin, 211
marinade for wild rabbit, 204
marinated black olives, 175
Marmande, 83
marrons, 165, *and see chestnuts*
  glacés, in pancakes, 165
marseillais, 188
Marseille, 21, 244
Mas, le, 169
Massif Central, 159, 198, 218, 227
meat, *and see separate headings*
  cold with figs, 134
melon with apple mint and honey sauce,
  53
melon à l'aigre-douce, 53
merguez, 217
merinjana, 95
mesclun, lou, au lard et aux croûtons, 112

Midi, 10, 20, 21, 217
midsummer green walnut liqueur, 150
milhas, 196, 221
mincemeat pies, 48
mint, 47
    spread with almond and anchovies, 53
    tea, 41
Mistral, Frédéric, 9, 181
mistral, 10, 169
mixed green salad with bacon and
        croûtons, 112
Mondragon, 233
Monique's
    cous-cous, 217
    fish soup, 23
monkfish stew with *aïoli*, 21
Mont Ventoux, 144, 227
Montauban, 159
morchella vulgaris, 189
morel, 189
moules
    au pastis, 47
    à la provençale, 178
Mouriès, 173
mousse
    chicken liver, 90
    chocolate, 244
mousseron, 189
moût, 145
mulberry liqueur, 149
mullet, red with tomatoes, 91
mushroom(s), 187
    with anchovies, 193
    with artichokes and peas, 195
    with bacon, 190
    baked garlic, 192
    beef stewed with, 196
    with cream, 191
    dried, 190
    fried, 191
    fritters, 242
    guinea fowl stuffed with, 196
    in hunter's pheasant, 197
    and leek tart, 193
    in omelette, 187
    raw
        with prawns and squid, 188
        salad, 188
    sauce, with little carrot pots, 194
    stuffed with chicken livers, 192
mussels
    stuffed, with olive oil, 178
    with pastis, 47
    to prepare, 48
must, wines from, 145
myrtle liqueur, 35

Nectar des dieux, 50
Nectar of the gods, 50
nectarine(s), 124
    liqueur, 149
    wine, 147
New World, 17, 221

nez de chat, 188
Nyons, 173, 174

Occitan (Oc), 10, 29, 34, 227, 232
œufs à la tomate, 83
oil(s)
    grape, groundnut, sunflower 174
    olive, 173
        béchamel sauce with, 241
        goat's cheese in, 231
        sandwiches with, 176
        stuffed mussels, with, 178
        olives in, 175
old has been's dessert, 124
olive(s), 173
    black
        in caviar Provençal, 176
        guinea fowl stuffed with, 179
        lamb or roast chicken with, 174
        in larks without heads, 181
        marinated, 175
        with squid or cuttlefish, 180
    green
        with duck, 182
        pickled and in oil, 175
        quail with, 182
        with rabbit, 181
        with sausages, 177
        with venison, 178
    oil, *see* oil
olives amères, cassées, d'été, à la grecque,
        picholines, piquées, taillées, 174
    vertes cassées and *à l'huile,* 175
    noires marinées, 175
omelette, 240
    a l'ail, 16
    with basil, 57, 84
    au chèvre, 229
    aux épinards et à l'oseille, 110
    garlic, 16
    goat cheese, 229
    mushroom, 187
    spinach and sorrel, 110
    aux tomates, 84
    tomato, 57, 84
    with a truffle, 199
    à l'ail, 16
onion(s)
    with aubergines and tomatoes, 98
    and chestnut soup, 161
    fritters, 242
    tart, 193
Orange, 3
orange
    liqueur in the window, 149
    peel, dried, 239
    wine, 147
orangé, 188
oreille de Jésuite, 188
oreillette, 188
oreillettes, 243
oronge and *oronge vineuse,* 189
oursin, 189

Oustelet Maëanen, 181
oyster mushroom, 187

pain
  aux abricots, 123
  à laillade, 14
  d'épinards ou de blettes, 104
  perdu, 242
pan bagnat, 176
pancakes, 241
  with *marrons glacés*, 165
papeton d'aubergines, 97
parasol, 188
parasol mushroom, 187, 188
Paris, 128
Parmesan, 58
partridge
  with mushrooms, 197
  with rosemary, 42
  in vine leaves, 152
paste, quince, 129
pastis, 47
  with beef stewed with fennel, 52
  in mincemeat pies, 48
  mussels with, 47
pastry
  anchovy, 70
  shortcrust, 240
  sweet, 240
  pizza, 85
pâte brisée, 240
pâté
  de coing, 129
  de foie gras, 218
  little pots of, 204
peach(es), 124
  liqueur, 149
  wine, 147
  in white wine, 124
pear(s)
  liqueur, 149
  pie, 139
peas, with mushrooms and artichokes, 195
pèbre d'ai, 29, 227
pêches au vin blanc, 124
peel, dried orange, 239
peeling chestnuts, 160
pélardon, 227
peppers
  sweet with anchovies, 72
  stuffed, 71
perdreaux, and see partridge
  aux feuilles de vigne, 152
  au romarin, 42
Périgord, 198
Persia, 95
persillade, 14, 230
Pesenti, Cathy, 4, 80, 146
pesto, 58
petit gris, le, 87
petit gris d'automne, 189
petits
  pâtés, 48

pots
  de carottes aux champignons, 194
  de pâté, 204
  poulets aux raisins, 152
pheasant, hunter's, 197
pickled
  bitter-sweet cherries, 122
  olives, 175
picodon, 227
pie(s)
  fig and honey, 136
  mincemeat, 48
  pear, 139
  pork with chestnuts and apples, 162
  squid, 91
  sweet
    pumpkin, 216
    spinach or Swiss chard, 108
pied de mouton, 189
pigeon with mushrooms, 197
pignen, pinen, pinet, 188, 189
pintade, and see guinea fowl
  aux anchois, 74
  farcie aux champignons, 196
  aux olives, 179
pistou, 58
  soup with, 59
pizza provençale (with pastry), 85
plum liqueur, 149
poêlon, 73
poivre d'âne, 227
pompes d'huile, 154
Pont St Esprit, 9, 70, 79, 117, 174
Pope's aubergines, the, 97
porc, and see pork
  au lait et à la sauge, 42
  au romarin et aux aubergines, 40
  aux pommes et au céleri-rave, 126
porcelet, 207
pork
  (or boar) chops with bitter-sweet sauce,
    211
  and chicken liver terrine, 205
  with grapes, 144
  jugging, 207
  in milk with sage, 42
  pie with chestnuts and apples, 162
  potatoes and thyme with, 33
  roast with apples and celeriac, 126
  with rosemary and aubergines, 40
porrosalda, 31
pot au feu de poissons, 51
potato(es)
  baked
    with garlic, 17
    cakes with cheese, 233
  fried, cake, 229
  gratin with thyme, 32
  and leek soup with thyme, 31
  with pork and thyme, 33
  salad
    with walnuts, 127
    warm with basil, 60

with a truffle, 199
potiron (mushroom), 188
potiron (pumpkin), 215
  au gratin, 216
poule verte, 223
poulet, and see chicken
  aux quarante gousses d'ail, 19
  au thym et à l'ail, 33
  sauté au basilic, 61
poussin grillée au romarin, 41
preserved
  basil, 57
  goat cheeses, 231
  duck, 218
provençal caviar, 176
Provence, 4, 9, 10, 13, 20, 33, 34, 48, 71,
    83, 85, 91, 95, 103, 121, 133,
    137, 154, 173, 203, 220, 227
prunes
  in bitter-sweet sauce, 211
  with cheese tart, 234
psalliota campestris, 189
psalliote champêtre, 189
puffballs, 190
pumpkin, 215
  au gratin, 216
  seeds, toasted, 215
  soup, 215
  sweet pie, 216
Puy, Le, 159

quail
  with grapes, 153
  with green olives, 182
  with juniper, 206
  with mushrooms, 197
  with sage, 42
  in vine leaves, 152
Queen Claude, 128
quichets, les, 66
quince(s)
  or crab apple jelly, 128
  liqueur, 149
  paste, 129

rabbit
  jugging, 207
  with juniper, 204
  with olives, 181
  in a piquant sauce, 72
  with savory, 36
  wild, marinade for, 204
radish soup, 111
ragôt, 211
raisiné, 153
raisins pendus, 154
Raoux, Madame, 42
rasimat or *raisiné*, 153
raspberry(ies)
  liqueur, 149
  syrup with red wine, 147
Rasteau, 143
ratatouia, 10

ratatouille
  auignonnaise, 100
  Avignon's, 100
  the gypsies', 98
  left over, 99
red mullet
  en escabèche, 75
  with tomatoes, 91
red wine with raspberry syrup, 147
redcurrants with honey, 138
reinettes, 126
Rhône, 3, 4, 9, 10, 143, 144, 198, 227
  the boatmen of, 73
  Alps, 5
rice salad, 66
riquiqui, 35
risto, 10, 96
roast
  chestnuts, 160
  duck with olives, 182
  kid, 34
  leg of boar, 210
  lamb with garlic sauce, 20
  pork with apples and celeriac, 126
Roche, Rosaline (Feijoo), 229
Rodrigo, Monsieur, 3, 4
rogeret, 227
Roquefort, 58, 227, 232
  with braised chicory, 234
  turnovers, 233
Roquefort-sur-Soulzon, 227
rose des prés, 189
rosehip tea, 41
rosemary, 39
  courgettes with, 40
  and herb teas, 41
  marinade using, 39
  partridge with, 42
  pork and aubergines with, 40
  spring chicken grilled with, 41
rosy
  cauliflower, 89
  fruit salad, 125
rôties à l'ail, 15
rouille, 22, 23, 24
  squid (or cuttlefish) with, 24
  Monique's fish soup with, 23
rouille de calmars, 24
roumanel, 189
rousdito à l'anchoio, 65
roussillon, 188
rousotte, 188
Rumtopf, 125
russula family, 190
russules, 190

sage, 39
  life-saving soup with, 43
  liqueur, 35
  pork in milk with, 42
  quail with, 42
  tea, 41
Sahli, Jean, 42

St George's mushroom, 189
St John's wort
    tea, 41
    liqueur, 35
St-Joseph, 144
St Marcellin, 228
St Martin d'Ardèche, 90, 117, 228
St Michel, 188
St Paulet-de-Caisson, 3, 35, 112
salad
    with anchovies, 65
    broad bean, 111
    chicken liver with thyme, 30
    courgette with basil, 57
    with croûtons, 14, 15
        mixed green and with bacon, 112
    cuttlefish (or squid), 49
    dressing, anchovy, 65, 68
    aux foies de volaille au thym, 30
    de fruits rouges, 125
    de houblons (hop shoot), 111
    aux lentilles (lentil), 224
    mixed green with bacon and croûtons,
        112
    niçoise, 60
    de Pâques, 65
    de pommes de terre
        au basilic, 60
        aux noix, 127
    potato
        with walnuts, 127
        warm with basil, 60
    de riz (rice), 66
    rosy fruit, 125
    de suppion, 49
    de tomates au basilic (tomato with basil),
        58
    with a truffle, 199
salt cod with *aïoli*, 21
sandwiches with olive oil, 176
sang de Christ, 189
sanglier, see wild boar
santons, 169
sardines, *en escabèche*, 75
Sarrasine, La, 30
sarrassou, 232
sarriette, 29
sauces
    aïoli, 20
    anchovy, hot with celery, 68
    basil (*pistou*), 58
    béchamel à l'huile, 241
    béchamel with olive oil, 241
    bitter-sweet, with prunes, 211
    aux châtaignes, 163
    cheese, *see* béchamel, 241
    chestnut, 163
    garlic, 20
    lemon with asparagus, 112
    mushroom, with little carrot pots, 194
    piquant
        Languedoc, 208
        rabbit in, 72

rouille, 22
sorrel, 107
tomato
    fresh, 89
    with chicken liver mousse, 90
    with snails, 87
saucisses
    à l'ail, 17
    aux olives vertes, 177
saucisson de montagne, de Toulouse, 134
saupiquet du Languedoc, 208
sausage(s)
    black with apples, 126
    with garlic, 17
    with green olives, 177
saussoun, lou, 53
sauvo-crestian, 145
savory, 29
    broad beans with, 35
    rabbit with, 36
scrambled egg(s), 242
    with basil, 57
    with chestnuts, 159
    with a truffle, 199
seiches, 24
Sète, 22, 91
shad, 107
shortcrust pastry, 240
Simply Fish, 6, 21, 51, 105, 107
snails
    in tomato sauce, 87
    purging, cleaning and cooking, 86
solitaire, 211
sorrel, 103, 106
    broad beans with, 107
    in Languedoc faggots, 109
    sauce, 107
    soup, 113
    and spinach
        omelette, 106, 110
        with trout, 106
sou-fassoum, 223
soups
    asparagus and sorrel or spinach, 113
    chestnut
        Ardèche, 161
        and onion, 161
    chickpea, 222
    drunkard's (cheese), 230
    eiderdown, 86
    fish, 23
    garlic, 15
    garlic croûtons with, 14, 15
    leek and potato with thyme, 31
    life-saving, with sage, 43
    with *pistou*, 59
    pumpkin, 215
    radish, top and tail, 111
    spinach or Swiss chard broth with eggs,
        105
    tomato, iced, 86
soupe
    d'asperges et d'oseille ou d'épinards, 113

aux châtaignes et aux oignons, 161
glacée à la tomate, 86
à l'ivrogne, 230
pelou, 111
au pistou, 59
de poisson, 23
aux pois chiches, 222
au potiron, 215
soupes and souper, 15
spearmint, 47
spiced wine, 146
spinach, 103
  broth with eggs, 105
  gratin, 103
  Languedoc faggots, 109
  loaf, 104
  and sorrel
    omelette, 110
    with trout, 106
  soup, 113
  sweet pie, 108
  tart, 193
spring chicken
  with grapes, 152
  grilled with rosemary, 41
squid
  with black olives, 180
  to clean, 91, 180
  pie, 91
  with rouille, 24
  salad with fennel, 49
Stilton, 232
strawberry(ies), 122
  liqueur, 149
  in wine, 122
strong cheese, 235
stuffed
  aubergines, 71
  cabbage, 223
  courgettes, 71
  eggs, 67
  guinea fowl
    with mushrooms, 196
    with olives, 179
  mushrooms with chicken livers, 192
  mussels with olive oil, 178
  peppers, 71
  tomatoes, 71
    with tuna, 84
sugar syrup, cherries in, 121
Sugocasa, 89
sunflower oil, 174
suppion, 49
Suze-la-Rousse, 144
sweet
  pastry, 240
  peppers, see peppers
  pumpkin pie, 216
  spinach or Swiss chard pie, 108
Swiss chard, 103
  broth with eggs, 105
  gratin, 103
  Languedoc faggots, 109

loaf, 104
  stalks with anchovies, 106
  sweet pie, 108

tapenado, 176
tapeno, 176
tart
  cheese with prunes, 234
  greengage, 128
  mushroom and leek, 193
tarte
  aux champignons et aux poireaux, 193
  au fromage frais aux pruneaux, 234
  de potiron, 216
  aux reines-claudes, 128
Tavel, 144
tawny grisette, 187, 189
teas, rosemary and herb, 41
terrine, chicken and pork liver, 205
thickened butter, 239
thirteen desserts, 154
thourin, 86
thyme, 29
  artichokes with, 30
  chicken
    and garlic with, 33
    liver salad with, 30
  with dried figs, 136
  leek and potato soup with, 31
  liqueur, 35
  potato gratin with, 32
  potatoes and pork with, 33
  roast kid with, 34
  tea, 41
tian, 50
  d'artichauts aux anchois, 70
  de blettes ou d'épinards, 103
  de courgettes et tomates au fenouil, 50
tielle, 91
tilleul, 41
tisanes, 41
toasts, garlic, 15
tomates, and see tomatoes
  à la provençale, 85
  au thon, 84
tomato(es), 83
  and aubergine
    and courgette gratin, 99
    and onions, 98
    ratatouille, 100
  baked or fried, 85
  courgettes and fennel with, 50
  with fried eggs, 83
  frogs' legs, 90
  green, fritters, 242
  omelette, 57, 84
  pizza, 85
  rosy cauliflower, 89
  red mullet with, 91
  salad with basil, 58
  sauce
    with chicken liver mousse, 90
    fresh, 89

snails in, 87
soup
    eiderdown, 86
    iced, 86
    squid pie, 91
    stuffed, 71
    with tuna (or tapenado), 84
Tomme d'Aligot, de Camargue, de Cantal,
    227
tomme de chèvre, 227
top and tail radish soup, 111
toudeillo, 221
Toulouse, 219
    sausages, 177
tourain, 86
tournesol, 174
tourril, 86
tourrin à l'édredon, 86
tourte
    à la cévenole, 162
    d'epinards ou de blettes, 108
Trescouvieux, 169
trichinosis (swine fever), 209
tricholoma family, 189
trompette de la mort, and des Maures, 190
trout with sorrel and spinach, 106
trufets à l'ail, 17
truffado, 229
truffe, la, 198
    du pauvre, 190
truffle, a black, 198
    ways to cook, 199
truites aux herbes, 106
trumpet of death, 187, 190
tuber melanosporum, 198
tuna, tomatoes stuffed with, 84
turkey with chestnuts, 159
turnips, duck with, 208
turnovers, Roquefort, 233

vache rouge, 188
vachotte, 188
Valbonne, 169
vegetables, see separate headings
    stuffed, 71
vendange, 117, 143
venison
    with bitter-sweet sauce, 211
    with green olives, 178
verbena
    tea, 41
    liqueur, 35
vesse de loup, 190
Vieux
    garçon, 124

Fusil, Au, 210
vin, and see wine(s)
    apéritif aux brugnons ou aux pêches,
        147
    d'aspic, 148
    de basilic, 62
    cuit, 145
    doux, 143
    d'Hypocras, 138
    de noix, 150
    d'oranges, 147
    de sautel, 146
vinaigrette with blue cheese, 232
vine leaves
    Greek in brine, 152
    partridge in, 152
vinegar with basil, 57
vineuse, 189
vineux, vinou, 189
vins de pays du Gard, 143
volcan, 163
volcano, 163

walnut(s), green
    liqueur, 150
    potato salad with, 127
    wine, 150
warm potato salad with basil, 60
white sauce (béchamel), 241
wild boar
    boar's head brawn, 210
    casserole, Angel's, 209
    false boar, 210
    with bitter-sweet sauce, 211
    roast leg of, 211
wine(s), 143
    alternatives in cooking, 144
    basil, pick-you-up, 62
    green walnut, 150
    harvest, 117, 143
    from the must, 145
    lavender, 148
    nectarine, 147
    orange, 147
    peach, 147
    peaches in white wine, 124
    red with raspberry syrup, 147
    spiced, 146
    strawberries in, 122
    white, with a truffle, 199
woodcock
    with mushrooms, 197
    in vine leaves, 152
wood hedgehog, 187, 189
wood pigeon, 197